Strategies for Success

TOOLS FOR THE SECOND-LANGUAGE CLASSROOM

Marcelle Faulds

André Charlebobis • Fiona Cogswell • Ann Golinsky • Caterina Sotiriadis

Foreword by John Ralston Saul

NELSON EDUCATION

NELSON EDUCATION

Strategies for Success

Senior Author
Marcelle Faulds

Authors
André Charlebois
Fiona Cogswell
Ann Golinsky
Caterina (Bueti)
Sotiriadis

Contributing Authors
Geoff Collins
Natalie D'Elia
Patricia Emerson
Brenda McKinley

Senior Consultant
Joan Irwin

Vice President, Publishing
Janice Schoening

General Manager, French
Lise Tremblay

General Manager, Marketing
Audrey Wearn

Publisher, French
Jodi Ravn

Associate Publisher, French
Laura Jones

Managing Editor, Development
Cheryl Turner

Product Manager
Lysanne Sévigny

Project Manager
Ananda Fulton

Developmental Editors
Andria Fogarty
Marie Turcotte

Assistant Editor
Véronique Boileau

Editorial Assistant
Jordana Camerman

Editorial Intern
Vanessa Nunes

CD-ROM
David Miller
Gord Rollason
ETraffic

Senior Content Production Manager
Sujata Singh

Copyeditor
Tanjah Karvonen

Proofreaders
Cathy Fraccaro
Doreen Bédard-Bull
Susan McNish

Indexer
Noeline Bridge

Production Coordinator
Susan Ure

Design Director
Ken Phipps

Interior Design
Greg Devitt
Peggy Rhodes
Liz Harasymczuk

Illustrators
Deborah Crowle
Dave McKay

Compositor
Zenaida Diores

Photo/Permissions Researcher
Joanne Tang

Printer
RR Donnelley

Reviewers
Rhéal Allain
Helen Coltrinari
Donna Daniel
Maria DiMauro
Susan Forward
Jennifer Sampson
Nicole Thibault
Paula Kristmanson

French-as-a-Second Language (FSL) is used throughout *Strategies for Success* as a global term to encompass all programs taught in Canada to students whose first language is not French.

Table of Contents

Foreword

For fifteen years now–almost half the life of many of the second-language programs in Canada–I've been following their evolution in defending the cause of bilingualism. Nobody can seriously deny that the last thirty-five years have seen an astonishing breakthrough in bilingualism and bilingual education in Canada. This has been true for French Immersion and Intensive French, for people who become interested in French through their Core French programming, and for Francophones who want to find new ways to become bilingual. This has also been a period in which French first-language students outside Québec have been offered new and energetic forms of education.

In other words, in spite of periodic statistics which may discourage some people, the last three decades have involved a breakthrough for bilingualism in Canada. I see this on a multitude of fronts by simply observing the use of the two languages by Anglophones and Francophones outside of Québec, and by traditional Québec bilingual graduates. I see this in political circles, national and provincial; in civil services; in theatre production and film-making; in dance companies and sports organizations; and in the general level of basic services offered to Canadians.

The newest breakthrough has come at the university level where an increasing number of universities–still not enough of them and still not fast enough–have come to understand that French is not merely something taught by the French literature department. There are more and more degrees across the country organized as bilingual degrees. There are more and more universities offering special adjustment programs to immersion graduates in their first year. And this is true right across the country, from Simon Fraser University to l'Université Sainte-Anne.

The biggest challenge to bilingualism in Canada is the need to constantly re-invent the way we teach languages in order to make them real, exciting, and applicable to students at all levels. This book is an attempt to put forward new ways of advancing bilingualism. I firmly believe that we cannot be aggressive enough or enthusiastic enough in ensuring that bilingual education really does lead to bilingualism, and that students carry their learning through from primary school to high school to undergraduate to post-graduate and on into the rest of their lives. This must be the primary motive of bilingual education–that continuity is the key to success. Success means that education shapes the lives of students. This means that there must be an ever-closer cooperation between the schools and the universities to ensure that the good done in the schools is carried on through progressive, bilingual university approaches. These progressive approaches must be championed in order to ensure that the outcome is bilingual adults who believe that the essence of bilingualism is that language is animated by culture. Only students filled with the sense of that culture here and now in Canada in both languages will be able to make full and proper use of their language skills.

John Ralston Saul
April 2009

About the Authors

Marcelle Faulds is the senior author of Strategies for Success.

As a life-long learner and educator, Marcelle Faulds studied Comparative Literature at the University of Toronto at both the undergraduate and graduate levels.

Since first entering the education profession, Marcelle has been immersed in curriculum development and implementation as a writer, reviewer, editor, facilitator and presenter at a systemic, regional and provincial level. She has presented on such topics as Multiple Intelligences, Differentiated Learning, Brain Research, and Literacy Strategies.

She is a respected member of the FSL teaching and learning community and has been involved at all levels of FSL education in her many roles as a teacher, program leader and coordinator. This valuable and valued experience has helped her to gain an understanding of current educational priorities across both panels.

She remains very proud to have been part of the original group of leaders hired to open a new school in Oakville, Ontario based on the global learner philosophy.

At all times, students have remained her central concern and focus. She is committed to excellence in education.

André Charlebois is a former FSL teacher and Language Coordinator who retired after a long career spanning 34 years with the Upper Canada District School Board, in Ontario.

Today, André is an Education Consultant who is currently working on a number of initiatives related to the teaching and learning of French as a Second Language in Canada.

Over the last several years, André has authored a variety of resources used across Canada in FSL and French immersion. As a consultant, André provides training for Intensive French program evaluators assessing oral and written competencies.

André is passionate about the learning of French and its culture. As a workshop presenter for publishers, CASLT, and SEVEC, he inserts elements of French culture into all of his presentations.

André is a part-time professor in the Faculty of Education, University of Ottawa, where he teaches French language, Social Studies and the Additional Qualification course in French as a Second Language.

André would like to dedicate this book to his father, a teacher of 41 years, who taught André his *Strategies for Success*.

Fiona Cogswell is an Intensive French Specialist for the Department of Education in New Brunswick. For a number of years she worked as a Faculty Associate at the Faculty of Education, University of New Brunswick, where her responsibilities included undertaking research, teaching a methodology course for secondary FSL students and supervising student teachers. Before being seconded to UNB, Fiona was Supervisor of French Second Language and· Differentiation for School District 17 in Oromocto, New Brunswick.

From 2001 to 2004, Fiona was seconded to the New Brunswick Department of Education where she served as Second Language Consultant in the Educational Programs and Services Branch with responsibility for French Immersion, FSL as well as the implementation of the Intensive French pilot project.

Fiona has taught in two New Brunswick school districts: District 10 and District 17. She has teaching experience in both FSL and French Immersion and has taught Grades 6 through 12 in both programs.

Ann Golinsky took her first French course at a small women's liberal arts college in Virginia. She fell completely in love with the French language and has been a confirmed Francophile ever since!

Ann has been involved with French language education in British Columbia since 1970 as a teacher, an author, and a coordinator. She has taught in both FSL and French Immersion at both elementary and secondary levels.

Since 1993, Ann has been the Languages consultant for the New Westminster school district. She contributes to the recruiting and hiring of staff for French Immersion, is in charge of staff development for both French Immersion and FSL, is responsible for District advocacy for language programs, is responsible for district curriculum development for French programs and manages federal funding for language programs.

Ann is the out-going president of the British Columbia Language Coordinators' Association, an association that she has headed for five years. She also finds time to teach Methodology courses at UBC.

Caterina (Bueti) Sotiriadis was French consultant/coordinator for the *Bureau de l'éducation française*, the Department of Education, Training and Youth for the province of Manitoba for over 25 years.

Currently an independent education consultant, Caterina provides training and consulting to various learning institutions, associations and bodies across Canada. As a published writer, Caterina has authored several educational works, journal articles and non-fiction pieces.

Caterina has taught modern languages (English, French, Spanish and Italian) from Kindergarten to Grade 12 in the public school system of Manitoba. She has also taught Italian and second-language methodology in the Faculties of Education and Arts at the University of Manitoba, at the University of Winnipeg, and at the University of Caen, in France.

Caterina has also served on numerous local and national volunteer boards, including as past-president of CASLT. Caterina is also a trustee on the Board of French for the Future.

As an advocate of the importance of education, languages and life-long learning, Caterina truly believes "Only the educated are free."

Introduction

How to Use *Strategies for Success* to Inform Your Teaching

Today, the role of teacher knowledge and skill is recognized as one important route to improving student learning. This principle is central to current professional learning programs and resources that highlight collegial efforts focused on what teachers know and do, and how students learn. Providing teachers with effective instructional practices for the second-language classroom is the primary goal of this resource. *Strategies for Success* is written from the perspective of teachers. The authors and contributors are currently teaching or have taught in FSL (French-as-a-second-language) classrooms; we are teachers who collaborate with other teachers to ensure that all students experience success in learning French.

We understand and appreciate the varied circumstances in which FSL teachers find themselves. Some of you often work as the only FSL teacher in a school; others are itinerants who travel from room to room (notably, over 40 per cent of FSL teachers in Canada do not have their own classroom); most of you have between 150 (typically) and 250 (rarely) students to teach in each cycle—not a typical situation in Grades 4 through 8 for other teachers. Despite the number of students you might be responsible for, you have an advantage over other teachers. You sometimes have the opportunity to teach and get to know the same students for many years. Attitudinal challenges from students, parents, homeroom teachers, or administrators are certainly present for many of you; however, you know and champion the fact that learning another language has significant benefits for students. Instruction in FSL classes engages students in a wide range of activities that stretch their minds, provide additional opportunities for them to become independent learners, and broaden their cultural perspectives.

Although FSL instruction is our focus, the resources in *Strategies for Success* have application in all second-language classrooms. Furthermore, many of the practices that we advocate are widely used in English Language Arts instruction. Because of the connections that exist between first language (L1) and second language (L2) learning, the resources in this work have the potential to support professional development activities across the school. The practices we describe that have universal applications include formative assessments to inform and differentiate instruction, modelling and scaffolding techniques to support students as they learn new strategies and concepts, lesson structures that enable students to understand purposes and expected outcomes, and strategies specific to listening, speaking, reading, and writing.

Features of *Strategies for Success*: Tools for the Second-Language Classroom

Linking professional knowledge and classroom practice is an essential feature of resources designed to support and sustain teachers. *Strategies for Success* has several elements that will enable you to synthesize and apply the information in your classroom as well as in conversations with your colleagues.

- **Quotations.** A quotation leads off each section and chapter of the resource. Quotations can serve to encourage reflection, challenge your assumptions, start conversations, and foster an exchange of opinions among teachers in a professional learning environment.

- **My Thoughts.** A series of questions or comments follow the opening quotations. Immediately, your attention can be drawn to personal insights or observations prompted by your reaction to the quotations.

- **Keys to Success.** This material highlights ideas that are central to each section and the subsequent chapter topics. It provides an overview that will facilitate the readers' thinking about the relevance of the content to their particular circumstances.

- **What I Am Thinking Now.** These activities, distributed throughout the chapters, represent the authors' efforts to engage in "conversation" with their readers. Comments and questions invite you to reflect on what you have read and how this relates to what you think about teaching generally, or your current instructional practices.

- **My Choices.** Following the chapter summary, My Choices provides additional comments or questions to foster reflection on teaching and learning.

- **Case Studies.** Teachers look for authenticity and can, without hesitation, spot "manufactured vignettes." These case studies are descriptions from real life in-class experiences of teachers and their students. Maybe you will picture yourself and your students in comparable situations.

- **From the Research.** The research base for second-language learning is impressive, but frequently teachers do not have easy access to this information. These summary statements describe the evidence that supports practices described in the resource.

- **Teacher Tips.** Practicality is important to teachers and that is what you will find in the Teacher Tips—activities that have been successfully used in FSL classes.

- **Blackline Masters (BLMs):** Placed at the end of each chapter, these resources provide hands-on activities you can use with your students.

- **References:** Throughout the resource, we have cited scholarly works that inform teaching and help shape our perspectives about what we can do to ensure that all students are successful in learning a second language.

- **CD-ROM.** The material here augments the content provided in the print material. Resources include:
  - Modifiable versions of the Blackline Masters.
  - Notebook Tutor Segments—Flash videos that model best practices including:

- A think-aloud of a teacher thinking through the development of a unit of study using the unit planning sheets. (See BLMs 2.3 and 2.4.)
- Guidelines of how to gather and organize anecdotal observations for assessment to inform instruction.
- Description of how to use think-aloud instructional strategy in a FSL classroom to help students apply reading strategies.
- Description of how to use shared writing experiences in FSL.

Strategies for Success offers a wide array of resources based in classroom practice and supported by research. The resource has two sections:

- Section One—Preparing for Success contains five chapters that examine essential concepts for success in second-language teaching.
  - Chapter 1: Creating a Language Learning Community
  - Chapter 2: Effective Instructional Planning
  - Chapter 3: Teaching the Learning Brain
  - Chapter 4: Facilitating Differentiated Instruction
  - Chapter 5: Assessing for Success
- Section Two—Literacy Development Strategies contains four chapters that describe instructional practices that demonstrate the inter-relationships among the four strands of language.

  - Chapter 6: Listening Strategies
  - Chapter 7: Speaking Strategies
  - Chapter 8: Reading Strategies
  - Chapter 9: Writing Strategies

The resource's conclusion, Keys to Success: My Thoughts and Choices, summarizes the content and invites readers to explore ways in which that content has contributed to their professional knowledge and influenced their practice.

Blackline Master Table of Contents and Usage Checklist

Blackline Master			Blackline Master Possible Use(s)							Strategy and Skill Development			
Number	Title	Page	For Parents	For FSL Teachers	For Your Colleagues	Getting to Know Your Students	Managing Group Work	Self-Assessment	Peer Assessment	Listening	Speaking	Reading	Writing
5.7	Ma réaction au portfolio	194							X			X	X
5.8	Auto-évaluation : J'écoute	195						X		X			
5.9	Auto-évaluation : Je parle	196						X			X		
5.10	Auto-évaluation : Je comprends	197						X		X	X		
5.11	Je réfléchis à mon travail	198						X					X
5.12	Grille d'évaluation par les pairs	199							X				
5.13	Fiche d'observation	200		X									
5.14	Fiche anecdotique	201		X									
5.15	Grille d'accompagnement pour interviewer un ou une camarade	202				X				X	X		X
5.16	Aider les élèves à réussir	203		X									
Section 2 – Literacy Development Strategies		205											
Chapter 6 Listening Strategies		206											
6.1	Tableau SVAP	232						X		X			X
6.2	La météo d'hier et d'aujourd'hui	233								X	X		X
6.3	Tableau de veille météorologique	234								X			X
6.4	Est-ce que tu écoutes attentivement ?	235						X		X			
6.5	Activité en Jigsaw	236								X	X		X
Chapter 7 Speaking Strategies		237											
7.1	J'évalue mon expression orale	263						X			X		
7.2	Un schéma circulaire pour organiser mes idées	264									X		X
7.3	Que penses-tu de ma présentation ?	265							X		X		X
7.4	Ma présentation	266									X		X
Chapter 8 Reading Strategies		267											
8.1	Comment te sens-tu face à la lecture ?	289						X					
8.2	Questionnaire sur la lecture	290										X	
8.3	Quand je lis	291						X				X	
8.4	Je me prépare à lire	292						X				X	
8.5	Chacun son tour	293										X	X
8.6	Survoler un texte	294					X					X	X
8.7	Guide de prédiction	295					X					X	X
8.8	Un parcours de lecture en équipe	296					X				X	X	X
8.9	La fiche d'identification d'un personnage	297										X	X
8.10	Qui est ce personnage ?	298										X	X
8.11	Un personnage qui me ressemble	299										X	X
8.12	Le compte-rendu	300										X	X
8.13	La pyramide d'un personnage	301										X	X
8.14	Trouver l'idée principale	302										X	X
8.15	Des pistes pour discuter à propos de nos lectures	303					X				X	X	X
8.16	Le scénarimage	304										X	X
8.17	Fiche de lecture	305										X	X
8.18	Le rappel d'un texte narratif	306										X	X
8.19	Mon compte-rendu de lecture	307										X	X
8.20	Un texte en diagramme	308									X	X	X
8.21	Voici ce que je vois de la lecture de mon ou ma camarade	309							X	X			X
8.22	J'évalue ma présentation au théâtre de lecteurs	310						X					
Chapter 9 Writing Strategies		311											
9.1	Fiche d'auto-évaluation: Mon opinion sur l'écriture	331						X					X
9.2	Le schéma du récit	332										X	X
9.3	Un napperon	333								X	X	X	X
9.4	Mon article de journal	334											X
Conclusion – Keys to Success: My Thoughts and Choices		335											
C.1	My Year in Review	338		X	X								
C.2	J'évalue mon année	340						X					
C.3	Annual Learning Plan - Template	341		X	X								

" Teachers who have a clear grasp of the relationship between educational ends and means are more likely to understand the importance of routinely verifying the quality of their instructional procedures (means) according to the impact those procedures have on student needs (ends). "
—W. James Popham

My Thoughts

- Reflect on your experiences in situations where student outcomes have been subject to intense scrutiny (from such sources as parents, school community, school administration, or the local media). How did this scrutiny affect you and your colleagues? What impact did this experience have on your instructional practices?

- In what ways do you examine your instructional practices? Do you think that your practices have changed over the years that you have been teaching? If so, what factors have contributed to these changes?

Section 1

Preparing for Success

Keys to Success

What teachers do and how students respond are inextricably related in every classroom. Schools and classrooms are complex social entities where a constellation of factors affect outcomes for both teachers and students. These factors are particularly important in FSL classes where the ultimate goal is to have students acquire sufficient capacity with French so that they can use the language in social situations.

- The teacher's leadership establishes a learning climate that enables students to use French with confidence even in the early stages of their learning.

- The teacher's instructional planning provides varying levels of support that guide students toward independence.

- The teacher's acknowledgment of students' intellectual and emotional development influences the social context for learning activities.

- The teacher's organizational skills and knowledge of students' learning needs are the driving forces for differentiated instruction.

- The teacher's confidence in using formative assessment ensures that improvements occur in student learning.

These factors are examined in the chapters that make up this section of *Strategies for Success:*

- Chapter 1: Creating a Language-Learning Community
- Chapter 2: Effective Instructional Planning
- Chapter 3: Teaching the Learning Brain
- Chapter 4: Facilitating Differentiated Instruction
- Chapter 5: Assessing for Success

Creating a Language-Learning Community

"If we were to devise theories of second language acquisition or teaching methods which were based only on cognitive considerations, we would be omitting the most fundamental side of human behaviour."
—H. Douglas Brown

My Thoughts

Educators are constantly reminded to take into account both the cognitive and affective aspects of learning. These concepts are alluded to in Brown's statement.

- How did you react initially to this quotation?

- What factors are included in "cognitive considerations" of language teaching? To what extent are these factors evident in your instruction? Do these considerations dominate your instruction?

- What aspects of instruction do you think are represented in the "most fundamental side of human behaviour"? To what extent are these factors evident in your instruction?

- Dealing with affective considerations (e.g., beliefs, attitudes) can sometimes be awkward. Reflect on situations in which you have dealt with either positive or negative factors related to FSL instruction.

In this chapter, we will discuss:

- Student Success Model

- Why Learn a Second Language?

- Creating a Positive School Atmosphere

- Creating a Positive Classroom Atmosphere

- Strengthening Home-links

Student Success Model

Making a positive difference in the lives of students motivates us all. Part of our work as educators is to create classroom settings that foster a desire for learning now and throughout students' lives. A key element to fostering life-long learning is the positive influence of all stakeholders on student experiences. As an open and influential French teacher, ongoing, quality communication with all stakeholders leads to involved parents and supportive administrators and colleagues. With strong adult support, students are more likely to be invested in their learning.

Open communication fostered by the French teacher is critical in the development of relationships with all stakeholders. Clearly and specifically expressing goals for learning a language and making connections between the languages spoken by students will allow for increased understanding in the value of learning French.

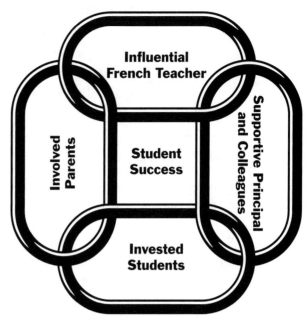

Figure 1.1: Student Success Model

Why Learn a Second Language?

Learning a second language is an important way of opening windows for our students: windows on other cultures, on our own history, and on the power of language as communication. Teaching a second language provides you with opportunities to apply best practice strategies that are informed by current brain research about learning, as well as demonstrating the benefits you derive from knowing French.

The pleasure and satisfaction we derive from being able to listen to French-language news or radio broadcasts, watch a movie, TV show, or Internet video in French, read a *bande dessinée* or book, or order food in a French restaurant are all rewards of successful learning in the FSL classroom. These are satisfactions that we can invite our students to share.

Second-language learning has been shown to benefit students by improving their problem-solving abilities, their short- and long-term memory capacity, and their abilities in other subject areas such as their first-language arts and even their math scores!

Increasingly, FSL educators are realizing that learning a second language has an impact on the first language. Research shows that second-language learning strengthens competencies in the first language. Second-language learning provides many benefits that everyone involved in education—students, parents, administrators, and colleagues from other disciplines—should know about.

What I Am Thinking Now

Having clarity about our own goals for teaching French (or any second language) is basic to achieving success with our students.

- Why did you choose teaching a second language as your discipline?

- What were your goals when you first started as a teacher? Do you still hold on to these goals? Have there been times when you felt that you were too idealistic?

- What new insights and skills are you trying to convey to your students through second-language learning? In what ways are these factors comparable to experiences that students have in other subjects?

- What challenges have you encountered in teaching a second language?

Look back at the Table of Contents in this guide to identify topics that are most relevant for your personal goals and instructional interests.

Teacher Tip

To delve deeper into these considerations, reflect on your own goals for teaching FSL.

1. What are my overarching goals for teaching French? To give my students:
   - ❑ an understanding of another culture through the medium of language;
   - ❑ a wider experience of life through learning about other cultural perspectives, e.g., through language, history, geography, art, literature, and music;
   - ❑ a deeper understanding of the French perspective in Canadian history;
   - ❑ a global perspective on the modern world;
   - ❑ the experience of empathizing with people from other cultures.

Other goals: _____

_____

2. What enduring understandings do I want my students to internalize as a result of their FSL education? I want my students to have:

❏ effective second-language learning skills;

❏ an appreciation of French language and French culture;

❏ a foundation for self-directed learning so that they can continue with French long after they have left my classroom;

❏ opportunities to experience the joy of being able to communicate in French with each other and with native speakers, whenever possible;

❏ a successful and enjoyable experience learning and communicating in French.

Other enduring understandings: _____

_____

3. What are my communicative and production goals for my students? They will be able to:

❏ describe themselves (e.g., family, friends, interests, school life);

❏ hold a conversation with a native speaker;

❏ read a text, view a movie, listen to a recording independently;

❏ write a text in French independently.

Other goals: _____

_____

4. What challenges do my students and I face in achieving these goals? Our challenges include:

❏ the lack of school and community support for FSL;

❏ the practical difficulties of being an itinerant teacher or not having a classroom.

Other challenges: _____

_____

What students believe about the value of learning French determines their degree of success in the FSL classroom. What are their attitudes about learning second languages? about learning French? What past experiences have they had? What do they know about French culture?

You can reinforce positive beliefs about bilingualism by sharing some ideas from a forum of Canadian teenagers on the subject. Participants discussed the advantages of learning other languages and came up with the following list.

You will notice that the students' list includes many advantages that are extracurricular and involve their future goals. But in order to gain some of these benefits, students must internalize effective learning skills as well as subject content and knowledge. Teachers do not just teach, and students do not just learn subject areas. Effective teachers teach, and successful students learn, the skills to become independent learners. In the FSL classroom, students are not only learning about language structures, vocabulary, and Francophone culture; they are also learning strategies for second-language learning and understanding how they learn. Have students complete BLM 1.1 to identify their goals for learning French.

What I Am Thinking Now

Brown's quotation at the beginning of this chapter highlighted the affective aspect of learning a second language (see p. 4). Take a moment now to reflect on that quotation in terms of your students' beliefs, attitudes, and behaviours.

- In what ways have you provided opportunities for your students to share their ideas about why they are learning French? How did results from these encounters influence your approach to instruction?

- Have you shared your goals about learning French with your students? How can you use your goals to help students determine personal goals for learning French?

- Do you have students in your FSL class who speak a language other than English? If so, how do you encourage these students to share their observations about the advantages of knowing more than one language?

• Do you think your students would identify with the advantages of bilingualism listed in the section "From the Research"? How could you use this listing to help your students talk about the advantages of knowing another language?

Creating a Positive School Atmosphere

Students will be more motivated to learn a language that is appreciated by all members of the school community. You can create a positive attitude for FSL in your school among your colleagues in other disciplines by reminding them of the benefits of second-language learning for brain development and its impact in student success in other academic areas.

FSL teachers face many challenges that teachers in other disciplines might not have to cope with. For example, many FSL teachers do not have a classroom dedicated to French or might even travel from school to school. If that describes your situation, ask the homeroom teacher for bulletin board space within the classroom. Negotiate for a section of the classroom where you can hang posters and Word Walls. Arrange for space in the classroom to put French-language resources such as dictionaries, atlases, and magazines. Ask the principal for hallway bulletin board space to exhibit student work.

Subjects such as social studies, language arts, and science can often be linked to topics in the FSL classroom. Ask your colleagues to outline upcoming topics so that you can identify connections to FSL or opportunities to make connections as you plan your lessons. For example, if students are learning about Francophone history in Canada or if they are learning about an area that has a large Francophone population (Québec, Acadia, northern and eastern Ontario, Manitoba, and northern Saskatchewan, Alberta, and British Columbia), then find information about those populations and areas and invite students to discover this information in French. Ask your colleagues about the topics of student projects so that you can identify cross-curricular connections to FSL. Are there ways of using the research for a similar FSL project? Ask about upcoming science and social studies topics and find non-fiction French-language books on those subjects.

French teachers can benefit from informing their colleagues about the topic or theme being explored in French class. The next step is to integrate that theme with what is going on in other subjects. It is impor-

As L.S. Vygotsky famously posited, common thinking processes are used across many disciplines.

tant for all members of the school community to know that language skills, learning strategies, and thinking processes cross disciplines.

Integrating skills, strategies, and processes across all disciplines helps students see and make connections. You can ensure that French is valued in your school by including French in any charts posted in staff rooms that list curricular links across subject areas. Imagine the power of the message in hearing every student and teacher sing the national anthem in both French and English at every assembly. If students are to see the value of learning a second language, then the whole school has a role to play.

FSL instruction can benefit from many of the same instructional practices and strategies used in the first-language (L1) literacy classroom. Literacy teachers also have to understand their students' learning profiles. Consider collaborating with the language arts teacher to find out if he or she has information on individual learning styles of your students. Conferencing with L1 teachers can provide you with useful information on areas where students can improve in their production skills, e.g., reading and writing.

See Section 2, Literacy Development Strategies, for BLM examples of attitudinal surveys.

Attitudinal surveys on reading and writing will reveal similar information in both the first language and the second, so consider collaborating with the L1 literacy teacher when you use these tools. Because the language of the surveys will be the first language, you will be able to find out much more specific information than if your students had to complete them in French.

Teacher Tip

Here are some suggested activities to raise the profile of FSL in your school:

- Request time during a staff meeting to share a strategy or teaching tip you are focusing on in your FSL teaching that is relevant to all teachers.
- Identify several students a month as the school's French ambassadors. Duties could include running a French contest on the morning announcements or greeting key visitors identified by the principal.
- Have students create signs to label school areas in French.
- Add curricular, activity, and homework involvement ideas to the homeroom teacher's parent calendar or newsletter. Or create your own newsletter to send to parents, your teaching colleagues, and the administrator.
- Institute a French Fact contest during the morning announcements highlighting culture, history, and language.
- Invite students to find Francophone e-pals and correspond with them. Ask for permission to post the correspondence. (Adhere to school Internet policies.)
- Find a French recording of *Ô Canada* and ask the school administration to play it during the morning announcements.
- Make sure your students know the French lyrics for *Ô Canada* and invite them to sing in French at school assemblies.
- Invite students to create a bilingual zone in your school by providing French-language signage.
- Ask for funds to buy and add French-language books to the school library.
- Rent or buy French-language animated DVDs from National Film Board of Canada, l'Office national du film du Canada.
- Research and share with students cool French expressions that students their own age would use.
- Research and share with students French expressions for cool equipment (e.g., MP3 players, video games, computer terms) and hobbies (e.g., sports terms, music) and encourage students to use these expressions.
- Put on a school play in French and invite other classes and parents.
- Create big books in French for students in lower grades.
- Host a French café for the school, profiling typical foods of la Francophonie (Québec, France, Belgique, Martinique, Haïti, Sénégal, etc.).
- Sponsor an exchange trip to Québec or to Francophone areas in your province.
- If students are visiting a French-speaking region on a school trip, invite the class to write a Visitor's Survivor Guide, covering such topics as: how to order food, how to ask for directions, how to make change, how to ask one question about a tourist attraction.

What I Am Thinking Now

Teachers, students, and visitors can pick up various messages about what happens in the school from the environment that exists within the building and individual classrooms.

- What do you think visitors to the school would notice initially? What do you think might be their first impressions of the school and the activities going on within it? Do you think all these impressions will be positive?

- What features of individual classrooms do you think best convey a positive learning environment? Are these features found consistently throughout the school?

- Talk with your students about features of their school or classroom that they find appealing as well as ones they find unappealing. What changes can possibly be made to change the climate/environment within the school/classroom?

Level of student motivation influences:
- Level of participation
- Level of engagement
- Persistence with activities

Creating a Positive Classroom Atmosphere

A positive learning atmosphere is one that respects every individual's need to feel wanted, accepted, and secure. When a positive emotional climate exists, students can explore new ways of thinking as they learn from one another and from you.

How the teacher behaves in the classroom affects the learning environment. You are a facilitator and role model for your students; you are also the weather vane. Students who learn with a teacher who is excited about learning will catch the same spirit of excitement.

Creating a positive learning atmosphere involves inspiring students as well as putting them at ease. Maintaining motivation levels, relieving anxiety, and encouraging risk-taking are all important components of a positive classroom setting.

When it comes to motivation, students typically begin their L2 learning with high levels of intrinsic motivation. They believe in their personal ability to succeed; however, as the tasks become more complex, students can experience a loss of sense of control and a decrease in immediate and observable learning achievements. Teachers are critical to ensuring that a sense of control and the ability to succeed remain within the grasp of students as they learn a second language. To maintain high levels of engagement, participation, and persistence, teachers must communicate the value and requirements of tasks so that students see them as controllable.

Motivation also relies on variety in classroom life. Vary the resources you use, vary the format of those resources (print, audio, video, and multimedia), and vary the classroom arrangement and décor. (For best results, have students produce the new posters, visuals, and flashcards.) Introduce themes that are relevant to students' lives and ensure that they are accompanied by activities that are age appropriate and relevant to their lives and skill levels.

Successful language learning integrates many skills: listening, speaking, reading, and writing (for a fuller discussion of teaching and learning strategies for the four strands, see Chapters 6–9). In an optimal learning environment for second languages, students should use and practise each skill during every class. Brain research shows that we need many, many opportunities to practise new skills and knowledge, so plan with the aim of providing students with many opportunities for practice and repetition.

You can create a positive learning environment by following a few simple guidelines.

- Work collaboratively with each student.

- Explicitly teach language-learning and metacognitive strategies.

- At the beginning of each class, review what students learned the previous day.

- At the end of each class, encourage students to reflect on what they have just learned.

- Provide opportunities for frequent peer- and self-evaluations to help students focus on the next steps to build on their learning.

Techniques for collaborative work and strategies for learning and metacognition are addressed in more depth throughout this resource.

An important consideration for early FSL teachers is to make sure that students get off to the right start at the beginning of their FSL education and at the beginning of each year. Early elementary students are often eager to learn all subjects and will take chances in speaking French. But as they get older, students often become more self-conscious and less willing to take risks in speaking French.

Key to Success

Create a classroom climate that is conducive to communication and in which experimentation is expected and honoured.

Creating a Language-Learning Community

Consider ways of creating a warm and inclusive environment where students will feel safe enough to take those risks. Students learn not only by interacting with you, the teacher, but by interacting and communicating with each other. Collaborative oral communication is especially critical to student success in the L2 classroom.

Teacher Tip

- At the beginning of each year, term, or semester, allow students enough time to become comfortable in their new surroundings. Take time during your first class to discuss expectations and answer questions.

- Make your classroom set-up physically inviting. Arrange desks and chairs in circle groupings to promote conversation. Provide French-language books, magazines, and posters. Post student work and exemplars, and anchor papers.

- Encourage appropriate behaviour while discouraging inappropriate behaviour indirectly, e.g., by moving closer to and addressing the student by name, or by placing a gentle hand on the shoulder.

- Praise students when they do well. Make sure that all students are praised. Be specific in your praise to allow growth on the part of students. (See BLM 1.2.)

(Adapted from Stratman, 2000)

Motivating Through Cultural Studies

Motivation, an important contributing factor in second-language acquisition, is explained as the learner's orientation to the goal of learning to speak a second language. Jacqueline Norris-Holt explains that, "motivation is divided into two basic types: integrative and instrumental. Integrative motivation is characterized by the learner's positive attitudes toward the target language group and the desire to integrate into the target language community…. Instrumental motivation is generally characterized by the desire to obtain something practical or concrete from the study of a second language… where little or no social integration of the learner into a community using the target language takes place, or in some instances is even desired." Integrative motivation is the more desirable type of motivation for a language learner because of the hope that the involvement of learning and speaking a second language is life-long. (Norris-Holt, 2001)

How can FSL teachers help students develop a positive attitude toward the French language and thus continue to develop integrative motivation? Language is the key to culture and the more students appreciate and value the language, the more they can unlock the intricacies of the culture. Culture is defined as a "general context and way of life. It is the behaviours and beliefs of a community of people whose history, geography, institutions, and commonalities are distinct and distinguish them to a greater or lesser degree from all other groups" according to the Syllabus Culture of the National Core French Study (LeBlanc, et. al., 1990, p. xii). The National Core French Study suggests that at the elementary level, students should focus on their own culture, the culture of their own family and region. Knowledge of another culture mitigates the ethnocentric view that our society is superior to all others.

Certainly there are difficulties inherent in the teaching of culture. Teachers typically cite not enough time and the belief in language structures first, and culture later. Many teachers feel they do not know enough about the Francophone culture. Some shy away from it because the study of culture deals directly with student attitudes. However, if teachers work on the recommendations of the National Core French Study and concentrate on students looking at their own culture, then the task seems less daunting.

Integrative Motivation: characterized by the learner's positive attitudes toward the target language group and the desire to integrate.

See Chapter 2 for more information on the National Core French Study.

Teacher Tip

- Begin this "cultural" journey by obtaining a French-language map of the world and of Canada. Ask students to find out where their parents and grandparents were born and pinpoint it on the map. Have students refer to BLM 1.3 and BLM 1.4 to celebrate their own cultural journey. Information from these forms will create the list of countries to teach in French for that class. The list of important countries that our students come from can be used during the study of other themes to help make deeper connections and emphasize that where they come from is honoured and valued. For example: *Quel temps fait-il au Japon?* when exploring a unit on weather or *Il est quelle heure maintenant au Manitoba?* when studying time. Students could draw the flags of the countries or provinces appropriate to the origins of their families and attach them to the maps.

- Ask students to survey the members of the class for birthdays: *Quelle est la date de ta fête?* (See BLM 1.5 for a *sondage*.) When their *sondages* have been completed, students share the information with the teacher. (See BLM 1.6 for a graphing opportunity with birthdates.) Students then draw the name of a classmate from a hat and make a birthday card using typical birthday card wishes (See BLM 1.7.) in French. The teacher files the cards and when a birthday arrives, gives the card to the celebrant and the class might join in and sing "Happy Birthday" *Bonne fête* in French.

- The book *Premiers poèmes* contains a very simple surrealist poem by Robert Desnos called *La Fourmi*. (See BLM 1.8.) Introduce unfamiliar vocabulary. Use the sentence strips provided on BLM 1.8 to introduce the poem. Have the students work with a partner and put the sentence strips in order as students read the poem aloud as many times as is necessary. Ask the students to guess the title of the poem or simply to provide their own title for the poem. Divide the class into seven groups. Each group will recite one line of the poem for a whole-class presentation. The whole class forms the chorus and repeats: « ça n'existe pas ». Students could draw one of the three pictures of an ant described in this poem. Drawings should include the three or four appropriate lines from the poem. For additional practice, 10 students could be given one line of the poem each. To get them up and out of their chairs, students try to arrange themselves in the correct order of the poem.

- Sometimes expressions in French are so colourful that they can create wonderful images for language students. (See BLM 1.9.) Students could try to figure out the sense of the expression in the left-hand column with the help of the definitions in the middle column (can be done with a partner) and then draw a picture illustrating what it means. Encourage students to keep the form with their personal dictionary or reference section in their *cahiers*. Have students attempt to use the expressions so that they become part of their regular communication. The BLM answers are

L'expression idiomatique	*La définition*
1. *Il a une faim de loup.*	*Il a envie de manger.*
2. *Elle a la chair de poule.*	*Elle a froid ou elle a peur.*
3. *Ne mets pas tous tes œufs dans le même panier!*	*Minimise tes risques!*

4. *Quel temps de chien!*   *Il fait mauvais.*

5. *Je baisse les bras.*   *Euh, je ne peux pas le faire.*

6. *C'est bête comme chou!*   *C'est facile!*

7. *Je fais chou blanc.*   *J'oublie complètement.*

8. *Il a deux mains gauches!*   *Ses mouvements sont sans élégances.*

Communicating in the L2 Classroom

Fostering communication among students involves laying a clear foundation for the development of social relationships through patterns of classroom interaction that enable them to talk with each other. Effective teachers build on the notion that meaningful teaching and learning acts on and responds to students' knowledge and their learning needs. By creating a safe, positive, and motivating learning environment in your FSL classroom, you will be giving students life-long strategies for success for second-language learning and all learning.

The types of activities and the language that you choose to use with your students are powerful tools in encouraging them to develop relationships with one another. Classroom talk that is clearly focused on learning strategies empowers students and encourages them to determine what is relevant in what they learn.

We should pause and consider the questions we have when we think about our students as individuals and learners. As Carol Tomlinson says, "asking the right questions has an enormous impact on how we pursue equity and excellence in our classrooms." (Tomlinson, 2003, p. 6) Excellence in teaching is found in a language that is clearly formed and informed by an educator's beliefs and practice. These observations help us to focus on the kinds of questions we should ask about our students as we strive to create a classroom atmosphere that encourages them to talk with one another. The following questions can help us better understand our students.

In a communicative classroom, a teacher asks...	rather than...
What are my students' interests and needs?	What labels do my students have?
What are their strengths?	What are my students' weaknesses?
What releases the motivation born in all humans?	How can I motivate these students?
How do I adapt the material to benefit my students?	What do I do if a student cannot accomplish my goals?

(Adapted from Tomlinson, 2003)

Creating a Language-Learning Community   **17**

Teacher Tip

How Well Do I Listen? Think about each question from the table below in the context of your interactions with your students during class. How do these questions describe you as a listener? Rate your listening behaviour—usually, occasionally, rarely. Provide comments about how you might change your listening behaviour.

Alternatively, you might also want to think about listening behaviour in the context of meetings with colleagues. How would changes in listening behaviour bring about changes in the way that such meetings function?

Listening Behaviour	Usually	Occasionally	Rarely	Changes I Can Make
Do you wait for the student to stop speaking before you say something?				
Do you listen attentively?				
Do you remain relaxed even though the student might be struggling and looking to you (or others) for guidance?				
Do you give the student your undivided attention?				
Do you send signals that encourage the student to continue talking?				
Do you resist the temptation to interrupt the student?				
Are you an effective model of listening behaviour for your students?				
Do you talk with your students about good listening behaviours?				

Implementing the Communicative Approach

The communicative approach goes well beyond the textbook. Topics that occur within the life of the school or in students' personal lives can be used to foster conversations that provide them with opportunities to practise speaking French. In the communicative approach, listening and oral skills are the foundation of all work in the strands. Reading and writing are not separate activities from listening and speaking; they are based on the foundation that you and your students build orally. Classroom activities should be structured to maximize opportunities for students to use the language to communicate a message in context, rather than to answer a question on grammar or vocabulary.

Use French for classroom management and instruction as much as possible. Studies have demonstrated, and current trends in FSL instruction such as Intensive French have also shown, that students' production abilities improve with more exposure to French when it is used as the primary language of classroom instruction and interaction.

Although oral skills are the focus in the communicative classroom, reading and writing skills are developed as well. For example, students could be given a passage to read then asked to talk about the most important part of the passage, or to summarize the passage first orally and then in writing.

The communicative approach incorporates grammar in a contextual way. As you are speaking, listening, or reading, ask students to notice grammatical or lexical items and then invite them to identify patterns.

The communicative approach recognizes that making errors is a necessary part of language learning. Encourage students to feel free to express themselves creatively and spontaneously. Successfully being able to convey a message, even if there are grammatical errors, is the goal in the communicative approach. Insisting on grammatical accuracy can often make students nervous or unwilling to take the necessary risks to speak in French.

Wherever possible, use authentic documents. Use the Internet as a source for documents and websites, e.g., news sites for weather reports and sports information. Many Francophone countries have websites that are accessible to a wide variety of learners. You can also

find Francophone sites on TV shows, movies, animals, and celebrities. Also be aware of the Francophone sites created by the federal government on many Canadian topics of interest such as history, geography, arts and culture, and government.

Excursions to the library to read French-language books or magazines can also help to keep students actively engaged in language learning. Students will need careful scaffolding and literacy strategies to access French texts.

Teacher Tip

Creating an Interactive Classroom Think about the ways in which you organize instruction to provide opportunities for your students to use French in a variety of situations. Rate your effectiveness on the 3-point scale (3 indicating a feature that is a routine in your classroom) and jot down suggestions for ways to make your classroom more interactive.

Interactive Features	1	2	3	Things I Would Like to Try
Use French for classroom routines and lesson directions				
Encourage students to greet each other in French—both in and out of French class				
Provide various models of spoken French and have students emulate these				
Encourage students to ask for assistance using as much French as they are able				
Show students how approximations in pronunciations are part of learning a language				
Use art and drama activities to foster students' confidence in using French				
Use read-aloud activities to help students become familiar with the sounds and cadences of French				
Use music (song and dance) activities that enable students to participate with language or actions				
Engage students in decorating a section of the classroom/school hallways with a French ambience				
Compliment students on their attempts to use French in various situations and activities				
Use think-aloud procedures to help students understand how they are learning				
Provide various opportunities for students to work together—in pairs or small groups—with follow-up in the whole class				
Have students repeat in French what they think they heard in various situations—lesson instructions, questions, another student's response, and so on				

Encouraging Risk-Taking

Students take risks in attempting to speak in the FSL classroom and must often overcome anxiety to do so. Teachers can reduce student anxiety by

- establishing a classroom climate that encourages student participation and builds confidence;

- modelling risk-taking;

- implementing low-stress classroom management techniques to prevent inappropriate student behaviour;

- using effective error-correction techniques.

Most FSL students want to avoid risk-taking. They define risk as the fear of giving a wrong answer, rather than not understanding or not being understood. You can help students redefine risk-taking in a positive way. Whenever students take a risk by speaking in French, they are testing a hypothesis about the appropriate thing to say in French in a particular context.

Model taking risks by taking some yourself. Use the word *défi* and associated expressions *relever le défi* and *prendre des risques* when you introduce new concepts or tasks. Try new ways of doing things and comment on the fact that you are doing so. Think aloud about how the new approach is working or not working.

Teacher Tip

To get a sense of how comfortable students are speaking in French, try the following activity.

- Write down the following statement: *J'ai peur de parler en français dans la classe de français. Je n'aime pas faire des erreurs devant mes amis.*
- Ask students to reflect on the statement and then respond by discussing with a partner or in groups and writing in their journals. After they have had time to think about their response, ask who agrees and who disagrees with the statement. Divide into groups based on their agreement with the statement and have them discuss and make notes on chart paper.
- Can students suggest ways of reducing anxiety about speaking in French?

Encourage activities that promote self-efficacy as a means to develop positive attitudes and motivation. As Mahatma Gandhi once exclaimed, "If I have the belief that I can do it, I shall surely acquire

Creating a Language-Learning Community

the capacity to do it even if I may not have it at the beginning." Student self-efficacy can be defined as what the student believes about his or her capacity to achieve the designated level of performance. An important aspect of this intrinsic motivation is autonomy. If students and teacher are all working toward a common goal, then both a sense of control and self-directed autonomy are present.

How students interpret past successes and failures can have a dramatic impact on their self-efficacy. Past performance is the single greatest contributor to students' confidence. Those self-efficacy beliefs determine what the student thinks and feels about the possibility of success, and thus greatly influences motivation. Students who doubt that they can succeed are much less motivated to learn. Students who feel assured in their capabilities approach difficult tasks as challenges to be undertaken rather than as obstacles to be avoided. It is certainly in the interest of FSL teachers to design lessons and incorporate strategies that build self-efficacy rather than weaken it.

Reinforcing effort and providing recognition will help students to develop beliefs of self-efficacy. (See BLMs 1.10, 1.11, and 1.12.) Recognition is most effective when it is contingent on the achievement of a certain standard of performance (Marzano and Pickering, 2001). When some kind of positive acknowledgment is given as students achieve something they have been striving for, a student's belief in his or her ability to reach the goal increases. Findings confirm that verbal praise (symbolic recognition) is just as or even more effective in increasing intrinsic motivation as tangible rewards. Rewarding students who have achieved certain performance standards can increase their achievement, but recognition is most effective when it is abstract (e.g., praise) or symbolic (e.g., certificates) and dependent on their attaining specific performance goals.

Varying Questions

Questions are not just tools for eliciting answers or gauging comprehension; they are also ways of extending student learning and promoting effective communication. One of the ways that you can increase student participation is to vary the way in which you invite students to respond to questions. Different forms of response enable students to interact with their peers, encourage risk-taking, and provide varied opportunities for you to observe their performance. Here are some ways to invite student response:

- Ask students to indicate agreement non-verbally through gestures, e.g., thumbs up for agreement, thumbs down for disagreement. *Levez la main si vous êtes d'accord. Ne levez pas le pouce si vous n'êtes pas d'accord.*

- Ask students to share their answers with partners or group members. *Ne levez pas la main pour répondre. Discutez de vos réponses avec les membres du groupe.*

- Give students time to think before answering. Then ask them to reply in one or both ways: share the answer with a partner; write a response. *Réfléchissez à vos réponses. Quand vous êtes prêts, partagez vos réponses avec un ou une partenaire. Écrivez vos réponses sur une feuille de papier.*

A well-prepared and supported student is more likely to feel confident and motivated to participate. Because the brain needs novelty and does not react well to stress, varying questioning styles is one way of ensuring productivity and improving student performance.

Teacher Tip

- Ask questions in non-threatening ways. For example, ask, *Qui veut discuter de sa réponse avec la classe?* instead of *Qui sait la réponse?*
- Allow for thinking time. After you ask a question or give instructions, give students time to process their thoughts.
- Dignify incorrect answers. Acknowledge students' efforts, and, if possible, relate the answer to the subject matter or give students another chance or a different format to answer correctly.
- Let student comments and answers stand on their own. If you repeat the answer, you will be training them to listen only to the teacher. If others did not hear, ask them to repeat rather than doing so yourself.
- Be a good listener because listening is such an important aspect of an effective communicative approach.
- Give students choices whenever possible. Choices empower and promote learning.

(Adapted from Stratman, 2000)

CASE STUDY

Setting a Positive Tone as an Itinerant Teacher

Like most FSL teachers, Monsieur Townsend wrestled with the various challenges of being an itinerant teacher for most of his career. Having taught students from Grades 4 through 8 for many years without ever having a designated French classroom, Monsieur Townsend resigned himself to always having to make the best of a difficult situation. Despite this, the same questions would regularly reoccur. How to create a positive French climate for 40 minutes a day in seven different classrooms? How to coax changes to desk arrangements, seating plans, available board or wall space, while causing minimal disruption to the homeroom teacher? Oh, and where on Earth had he left his flashcards?

Over the years, Monsieur Townsend acquired a number of strategies to help alleviate the problems inherent in his situation. At the beginning of every school year, he negotiated with each homeroom teacher to get a French corner in all the classrooms. He made a point of regularly praising homeroom teachers on the effectiveness of their classroom lay-out and seating plans, while subtly making suggestions for possible changes. His lessons included as many engaging, communicative, and differentiated activities as possible. However, one particular class in late September showed him that he had succeeded in creating a climate conducive to learning French that could be continued throughout the year and replicated, with a few modifications, in all his other classes.

Armed with his recently purchased cart, Monsieur Townsend entered Monsieur Nelson's Grade 6 classroom to a sea of hands and a chorus of «Est-ce que je peux vous aider?». Opening activities were now firmly established and the first volunteer fired up the CD player while the second popped Monsieur's memory stick into Monsieur Nelson's computer and brought up the PowerPoint that accompanied the song. After some enthusiastic singing, two more volunteers led the class in the familiar oral warm-up activities while a third circulated around the class stamping "Bravo" onto students' oral participation calendars. The next 15 minutes saw the class practise a play in small groups aided by an array of props eagerly taken from the cart. This was cut short so that the class could end with a rousing rendition of their latest favourite game, «Cache le cochon». Monsieur Nelson then returned to find a student removing a stuffed toy pig from behind his computer and the class was over.

Monsieur Townsend left Monsieur Nelson's classroom that day with a broad, satisfied smile on his face and a real sense of having spent 40 minutes with a class for whom French was a completely positive experience. It also dawned on him that in the course of the whole lesson not one student had needed to be redirected and not one word of English had been uttered. The daydream was swiftly interrupted by the realization that he now had to jettison his cart into the French office, grab his bucket of Grade 7 materials, walk the length of the school to the staircase that would take him down to his next class that began three minutes ago, and do it all over again. C'est la vie!

What I Am Thinking Now

"Genuine learning always involves dialogue and encounter."—*Clark E. Moustakas*

The implications of this statement are relevant for instructional activities that foster interaction. Reflect on your practice in relation to the Case Study: Setting a Positive Tone as an Itinerant Teacher.

- Take a few moments to visualize what happens during your FSL classes. What do you see? Who is talking? Who is engaged? Who is distracted? Who is creating distractions? What does the noise level reveal about student engagement?

- How do your classroom routines facilitate student communication and interactions? Do you think you need to make changes in any of these routines? If so, what would you like to change?

- Like in the case study, if you are an itinerant teacher, you might encounter unique challenges in creating an inviting FSL learning environment. What are these challenges? What success have you had in dealing with these?

Strengthening Home-Links

Involved parents and guardians are critical to student success. Home value systems correlate directly to values students bring to a learning environment.

Advocating for the importance of learning a second language is often the exclusive role of the FSL teacher in a school. Teachers must work to involve school colleagues and administration in assisting to communicate the value of learning another language. (See BLM 1.13.) Communication on the part of the French teacher and the school administration is key to ensuring parental involvement in FSL programs. (See BLM 1.14.)

An immediate barrier can exist for the parent due to the language of instruction. Parents might not know how to support their child's learning and might not immediately see the value in the learning. Teachers need to establish early communication with parents to outline:

- Benefits to learning French

- Goals for the FSL class

- Overview of units-of-study

Contact your provincial chapter of Canadian Parents for French (CPF) to receive promotional materials for your classroom and for distribution to parents. CPF can provide additional tips on promoting French language and culture in your community and school.

Refer to your school or school district's homework policy prior to implementing any form of homework program.

- Tips on supporting discussion of unit themes at home (See BLM 1.15.)

- Connection between L1 and L2 strategy focus for a unit

- Tips on assisting with FSL homework (if a homework program is part of FSL initiatives)

Teacher Tip

To assist in communicating with parents, try some of the following:

- Send an introductory letter home in June with students who will be starting FSL for the first time in September. Outline the benefits of learning French and provide a tip or two to encourage parents to be actively involved in their child's learning.

- Join forces with homeroom teachers to communicate learning goals and units of study via homeroom newsletters.

- Use the school-home voice-mail system or use parent e-mail addresses to correspond directly with parents on a regular basis.

- Create a simple FSL web page as part of the school website to post information relevant to parents and students. Regular updates will encourage parents to check the site periodically.

- Encourage the administration to allow you to speak to the large assembly of parents at the beginning of curriculum night. Make links from L1 to L2 learning.

- Provide handouts outlining the links between learning outcomes and activities in the classroom so that parents have a better understanding of the importance and educational value of the activities in FSL.

- Participate in student-parent-teacher conferencing with the homeroom teacher(s) as often as possible so that the message about student achievement and learning habits is strengthened. (Priority will need to be set as FSL teachers will not be able to attend meetings with all parents during meetings with the homeroom teachers.)

- With the school administration, outline an action plan for involving parents and the wider community in the school's FSL program. Include action statements that are measureable and reasonable and focus on improving communication, volunteerism, home-learning programs, joint decision making, and collaboration with the extended community.

Summary

A positive learning environment fosters self-esteem and focuses on the development of the whole student. Your role involves

- building a community of learners
- promoting the profile of French in the school

A positive learning environment is a stimulating one. You can create this environment by

- creating an attractive classroom or space within the school
- empowering students
- speaking less and listening and observing more

A positive learning environment encourages interaction and values relationships. You can achieve this by

- incorporating small group or partner work into each class
- finding ways to continue learning and practising French outside the classroom

A positive learning environment encourages risk-taking and values student voice in class decisions. You can support students by

- honouring risk and minimizing anxiety
- incorporating student suggestions into activities and techniques
- celebrating all successes along the way

My Choices

In creating a learning environment that facilitates language use, the teacher assumes a variety of roles including model, facilitator, motivator, listener, explainer, monitor, and organizer.

- Talk with a colleague about how you see yourselves in these roles (or others that you add to the list). Describe instructional situations in which these various roles are played and the instructional purposes they serve.

- Which of these roles comes into play when you are communicating about the FSL program with other teachers? with individuals in the community?

Cette année, je veux...

Nom : _____ Classe : _____ Date : _____

Il est temps de choisir tes objectifs pour le cours de français. Choisis deux ou trois objectifs par section.

Section A – Améliorer mon français

Pour améliorer mon français, je veux...

- ❏ apprendre à lire en français
- ❏ apprendre à utiliser des stratégies pour m'aider
- ❏ parler français tous les jours
- ❏ parler français avec l'enseignant(e)
- ❏ parler français avec mes amis
- ❏ faire de bonnes présentations
- ❏ corriger mon travail écrit
- ❏ ajouter des mots sur le mur de mots
- ❏ utiliser l'ordinateur pour faire des recherches en français
- ❏ jouer à des jeux en français
- ❏ étudier une unité sur _____
- ❏ bien travailler dans mon groupe
- ❏ m'amuser quand je travaille dans la classe de français
- ❏ aider mes camarades de classe quand je peux
- ❏ respecter mes camarades de classe

Un autre objectif personnel est :

_____

_____

_____

Section B – Comprendre la culture française

Pour mieux comprendre la culture française, je veux...

- ❏ créer et participer à un café français dans la salle de classe
- ❏ goûter à de la nourriture française
- ❏ planifier un voyage dans un pays ou une région francophone
- ❏ commander de la nourriture dans un restaurant français
- ❏ acheter quelque chose dans un magasin où on parle français
- ❏ célébrer l'anniversaire d'un ami ou d'une amie en français
- ❏ chanter des chansons de langue française
- ❏ écrire un menu, une affiche, une brochure, une bande dessinée en français
- ❏ regarder un film de langue française

Un autre objectif personnel est :

_____

_____

_____

Tes réactions aux travaux des autres

Nom : _____ Classe : _____ Date : _____

À l'oral, fais part à tes camarades de classe de tes réactions à leurs efforts et travaux.

Comment utiliser la fiche :

1. **Identifie l'objet de ta réaction (Partie A, B, ou C).**

2. **Choisis un commentaire approprié à échanger avec les autres.**

3. **Sois expressif / expressive en échangeant ton commentaire.**

Partie A – Le message

Bien réussi
• *Tu respectes très bien / bien / assez bien les consignes données.*
• *Ton message est très bien / bien / assez bien structuré.*   *(l'introduction, le développement, la conclusion)*
• *Les informations données sont très suffisantes / suffisantes / assez suffisantes.*
• *Les informations s'enchaînent de manière très cohérente / cohérente / assez cohérente.*
• *Tu as fait un très bon / bon / assez bon lien à tes expériences personnelles pour ajouter des idées à ton message.*

Partie B – La langue

Bien réussi
• *Tu exprimes très clairement / clairement / assez clairement ton message. (les phrases bien construites)*
• *Tu utilises très bien / bien / assez bien un vocabulaire juste et précis.*
• *Tu respectes très bien / bien / assez bien les règles linguistiques.*   *(l'orthographe, l'accord, la conjugaison, la syntaxe)*
• *Ta prononciation, ton articulation, et ton débit sont très appropriés / appropriés / assez appropriés.*

Partie C – L'attitude

Bien réussi
• *Tu regardes très bien / bien / assez bien le public.*
• *Tu démontres une attitude très positive / positive / assez positive.*   *(le sourire, le visage expressif)*
• *Tu suscites très bien / bien / assez bien l'intérêt du public.*   *(l'intonation, le débit, les gestes, les mimiques, l'usage de l'espace)*

D'où viens-tu? D'où viennent-ils?

Nom : _____ Classe : _____ Date : _____

1. **Demande à tes camarades d'où ils ou elles viennent. Essaie d'identifier la région sur la carte du monde. Essaie aussi de trouver comment on appelle les personnes de ces régions et la langue qu'ils parlent.**

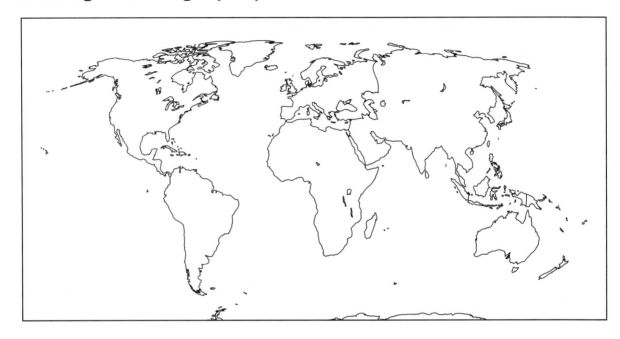

Régions	Habitants	Langue
Canada	Canadien / Canadienne	Anglais et français

2. **Connais-tu des pays où on parle français? Avec un camarade ou une camarade essayez de trouver 5 pays où on parle français. Identifiez ces pays sur la carte. Écrivez le nom de ces pays sur la ligne ci-dessous et coloriez-les en bleu sur la carte.**

Ta fête culturelle préférée.

Nom : _____ Classe : _____ Date : _____

Chaque pays a des fêtes culturelles. Parfois ce sont des fêtes religieuses comme Pâques ou Noël, parfois ce sont des fêtes civiles comme le Jour de l'An ou la Fête du Canada.

Fais découvrir à tes camarades ta fête culturelle préférée! Réponds aux questions suivantes, puis présente à tes camarades cette fête.

1. Comment s'appelle ta fête culturelle préférée ?

_____

_____

2. À quel moment dans l'année célébrez-vous cette fête ?

_____

_____

3. Quelle est la signification de cette fête ?

_____

_____

4. Est-ce que vous mangez quelque chose de spécial ?

_____

_____

5. Est-ce que vous portez des vêtements spéciaux ?

_____

_____

6. Est-ce qu'il y a de la musique spéciale ?

_____

_____

7. Est-ce qu'il y a des choses à faire avant la fête ? (Exemples : jeûner, décorer la maison)

_____

_____

8. Comment se déroule la journée, le jour de cette fête ?

_____

_____

Sondage : C'est quand ta fête?

Nom : _____   Classe : _____   Date : _____

Demande à un ou une camarade de répondre aux questions suivantes. N'oublie pas d'écrire les réponses sur ta feuille.

Le nom de la personne que j'interview est _____

1. Quelle est ta date d'anniversaire?

Elle est née / il est né le _____

2. Est-ce que tu invites des amis ou amies pour célébrer ta fête?

Oui, elle / il _____

Non, elle / il _____

3. Quel est ton gâteau préféré?

Elle / Il préfère le gâteau _____

4. Qu'est-ce que tu préfères le jour de ta fête?

❑ Aller au restaurant

❑ Être avec ta famille et tes amis

❑ Avoir des cadeaux

❑ Manger du gâteau

5. Aimerais-tu avoir une fête-surprise pour ton anniversaire?

Oui, elle / il aimerait _____

Non, elle / il n'aimerait pas _____

6. Est-ce que tu aimes les fêtes-surprise?

Oui, elle / il aime _____

Non, elle / il n'aime pas _____

7. Qu'est-ce que tu aimes le plus à ta fête?

Elle / Il aime _____

Défi
Partage les réponses avec la classe pour créer un diagramme de plusieurs questions. Fais une analyse brève des résultats. Qu'est-ce que tu observes dans les diagrammes?

Dates d'anniversaire de mes camarades de classe

Nom : _____ Classe : _____ Date : _____

Pour chaque saison, inscris les mois de l'année correspondant. Ensuite, demande à tes camarades leur date d'anniversaire. Inscris la date et le nom de ton camarade dans le carré correspondant au mois de son anniversaire.

Mes camarades nés / nées en **automne** sont :

Mes camarades nés / nées en **hiver** sont :

Mes camarades nés / nées au **printemps** sont :

Mes camarades nés / nées en **été** sont :

Une carte d'anniversaire — un modèle

Nom : _____ Classe : _____ Date : _____

Utilise cette fiche comme modèle et brouillon de ta carte d'anniversaire pour un ou une camarade. Insère les noms appropriés. Choisis les expressions en italique que tu veux utiliser dans ta carte pour ton ou ta camarade.

Cher David,
Chère Marie,

Pour ta fête, je te souhaite *du bonheur / du plaisir / du succès à l'école / du succès dans tes loisirs / de la joie / de la tendresse / de l'amour / de beaux cadeaux / des surprises / de bons moments avec tes amis / une belle journée / une belle fête / de t'amuser beaucoup / d'être heureux ou heureuse.*

Je veux te dire que tu es *gentil / souriant / sympathique / mon meilleur ami / ma meilleure amie / une personne courageuse / une personne patiente.*

Avec toi, j'aime *jouer au soccer / dessiner / aller au cinéma / jouer aux jeux vidéo.*

Profite de ta journée de fête *pour jouer avec tes amis ou amies / te laisser gâter / t'amuser.*

Bonne fête,

Ton ami Daniel XXX
Ton amie Anne XXX

Prépare une version finale et donne-la à ton enseignant(e) qui va la remettre à ton ou ta camarade le jour de son anniversaire.

Un poème de Robert Desnos (1900–1945)

Nom : _____ Classe : _____ Date : _____

Robert Desnos est un poète français surréaliste. Il mélange le réel et l'irréel. C'est comme dans les rêves, tout est possible!

Quoi faire...

Découpe les parties d'un poème de Robert Desnos. À deux, essayez de refaire les phrases du poème. Incluez le titre du poème. Dessinez une illustration pour chaque stanza du poème.

Le poème	Les illustrations
Le titre : _____	

Parlant latin et javanais,	Ça n'existe pas, ça n'existe pas.
Une fourmi traînant un char	Plein de pingouins et de canards,
Avec un chapeau sur la tête,	Une fourmi de 18 mètres
Ça n'existe pas, ça n'existe pas.	Eh! Pourquoi pas?
Ça n'existe pas, ça n'existe pas.	Une fourmi parlant français,

Des expressions idiomatiques

Nom : _____ Classe : _____ Date : _____

Étudie l'expression dans la première colonne et essaie de trouver des indices pour en deviner le sens. Écrit la bonne définition à la bonne endroit dans la deuxième colonne. Illustre l'expression dans la troisième colonne.

Les définitions possibles…		
· Il fait mauvais.	· C'est facile !	· Il a envie de manger.
· Minimise tes risques !	· Elle a froid ou elle a peur.	· Euh, je ne peux pas le faire.
· J'oublie complètement.	· Ses mouvements sont sans élégances.	

L'expression idiomatique	La définition	L'illustration
1. Il a une faim de loup.		
2. Elle a la chair de poule.		
3. Ne mets pas tous tes œufs dans le même panier !		
4. Quel temps de chien !		
5. Je baisse les bras.		
6. C'est bête comme chou !		
7. Je fais chou blanc.		
8. Il a deux mains gauches !		

Quelle expression est-ce que tu vas utiliser demain en classe ?

_____

Casse-tête d'un ou d'une élève efficace

Casse-tête (suite)

- Bien écouter — pièce n° 1

- Bien se concentrer — pièce n° 2

- Se préparer et s'organiser pour apprendre — pièce n° 3

- Prendre l'habitude de faire ses devoirs — pièce n° 4

- Connaître le monde extérieur — pièce n° 5

- S'autoévaluer de façon efficace — pièce n° 6

- Pouvoir régler ses problèmes et savoir quand il faut demander de l'aide — pièce n° 7

Un certificat pour

_____ est un(e) apprenant(e) efficace

(Nom de l'élève)

parce que

_____

_____

_____

_____

_____

_____

Signature : _____ Date : _____

The Value of Learning Another Language

Dear Parents, Guardians and Colleagues,

Research shows that learning a second language is an asset that few of us can ignore in today's global world. We are fortunate in Canada to have excellent programs designed to teach French to our students. Whether students take a Core/Basic French, an Extended, or a French Immersion program, their exposure to French language and culture helps them understand our Canadian heritage, and the world we live in. By studying French, students develop a much greater understanding of other cultures and the multicultural mosaic that is Canada today.

There are many reasons to learn a second language in today's world. The following list identifies some worthwhile reasons for studying French.

Reasons for Studying French

- French is recognized by the United Nations as one of the most widely used languages in the world.
- There is not a continent on Earth that does not have at least one French-speaking country on it.
- Speaking French is as unique a skill as the bilingual Canadian culture that it celebrates.
- Canada's reputation in the world is as a population that embraces multiculturalism, diversity, and mutual acceptance.
- International travel requires knowledge of more than one language.
- All Olympic events are announced in English, French, and the language of the host country.

Scholastic Achievement:

- Second-language students have higher test scores in reading, language, and mathematics.

Effects on First Language:

- Second-language education significantly strengthens first-language skills in areas of reading, vocabulary, grammar, and communication skills. Research proves that providing links from students' first language of study to the second language affords them opportunities to develop better skills in each language.

Economic Potential:

- There is an urgent requirement for qualified speakers of languages other than English in areas of science, technology, medicine, and global commerce.
- Since Canada is officially a bilingual country, adults are required to be bilingual (English and French) in order to be offered a government position.
- Most adults, at some point in their lives, need some measure of French to communicate with other Canadians, no matter what their field of work.

Health Benefit Potential:

- Learning a second language creates more synapses in your brain and is likely to reduce your chances of diseases that affect the minds of older individuals, like Alzheimer's.
- Bilingual stroke patients have been observed to retain language in the undamaged areas in brains.

As the adults responsible for the education of our children, it is important that we encourage young people to continue their French studies as long as possible. Many Canadian adults regret not having continued their French studies beyond Grade 9; today, they see the value of having a second language.

The benefits of studying French are overwhelming. I look forward to working closely with you as we provide these wonderful and exciting opportunities for our students.

Yours sincerely,

Record of Communication

Use this chart to record details of all communication with parents and guardians.

Student	Date	Communication Method	Contact	Strengths, Needs, Next Steps	Follow-up Actions/Dates

How to Support Learning Another Language

Dear Parents or Guardians,

This year, [once again], your child will be learning French. I'm sure you are asking yourself how you can help with French homework when you might not know French yourself. Rest assured that you don't need to know French in order to support your child in learning and appreciating the French language.

The secret to helping your child learn another language is to make him or her comfortable working in another language. This year we will focus on a variety of learning strategies that will make it easier for your child to learn French. You might consider doing any of the following to support the learning of those strategies:

- Invite your child to talk about what he or she did in French class during the day. Asking this question at the supper table can involve the whole family. It also allows your child to reflect on and solidify the learning.

- Post your child's writing projects somewhere in the house where everyone can see them (you might want to place a bulletin board in a hallway for this purpose). In this way you recognize the accomplishments of your child and encourage greater participation.

- Watch a few minutes of French television with your child, e.g., children's programs, a cartoon, a weather report, and work together to determine what it's about. This type of activity teaches your child to infer, predict, and consolidate meaning. Your child will likely not know all of the details, but he or she might be able to use the visuals, the facial expressions of the characters, and some French words to determine the main idea.

- Access some age-appropriate reading material at the local library or book store and have your child read something to you at night, before he or she goes to bed (one or two pages of a text would be enough for one evening). Invite your child to predict what might happen in the reading using the visuals. You can both have fun looking for words you each recognize. You might even find some reading material that is accompanied by a CD.

- Purchase some French CDs or DVDs of songs or borrow some from your local library and listen to them with your child. Get him or her to create actions to the music and do the actions with your child.

- Check the Internet for games and activities that exist in French for students at this age group. Watch your child play and do the activity as he or she works in French. I can provide you with some appropriate websites, if you wish.

- Have fun looking for words in English or French texts (in recipes, in the newspaper, in your child's English textbooks, etc.) that are cognates (words that are used in both French and English—e.g., *machine, téléphone, orange*). Making connections between languages strengthens children's abilities in both languages.

I hope that your child will enjoy his or her French experiences, and with your help, we can ensure that the experience is a positive and rewarding one.

Merci beaucoup!

Au plaisir,

Chapter 2

Effective Instructional Planning

"Education is not the filling of a pail, but the lighting of a fire."
—W. B. Yeats

My Thoughts

- Tell a friend or colleague about a teaching experience that you were reminded of as you read this quotation.

- Motivation (i.e., "the lighting of a fire") is an important factor in learning another language. What do you think are effective ways to foster motivation in your students?

- How can you use the ideas expressed in this quotation to help students and their parents understand and appreciate the value of learning French?

In this chapter, we will discuss:

- Gradual Release of Responsibility

- Modelling the Strategy or Skill

- Instructional Approaches

- Principles of Instructional Planning

How do we ensure that our students derive the most benefit from learning a second language? What kinds of experiences do we want them to have? What kinds of resources will we provide so that they can have those experiences? Current research in effective instruction shows that explicitly teaching strategies that help students think about new ideas in light of their prior knowledge, and then apply and transform that knowledge for their own use and in other situations, results in students who are actively engaged in their own learning.

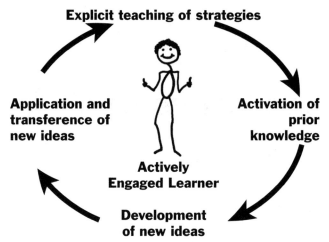

Explicit teaching of strategies

Application and transference of new ideas

Actively Engaged Learner

Activation of prior knowledge

Development of new ideas

Figure 2.1: Actively engaged students are explicitly taught learning strategies to activate prior knowledge in order to develop new ideas. Using learning strategies, learners then apply and transform the new ideas for their own use and in other situations.

To actively engage students, educators must reflect continuously on the role that they play in today's classrooms. This reflects a critical shift in instructional pedagogy. Today's classrooms should no longer encourage rote memorization of new knowledge, but instead expose students to instruction that emphasizes learning how to learn through inquiry-oriented activities. In the L2 classroom where oral communication is the focus, a learner-centred approach will have a greater impact than an approach based on learning in isolation. In this environment, teachers are facilitators of learning and students are collaborative participants, engaging in learning that is connected to the real world. This active engagement with ideas can lead students to make knowledge their own and empowers them to acquire a level of understanding that will serve as the foundation for life-long learning.

Gradual Release of Responsibility

The process by which teachers and students collaborate to create autonomous student learners is called the Gradual Release of Responsibility (GRR). At the beginning, the teacher is the focus of the instruction and leads the learning. But over time, and by modelling how to learn and by giving students many opportunities to practise, students can become independent learners and guide their own learning.

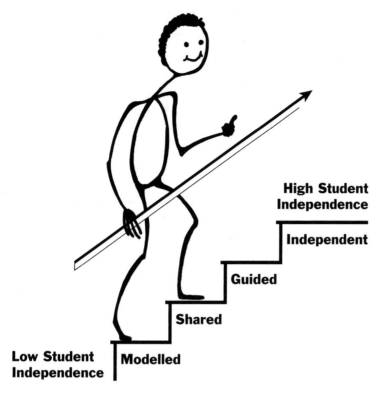

Figure 2.2: Gradual Release of Responsibility (GRR) Model

The steps in the Gradual Release of Responsibility teaching approach are:

1. Explain and model the strategy.

2. Continue modelling the strategy through shared practice.

3. Help students to use the strategy through guided practice and by providing scaffolding.

4. Now students are ready to use the strategy independently.

There are general strategies for learning and metacognition and skill-specific ones as well. Strategies can be classified by the point at which they are applicable in an activity:

For a fuller discussion of the skill-specific strategies, see Chapters 6–9.

1. Before-Activity Strategies

2. During-Activity Strategies

3. After-Activity Strategies

Before	During	After
· Make predictions. · Think of questions that you would like to have answered. · Make connections to your prior knowledge. · Make connections to your personal experiences. · Think about your purpose for doing the activity.	· Does the activity (the reading or listening) make sense? · Re-read or listen again. · Ask questions. · Ask for help. · Are your predictions being answered? · Do you have any more questions?	· Were your predictions accurate? · Which strategies helped you to understand? · Which strategies would you use next time? · Is there a main idea? Can you explain it?

Modelling the Strategy or Skill

At all stages of modelled, shared, and guided practice outlined below, you will be providing scaffolding in the form of support (providing resources, answering questions, supplying mini-models for skills practice, etc.).

In the modelling stage, the teacher models the activity for students. As you demonstrate, you comment aloud on the process through a think-aloud. For example, during a think-aloud, you might

- discuss where you are having difficulties understanding a reading text;

- discuss which strategies could be helpful in understanding the text;

- discuss what predictions or questions you have about a listening activity;

- discuss the necessary steps for completing a writing task, presentation, or group work.

Modelling the activity is almost exclusively teacher led. Students are learning through observing and are preparing for the next step, Shared Practice.

Shared Practice

After the students have become familiar with the process through observing your model, involve them in the process through shared practice. In this step, you will still provide the model to be worked on, but as you do so, ask questions to engage students. For example, instead of telling them which strategies you are going to use or steps you will follow, ask them to provide suggestions (*Je ne comprends pas cette partie… Qu'est-ce que je vais faire pour comprendre? Qui peut suggérer une stratégie utile… la première étape… ?*).

Guided Practice

After students have observed and contributed to the activity through shared practice, give them opportunities to experience the learning more intensively through guided practice. In guided practice, group students to work on short tasks and activities. For example, have them read part of a reading selection; have them work on a mini-task that involves skills they will use for the final task; have them do a jigsaw-listening activity, and so on.

Circulate among them and check to make sure that they are on track and on task. Facilitate the discussion by answering questions, helping students practise necessary skills for successful comprehension or completion of the task.

When students have completed these stages, they should be ready to move to independent work.

Using Metacognitive Strategies

At all stages of the GRR approach, you are either reflecting on your use of strategies (during modelling) or asking students to reflect on their own use of strategies (during shared and guided practice). The ability to use metacognition, that is, to choose and use strategies, will greatly increase students' success and enjoyment in the FSL classroom.

Metacognition is the ability to think about thinking. For example:

- How do we learn?

- What are the optimal ways to learn?

- Which strategies or techniques complement which skills?

Learners who can reflect on how they learn develop awareness of how they can monitor and repair their learning; how they can figure out what to do when they are not sure what to do. To think metacognitively, students must ask themselves the following questions during an activity:

- Do I understand what is happening?

- At what point did I stop understanding?

- Have we discussed a strategy (in the before-activity discussion) that might help me understand?

After an activity, the key questions students should ask are:

- What strategies worked (helped me understand)? Why?

- Which strategies did not work and why not?

- What will I do next time to improve my work?

Focus on helping students learn about learning strategies in a variety of contexts so that they will know which strategy is the most appropriate for their current learning situation. If students know of strategies that have helped them make sense of and expand their learning, they are better equipped to set goals and improve and continue their learning.

What I Am Thinking Now

The Gradual Release of Responsibility (GRR) model is reflected in well-designed lesson plans.

- Review several of your current lesson plans to determine how you have applied this instructional process. In what ways has this process helped you to assess your students' progress in learning French? to differentiate instruction based on your observations of their progress?

- Learning how to learn is an important factor in students' metacognitive development. Strategy instruction in L1 often provides opportunities for students to use behaviours that lead to metacognitive awareness: defining what they are learning, identifying difficulties, knowing some ways to deal with difficulties, and describing what they have accomplished.

- Talk with the literacy teacher(s) about metacognitive strategies they are using with students.

- In what ways do you think the strategies students learn in L1 can help them in French class?

- How have you structured activities so that students have opportunities to think and talk about their learning?

Instructional Approaches

As we gain more experience as teachers, we develop a repertoire of teaching and learning strategies in our professional toolkit. It is important to remember that students need the same opportunities to determine their preferences in teaching and learning styles.

The range of learners in our FSL classrooms underscores the need for careful planning. Instructional activities can be designed in various ways to meet students' learning needs. While certain methodologies, such as physical response approaches, appeal to kinesthetic and creative learners, other practices with a strong oral component might interest the more social and verbal students.

There are a variety of instructional options available. All of them share the common goal of developing language skills in a meaningful and relevant way. They all elaborate on the key principles of the National Core French Study, which revolutionized FSL instruction in Canada.

The National Core French Study (NCFS), initiated by H.H. Stern in the 1980s, introduced the idea of a communicative-experiential approach to the study of French. Along with other educational movements in disciplines such as literacy, the NCFS has had a profound and pervasive effect on French-as-a-Second-Language education across Canada. The NCFS teaching units are created through the integration of four syllabi (Communication, Language, Culture, and General Language Formation). This multidimensional approach focuses on authentic communication and is based on and shaped by a learner's experiences.

The founding principles of the NCFS have helped to define the goals of most successful second-language instructional approaches developed since the 1990s.

These principles include

- using fields of experience (e.g., food, physical education, clothing, school, family, friends) that are relevant and appropriate for learners of different ages;

- providing authentic communication opportunities;

- drawing on learners' experiences;

- defining learning goals clearly at the outset of instruction;

Significant correlations can be made between the National Core French Study, the National Standards for Foreign Language Learning (American Council on the Teaching of Foreign Languages), and the Common European Framework of Reference (Council of Europe). All promote the learning of language to foster greater understanding of community and culture.

- providing opportunities for collaborative work and interaction;

- creating a classroom environment that fosters and supports learning;

- using a final task as a goal of the learning.

The following instructional approaches to authentic and interactive second-language learning are explored in this chapter:

- Project-Based Pedagogy

- Total Physical Response

- Differentiated Instruction

- Constructivist-Based Pedagogies

Providing the appropriate supports for a variety of different types of learning experiences enhances the delivery of sound FSL programming.

Project-Based Pedagogy

Project-based pedagogy (PBP) allows students to develop language skills by proposing a collaborative project. The project is usually connected with the school community or the larger community, and highlights real-world issues and skills and, if possible, involvement from other community members (other school staff, parents, community members with skills relevant to the project). A project-based approach emphasizes the process of learning rather than the final task.

In project-based pedagogy, students play an integral role in deciding what type of project they wish to undertake. Critical thinking skills, discussing, brainstorming, and negotiating are all part of the process of learning in PBP.

There are four phases in PBP:

1. In the **global phase**, students express preferences and interests, in consultation with the teacher, if necessary.

2. In the **analytical phase**, students research the topic of their project.

3. In the **synthesis phase**, students categorize, summarize, and arrive at a new interpretation or presentation of their project research.

4. In the **communication and action phase**, students present their project in the format of their choosing.

(Francoeur-Bellavance, in Howden and Kopiec, 2002)

In the L2 context, this pedagogy presents challenges as learners do not always have the necessary vocabulary and experience to negotiate or even consider alternatives. However, careful and meaningful scaffolding can allow this type of PBP to happen successfully.

Project-based pedagogy incorporates

- curricular content (e.g., specific communicative goals, development of skills such as problem solving, cultural goals);

- cross-curricular links (e.g., to language arts, social studies, multimedia);

- student involvement and responsibility for choosing a project, planning, budgeting, and assigning group responsibility;

- real-world connection (in the school, larger community, other school staff or students, people outside the school);

- ongoing assessment and conferencing among group members and with teachers.

Some examples of project-based pedagogy projects could be

- developing a school website or newsletter;

- connecting with Francophone communities in Canada or abroad, as part of a cultural or social studies unit of learning;

- fundraising for a community or school cause (e.g., raising money for French-language library resources);

- mounting and presenting a play for the school community;

- hosting a school café, or a Francophone-related festival (e.g., Mardi Gras);

- creating a school or community garden.

Principles of project-based pedagogy include

- empowering students to make choices;

- emphasizing collaboration and collaborative projects with action-oriented results for the school community or larger community;

- involving real-world skills and connections to the larger community within the school or outside;

- assessing with emphasis on the quality of student participation rather than on the quality of the end product.

What I Am Thinking Now

- Which topics have you used successfully for project work with your students? In what ways are these topics related to those your students encounter in other classes?

- What strategies did you use to guide your students in developing a collaborative project? What strategies have you found effective in streamlining project work with your students?

- Which parts of the project do you think were most effective for the students? What did you learn about the students' use of French as they participated in the project?

- What changes would you make in developing another project with your students?

Total Physical Response

In the Total Physical Response (TPR) approach, students are encouraged to demonstrate understanding through movement. Developed by James Asher in 1977, TPR was used initially in ESL instruction, but the method has proven to be effective in language learning of all kinds. In its simplest form, the TPR approach involves a physical response to a specific request, such as "stand up," "sit down," and "clap your hands." TPR is most effective with beginning language learners who are at the pre-production phase of language acquisition and are not yet able to verbalize. A TPR approach is an effective way for you to monitor student comprehension. Students can nod "yes" or "no" and can point to information. If the learner is not doing the designated response or movement, you can provide immediate support.

TPR is effective because it connects an external stimulus—an action—with an internal stimulus—the site in the brain where a particular item of knowledge is stored (Markowitz and Jenson, 1999). Invite students to think of actions to accompany the expressions. For example, point to yourself for *je*, point to a boy for *il*, cup your ear for *écoute*, etc. Or try the following ideas:

- Call out a verb and have students respond by miming the action.

- Play charades. Write a phrase on a card (so that the class cannot see it) and have a volunteer act out the phrase as the class tries to guess the meaning.

- Incorporate simple movement songs such as *Tête, épaules, genoux, orteils.*

- Incorporate games like *Simon dit*, or games where students have to mimic a series of actions.

TPR activities work well as transitions between activities or as warm-ups to motivate and focus students. Adding movement increases stimulation and motivation and adds novelty to your activities. This active engagement in the learning process is well received by learners.

The principles of TPR include

- involving students in movement;

- associating actions with corresponding words.

Teacher Tip

Many games can be adapted to reflect TPR principles. The following are easy-to-use and brief examples that could be incorporated as warm-ups to access prior knowledge or as fun ways of reinforcing previously learned vocabulary and structures.

Identify the ...: Divide students into small groups. Distribute illustrations or flashcards that show previously taught concepts or vocabulary (e.g., actions, emotions, objects, places, etc.). Comment on what the illustrations show and have students point to the cards that match your verbal descriptions. *Indiquez la personne qui fait du vélo, Indiquez la personne qui a peur*, etc. This is a low-risk activity, as students will have time in their groups to verify their choices with one another.

Bouncing the Ball: Concepts such as numbers, days of the week, and months of the year are reinforced by having students perform an action (e.g., bouncing a ball) at the same time as they use or hear it. (Richard-Amato, 2003) For example, each one of twelve students in a circle represents a month of the year. The « *mars* » student is directed to bounce the ball and call out « *mars, juin* ». The student who is « *juin* » has to catch the ball before it bounces a second time. Conscious attention is centred on the act of catching the ball while the language itself is being internalized at a more or less peripheral level of consciousness. You might want to have students experience this activity outdoors or in the gymnasium.

Information Gap Activities: In an Information Gap activity, only one or some students have information that other students must then find out. For example, organize students into partners or small groups and have one partner or some group members perform an action (make, build, or draw something, rearrange classroom objects, etc.), making sure that the partner or other students cannot see what is going on (by having them face the opposite direction, by leaving the space or room, or by using a screen to block the view of the other group's or partner's actions). Then the partner or group members who have performed the actions give directions to the group members who did not see what was done so that they can perform the same actions.

Miming Actions: Ask students to act out emotions when you read aloud sentences, for example:

· *J'ai gagné à la loterie ! (la surprise)*

· *J'adore mon chat ! (l'amour)*

· *Youpi ! Les vacances commencent ! (l'enthousiasme)*

· *Je ne veux pas arrêter de jouer. (la tristesse ou la colère)*

· *Chut ! J'entends un bruit… Qui est là ? (la peur)*

· *Un cadeau pour moi ? Pour ma fête ? Merci beaucoup ! (le bonheur)*

What I Am Thinking Now

· To what extent do you use TPR activities to support direct instruction of vocabulary? to make transitions between lesson parts? to motivate and engage students?

· How do you assist students who might be somewhat hesitant to participate in TPR activities?

· At what point in your students' learning do you think it is appropriate to begin to reduce the frequency of TPR activities?

Differentiated Instruction

The key idea behind differentiated instruction (DI) is that students are individuals and they have individual needs as learners. Each student learns at a different pace and in a different way. The teacher's role is to plan a variety of different learning opportunities, to organize students in flexible grouping arrangements, and to use time in a flexible way.

Differentiation can occur for content, process, and product in a second-language context. Providing choices, considering multiple intelligences, and focusing learning on students' readiness are all appropriate and recommended.

Before you can determine what types of DI might work best for your students, it will be necessary to assess their stage of development, and, if possible, identify their learning profiles.

Certain types of differentiation are most appropriate for the second-language classroom. "Considering the primary importance of developing the students' ability to interact with others using their second language, the FSL context does not lend itself easily to more independent styles of differentiation such as learning contracts. Tasks involving roles where each student has a contribution to make and where the contribution of each is needed and valued are very appropriate." (Cogswell and Kristmanson, 2007)

A more detailed explanation of strategies to differentiate instruction is provided in Chapter 4.

Three Ways of Differentiating Instruction		
Content	**Process**	**Product**
Use a variety of different instructional techniques, of varying levels of complexity	Extend topics of interest	Use graduated projects
Use a variety of resources, in different formats (print, audio, video, etc.)	Allow optional studies, topics, tangents	Allow individual learning
Use questions and activities based on Bloom's Taxonomy	Use activity centres	Tasks based on multiple intelligences and different learner preferences
Activities graduated by level, degree of challenge	Use literature circles	Different presentation methods
Model activities	Vary teacher materials (blackline masters, audio resources, songs)	Products in different genres or formats (oral presentations, written, illustrated, multimedia)

Effective Instructional Planning **55**

Three Ways of Differentiating Instruction		
Content	**Process**	**Product**
Allow guided practice	Use a variety of delivery formats (audio, DVD, SMART Board)	Group discussions
Vary the content	Base tasks on multiple intelligences and learner preferences	
	Group or individual work	
Variety of resources Following Bloom's Taxonomy Graduated activities Modelling activity Guided practice Varied content	Extending topics of interest Optional studies Activity centres Literature circles Varied teacher materials Varied formats for delivery (audio, DVD, SMART Board) Tasks based on multiple intelligences and learner preferences Group or individual work	Graduated projects Individual learning Tasks based on multiple intelligences and different learner preferences Projects in different genres and formats Different presentation methods Group discussions

Teaching Strategies		
Discussion	Oral presentation	Conferencing
Collaborative learning	Group work	Note taking
Role-play	Pair work	Demonstrating
Debate	Brainstorming	Modelling

DI principles include

- assessing and adjusting instructional practices on an ongoing basis;

- ensuring that work is respectful;

- using flexible grouping;

- encouraging risk-taking;

- providing opportunities for collaborative and co-operative learning.

Co-operative Learning Techniques

Co-operative learning focuses on grouping strategies that support the principles of differentiated instruction. In small groups, students use a variety of learning activities to improve their understanding of a subject. Helping students develop these skills contributes to positive and productive group interaction. Research has shown that co-operative learning techniques optimize student retention and enhance student satisfaction during the learning experience. These techniques help students develop important social skills while improving their self-esteem.

In a co-operative group, each member is responsible not only for his or her own learning but also for the learning of all the group members. In this way, all members are accountable, involved, and learning, thus creating an atmosphere of success and achievement. This sense of positive interdependence among group members confirms and validates everyone's unique contribution and enables students to move forward together from receiving knowledge to generating knowledge. Strategies that elicit cooperation are key to creating a community of learners.

Carefully structured teacher and student talk is central to creating a classroom environment that fosters communication and enables learners to use French for a variety of purposes. Incorporating flexible groupings and co-operative learning strategies will provide a first step in this process.

Co-operative learning provides the time for teachers to observe and get to know their learners' interests and strengths. In this process, students are taught to self-talk and self-reflect and generate meaningful questions and statements. Teachers respond to student responses in a way that shapes the talk around successful learning and performance. To continue to stretch and challenge students in this process of discovery and make connections, interactive and co-operative activities are recommended for a communicative classroom.

An important daily routine involves working with a partner or in a small group. Language is social. Time needs to be allotted in every language class for students to interact with one another.

Co-operative learning is a type of grouping strategy that increases student achievement. Johnson and Johnson (1999) identified three types of co-operative learning groups: informal, formal, and base groups. The informal group is formed for a specific purpose and for a relatively short period of time. Examples of how informal co-operative grouping could be used in the FSL class include: turning to a neighbour in class to play a quick card game to reinforce new vocabulary/structures; working with a partner to review a homework assignment prior to discussing it in class, and a think-pair-share (Kagan prefers a timed think-pair-share) at the end of class about what was important and why. Formal groups are naturally more structured and last longer than the informal groups. An example of how formal groups can work in the FSL class is by forming groups to collaborate on a final project. Base groups or home groups are long-term groups, perhaps lasting for a semester or even a whole year. These groups are formed to allow students to give long-term support to one another. In the FSL class, students could meet briefly in their base groups to monitor/review homework assignments or at the end of the class to see that everyone has what they need to review for a test. Base grouping has been shown to increase students' general sense of belonging.

Co-operative learning activities are only effective when part of a well-devised lesson plan or unit of study.

Effective co-operative grouping means more than simply asking students to work together. According to Johnson and Johnson (1999), there are five basic components for an effective co-operative activity:

- positive interdependence

- group processing

- appropriate use of social skills

- face-to-face promotive interaction

- individual and group accountability

In a second-language class-setting, each member must have a specific role like *l'animateur ou l'animatrice, l'analyste,* etc. (See

BLMs 2.1 and 2.2. Each group can have more than one student assigned a role as necessary.) Initially the teacher can assign these roles, but once students are familiar with the routine, they can be involved in assigning different roles within their groups.

See Section 2, Literacy Development Strategies for specific co-operative learning activities that can be incorporated into unit and lesson plans.

Learners need to clearly understand the social skills necessary to perform effectively in a group. Both teacher and student should monitor individual, group, and self as to demonstrate social skills, proper use of strategies, and promotive interaction. Students need frequent opportunities to peer- and self-assess on specific skills and teachers need to build in reflective time to review and reassess their instructional practice. Effective co-operative grouping requires thorough planning.

What I Am Thinking Now

- What factors do you take into consideration when organizing your students into groups?

- To what extent and for what purposes do you use informal groups? formal groups? base groups?

- What strategies do you use to help your students understand what is required of them to function successfully in a group?

Constructivist-Based Pedagogies

Constructivism is a theory that asserts that individuals construct their own personal understanding of the world. In a constructivist classroom, students are encouraged to engage in a discovery-based approach to learning. They are encouraged to participate actively in the learning experience by learning through doing. The role of the teacher is to help students to learn how to learn.

Constructivism emphasizes the learner's background, needs, and interests. It also places responsibility for learning on the learner. Students do not passively receive knowledge from teachers, but should be engaged independently and with each other in constructing meaning. Constructivist theory also stresses the role of motivation in learning. Learners must be challenged to learn actively, but it is crucial that they experience success in their efforts to learn by doing. Learners must have confidence in their own abilities to learn.

In the constructivist classroom, building on the student's prior knowledge is essential. In the L2 classroom, students will most likely have developed first-language literacy skills upon which they can draw as part of their learning background. Most pre-activities in a second-language constructivist classroom should connect with students' prior experiences.

In the constructivist classroom, the role of the teacher is to guide and facilitate instruction rather than lead it. Typically, teachers using constructivist-based pedagogies ask questions rather than provide answers. They also provide scaffolding as needed, and ask thought-provoking questions to help steer the learning process as necessary.

Learning in a constructivist environment will encourage the development of many skills: collaboration, peer interaction, reflection, and problem solving. This approach aims to create a stimulating learning environment where learners are actively engaged in their development of knowledge and understanding.

The constructivist approach is often used across disciplines to help students find solutions to problems specific to that discipline. In science, students might be invited to propose a hypothesis and conduct experiments to verify their hypothesis. In social studies, students interested in understanding the implications of building the Canadian national railway might actively seek information that will allow them to draw conclusions to the query.

In the L2 classroom, simple problems to be solved might include

- having students infer grammatical and language convention structures from examples or from texts;

- inviting them to think of alternative endings to fictional stories they are reading; to historical events involving Francophones;

- inviting them to find real-world solutions to school problems (e.g., by creating rules of conduct and justifying them; by proposing classroom rules; by suggesting new procedures for school routines such as assemblies, library privileges, and using the computer lab.).

Constructivist principles include

- Using a student-centred approach

- Grounding instructional activities on learners' prior experiences and knowledge

- Having students learn by doing

- Providing opportunities for collaborative work and interaction

- Basing learning and activities on real-world applications

What I Am Thinking Now

· Interaction and collaboration are characteristics of constructivist-based pedagogy.

· What limitations have you had to overcome in using a constructivist approach in your class? How have you addressed these limitations?

· How do you organize instruction so that all your students—no matter what their level of proficiency in French—can contribute to the activities?

Principles of Instructional Planning

When you plan instruction, keep in mind these overarching considerations that address learning goals and their relevance to the students' current situation.

Key to Success

Planning instruction with both short-term and long-term goals in mind—today's lessons are the foundations for future success.

Integrating the Four Skill Areas

Plan instruction with a view to integrate all four skill areas: listening, speaking, reading, and writing. Oral communication should be the focus of L2 learning, but all strands must be practised for successful learning. Make sure that all learning has a solid oral basis, during which students hear and say what was just learned many times, with you, as a class, and with a partner or in groups.

Oral Participation

Encourage students to take responsibility for their daily oral participation. Consider criteria for daily oral participation that are both age appropriate and appropriate for the language-learning stage of your students. Discuss the criteria with the class, and then establish no more than five criteria for oral participation.

Active listening is an important language-learning strategy. If students are actively listening, they are comparing and contrasting what they are hearing to what they already know, and they are linking this new information to their own experience.

Metacognition

Teach students how to set goals and how to reflect and assess evidence of skills on an ongoing basis. Encourage students to reflect on their goals, to think about what they might do better next time, to write down what was most important, and to share with a partner their thoughts on how what they have learned fits into what they already know and their own experiences.

Teach students to manage their own learning processes by helping them to form precise goals that relate to how they will spend their time during class. The other side of setting goals at the beginning of class is reflecting on them at the end of class. Model what this reflection would look like. Always include thinking about the next time, «*pour la prochaine fois*» in the reflection time. Asking students to reflect on questions they might have stemming from the lesson can also be part of the reflection process.

Teach students how to reflect on how their new learning connects with prior knowledge and personal experiences. Encourage students to think of connections to previous learning in the L2 class and in other subject areas as well. This relates not only to content, but to learning new skills and strategies.

Language-Learning Strategies

Explicitly teach students how to use strategies to access prior knowledge; for example, identifying cognates and familiar vocabulary; making inferences or predictions by skimming text and examining titles, captions, and visuals; thinking of relevant personal experiences.

Explicitly teach language-learning strategies.

Teach students to monitor their learning during an activity or task, for example, by asking themselves such questions as

- Do I have a purpose for doing the activity? *Est-ce que je sais pourquoi je fais cette activité?*

- Can I identify the idea? *Est-ce que je peux identifier l'idée?*

- Do I understand the activity (listening, speaking, reading, or writing)? *Est-ce que je comprends l'activité (écouter, parler, lire, ou écrire)?*

- If I do not understand, can I identify what elements are causing difficulty for me? *Si je ne comprends pas, est-ce que je peux identifier les éléments qui sont difficiles à comprendre?*

- Are my predictions correct? *Est-ce que mes prédictions sont exactes?*

- Which strategies did I use during the activity? Were they helpful? *Quelles stratégies est-ce que j'ai utilisées pendant cette activité? Est-ce qu'elles m'ont aidé/e?*

- Which strategies would I use next time? *Quelles stratégies est-ce que je vais utiliser la prochaine fois?*

- Are there resources in the classroom that I can use to help me (e.g., dictionaries, posters, reference books, asking my teacher or my classmates for help)? *Est-ce qu'il y a des ressources dans la classe qui peuvent m'aider (p. ex. des dictionnaires, des affiches, des livres de référence, demander de l'aide à mon prof ou à mes camarades de classe)?*

See Chapters 6–9 for more information on language-learning strategies.

Higher-Level Thinking

Provide classroom activities that emphasize reasoning, decision making, and expressing opinions. Teach students how to develop the skills to formulate, discuss, and solve problems together.

See Chapter 3 for further information on developing higher-order thinking by incorporating the principles of the revised Bloom's Taxonomy in L2 settings.

Student Choice

Allow for choice in activities as often as possible in order to accommodate the different learning styles and preferences of your students. For example, provide a variety of activities that are appropriate for verbal/linguistic learners; for kinesthetic learners; for logical/analytical learners, etc. Wherever possible, allow students to complete tasks or projects in a format that makes the most of their strengths as learners. At the heart of this principle is understanding how your students learn and providing them with tasks that allow them to succeed.

Collaboration and Interaction

Provide learning experiences that are socially interactive. Oral communication with a partner and in groups is key in the L2 classroom. Vary student groupings: partner, small groups, whole class, jigsaw groupings; and vary group makeup (depending on student personalities, abilities, and the task).

Feedback and Scaffolding

Give meaningful and relevant feedback to support learning and provide scaffolded support as needed.

Teacher Tip

Reflect on your key considerations in planning instruction in the L2 classroom. For example, what are your key considerations regarding

- students' language level and interests;
- communicative purpose;
- curriculum requirements;
- theme and format;
- classroom interaction?

Students' Language Level and Interests
Where, in the three stages of language development, are your students?

1. Beginners at the pre-production stage cannot yet speak but can understand simple sentences and words with visual prompts and gestures, and can nod yes or no.

2. Intermediate beginners at the early production stage can understand and produce simple statements or speech fragments with familiar words and structures.

3. Late beginners at the speech emergence stage can communicate in sentences; have increased comprehension; and can take part in scaffolded discussion and conversation. (Krashen, Terrell, 1983)
   - Have you chosen goals that are age appropriate and that students are ready to undertake?
   - What are the appropriate skills for students at this level?
   - What are your students' interests?

Communicative Purpose
- What is the communicative purpose of the learning?
- What should students be able to say or understand during listening?
- What should students be able to read or write?
- How is the vocabulary to be incorporated and spiralled throughout?

- How are the language structures to be introduced, re-introduced, and practised in context?

Curriculum Requirements

- What are the curriculum requirements?
- Are there cross-curricular connections?
- What are the key concepts of the new learning, e.g., language-learning skills, curricular, cross-curricular, thematic, higher-level thinking skills, language structures?
- What are the key language elements, e.g., vocabulary, language structures, and conventions?

What is the theme or topic?

- What are the genres or formats most suited to that theme or topic?
- What supplementary and secondary resources would be ideal?

Are there opportunities for classroom interaction: individual, partner, group, and whole-class work?

- What opportunities are there for work in each strand (listening, speaking, reading, and writing)?
- What opportunities are there for homework as practice and as application?
- What opportunities are there for activities for different learning styles and preferences, e.g., auditory, verbal/linguistic, analytical/logical, kinesthetic, musical, analytical, practical, and creative?

Using Backward Design Principles

In order to determine the educational path of your L2 students, it is important to identify the end result. This means knowing what the goal of lesson planning will be, a process called backward design. Backward design encourages the idea of starting with the end in mind, sharing with students the goals and outcomes to be achieved and the assessment instruments to be used before undertaking a project or unit. As you begin a unit, review curriculum expectations and communicate the unit's "desired results" to students. Identify what students should **know**, **understand**, and be able to **do** as a result of their learning (identify the K.U.D.). Do this within the context of student and teacher goals, learning profiles, and interests.

Provide a clear description of the final task that students are expected to complete. In this initial period, discuss with students the various forms of assessment included in the unit.

Before planning instruction, consider planning from three perspectives: curriculum, assessment, and instruction. Ask yourself the following three questions:

K.U.D.
When applying the principles of backward design to planning your year, unit, and lessons, make sure to identify what your students should KNOW, what you want them to UNDERSTAND, and what you want them to DO following the period of learning.

Effective Instructional Planning

1. What are the curriculum requirements? What do I expect students to know and be able to do at the end of this unit, term, or year?

2. How will I assess? How will I determine whether they have learned these things?

3. What instructional means and format will be most effective in enabling students to demonstrate they have learned these things?

(Cooper, 2007)

When you are determining how students will demonstrate that they have understood what they have learned, consider whether or not students

- can explain it;

- can interpret it;

- can apply it;

- have a perspective about it;

- can empathize with it;

- have gained self-knowledge because of it.

(Wiggins and McTighe, 2000)

These six facets of understanding are emphasized at each stage of the design process. However, they are of critical importance at the stage of determining evidence for assessment. Wiggins and McTighe emphasize that before planning learning experiences, teachers must first determine their choice and range of assessments. Although the emphasis is on developing performance tasks, they promote a balanced use of assessment tools to help students develop and demonstrate understanding. (Wiggins and McTighe, 2000)

CASE STUDY	Planning a Unit of Study

Mme Comeau is preparing some lessons on shopping. This is a popular topic with her Grade 6 Core FSL students, many of whom have allowances or have begun to make money through babysitting and performing tasks and chores at home. Like all Grade 6 students, Mme Comeau's students are interested in fashion, accessories, and electronic equipment such as cellphones, computers, and video games.

Mme Comeau is proposing a series of lessons in which students will pick an item that interests them (clothing, electronic) and decide to buy it. Students will consider and discuss which item they wish to buy, why, their budget, and how they will earn the money to buy it. Students will describe their purchases or desired items to each other, explaining why they want or need that item. The theme will involve numbers; how to use persuasive language; how to use descriptive language (to describe the item); and how to ask questions of a sales person.

Communicative Goals

Listening: to listen to conversations about making purchases, and radio and TV ads for purchases

Speaking: to explain a shopping budget, to persuade a parent to agree to one big-ticket item; to ask a sales person questions about the item

Reading: to read and understand main ideas from ads for items to be bought, and product websites

Writing: send brief messages to explain purchases; to arrange to meet friends at the mall

---

What I Am Thinking Now

Refer to the Case Study: Planning a Unit of Study.

· How do Mme Comeau's ideas reflect keys to successful instructional planning?

· What types of assessments would you pair with a unit of study similar to Mme Comeau's?

In your own planning of units of study, what factors have been present in your most successful units? (See BLMs 2.3, 2.4, and 2.5 for unit-planning templates.)

Using Marzano's Nine Strategies for Planning

Robert Marzano and colleagues investigated the research on the most effective teaching strategies. They found nine strategies that were most effective in promoting student success and that could be used as the foundation of instructional planning. The strategies are listed below.

1. Identify similarities and differences.

2. Summarize and make notes.

3. Recognize and reinforce students' efforts.

4. Do meaningful homework.

5. Use ways other than language to extend students' learning.

6. Work co-operatively with groups and partners.

7. Set goals.

8. Make and test hypotheses.

9. Use cues, questions, and organizers to identify prior knowledge.

Strategy	How to Apply the Strategy
1. Identify similarities and differences.	• Use graphic organizers (e.g., Venn diagrams, charts). • Have students compare and classify. • Have students create similes (A is like B) or metaphors. • Ask questions in group discussions to help students identify similarities. As an extension, ask questions to consider the reasons for similarities or differences.
2. Summarize and make notes.	• Create procedures or templates to help students learn the necessary steps for taking notes and summarizing (e.g., deciding what is important, deleting or not including material, making substitutions, etc.).
3. Recognize and reinforce students' efforts.	• When students achieve goals, stay on task, or perform well, give specific praise. • Personalize praise (through a reward system, through comments or stickers on work). • Pause when a student is having trouble, offer help, and then praise when the task or answer is successfully completed. • Encourage students to develop metacognitive strategies (reflecting on what worked and what did not; next steps).

Strategy	How to Apply the Strategy
4. Do meaningful homework.	• Assign homework that allows for practice, review, and application. • Establish clear procedures for homework (e.g., deadlines, research requirements, etc.). • Explain the purpose of the homework (e.g., for practice or to prepare for upcoming work).
5. Use ways other than language to extend students' learning.	• Encourage students to use mental images as aids to learning (e.g., visualization, illustrations, symbols). • Encourage students to create pictorial ways for representing their learning (symbols, icons, emoticons, graphics). • Invite students to act out words, sentences, and stories.
6. Work co-operatively with groups and partners.	• Vary group size and membership as necessary. • Incorporate a group-work step in class work or in projects (e.g., have students access prior knowledge as a group; have students summarize findings, draw conclusions, and make recommendations, in groups).
7. Set goals. Provide feedback on how students have attained those goals.	• Introduce the overarching goals (of a unit of learning, a lesson, text, listening or viewing activity on audio CD or DVD) and encourage students to find ways of creating their own personal goals. Invite students to ask K.U.D. questions such as: What do I want to know or find out? • Use entrance passes as aids for goal-setting. • Vary the way in which you provide feedback on goal achievement, on areas of improvement, on class work, homework, projects, and presentations.
8. Make and test hypotheses.	• Encourage students to make predictions about reading, listening, and viewing activities, and then monitor their predictions during the activity, and verify them afterward (and make changes or corrections).
9. Use cues, questions, and organizers.	• Use cues, questions, and graphic organizers to elicit students' prior knowledge. • Vary the way in which the cues are presented (e.g., skim text, show illustrations or photos from a text or DVD, discuss the cover, title, captions, etc.). • Model reacting to cues by doing a think-aloud before reading, listening, or viewing. • Allow students time to think after you have asked a question. • Use entrance passes as aids for accessing prior knowledge.

Summary

Effective instructional planning is the key to a classroom that offers students a variety of learning experiences that keep them engaged, interested, and motivated. Just as important, such planning is the means through which teachers sustain their creativity and motivation as they work with students whose learning needs might differ widely.

FSL instruction is centred on the communicative-experiential approach. This approach is characterized by a range of activities designed not only to build students' capacity to communicate in French, but also to develop their ability to use familiar learning strategies to support acquisition of French. The challenge for teachers in planning FSL instruction is to strike a balance between authentic communication activities and strategy instruction. Many of the strategies described in this chapter are also used in L1 classes; consequently, FSL teachers can help their students see how what they have learned in English language arts can be used to support their learning in French. Effective instructional planning for FSL classes takes these factors into account: students' language level, interests, and experiences; the communicative purposes of individual lessons; and established routines that provide for interactions through listening, speaking, reading, and writing.

My Choices

Effective instructional planning takes into account several factors:

1. the learner's background (educational, cultural, stage of language development);

2. the learners' needs, interests, and preferences;

3. varied instructional approaches that accommodate learners' needs and interests.

   - Of the instructional approaches described in this chapter, which one(s) have you used? How would you rate your success in implementing the approaches? What worked well? What would you like to change?

   - What factors in your school setting influence the extent to which you can effectively implement approaches that foster student interaction and collaboration? What do you think can be done to deal with these factors?

   - In which approaches do you think your students experienced the greatest success? What factors contributed to their success?

Les rôles du groupe

L'animateur / l'animatrice

Objectif :

Aide le groupe à avoir une idée générale du sujet et à la partager.

Tâches à compléter :

- Dresse une liste de questions et d'idées;
- Encourage;
- Écoute attentivement;
- Fais le reportage oral.

Expressions à utiliser durant le travail du groupe :

- Qui a des suggestions ?
- Bonne idée. Est-ce qu'il y en a d'autres ?
- C'est à ton tour …
- Je ne comprends pas. Peux-tu répéter, s'il te plaît ?
- À notre avis, …
- Notre groupe a déterminé …

Le magicien / la magicienne des mots

Objectif :

Recherche les mots nouveaux, les mots intéressants, et fournis la définition. Repère les points spécialement importants.

Tâches à compléter :

- Écoute attentivement;
- Encourage;
- Partage la définition du mot trouvé;
- Écris les mots et expressions utiles.

Expressions à utiliser durant le travail du groupe :

- C'est un bon mot.
- Veux-tu que j'écrive ce mot ?
- Bravo, nous avons trouvé de bonnes idées et des mots-clés pour les exprimer.

Les rôles du groupe (suite)

L'analyste

Objectif :

Trouve les liens entre le sujet et le monde extérieur.

Tâches à compléter :

- Lis les directives
- Encourage
- Écoute attentivement
- Cherche des liens entre le sujet et ce qui se passe à l'école, dans la communauté, etc.

Expressions à utiliser durant le travail du groupe :

- Est-ce que tu peux clarifier ton idée ?
- Oui, c'est un lien clair.
- Ah, je comprends ce que tu veux dire.

Le synthétiser

Objectif :

Responsable de la récapitulation et de formuler un bref résumé.

Tâches à compléter :

- Écoute attentivement
- Encourage
- Parle aux membres des autres groupes
- Fais la récapitulation à l'écrit des points essentiels de la discussion et des points essentiels à retenir

Expressions à utiliser durant le travail du groupe :

- Veux-tu que j'inclus ça dans le résumé ?
- Je ne comprends pas. Répète-le.
- Oui, je vais l'écrire. Bonne idée.
- Qu'est-ce que vous pensez du sujet ?
- Mon groupe a les mêmes idées.
- Mon groupe n'est pas d'accord.

Unit Curriculum and Assessment Plan

Unit/Strand:

Big Ideas and Essential Skills:

Focus for Learning:

Title/Description of Culminating Task:

Enabling and/or Other Assessment Tasks

	Title:	
Learning Habits:	Diagnostic/Formative	Write/Do/Say	Curriculum Outcomes/Content Standards:

| **Learning Habits:** | **Title:** Diagnostic/Formative | Write/Do/Say | Curriculum Outcomes/Content Standards: |

| **Learning Habits:** | **Title:** Diagnostic/Formative | Write/Do/Say | Curriculum Outcomes/Content Standards: |

| **Learning Habits:** | **Title:** Diagnostic/Formative | Write/Do/Say | Curriculum Outcomes/Content Standards: |

Unit Culminating Assessment Task Plan

Assessment Task Title:

Unit:

Description of Task:

Curriculum Outcomes/Content Standards:

Big Ideas:

Essential Skills:

Student Products and Processes

Assessment Strategy 1:

Assessment Strategy 2:

Assessment Strategy 3:

Assessment Tool:

Assessment Tool:

Assessment Tool:

Assessment Criteria:

Assessment Criteria:

Assessment Criteria:

Resources/Technology Integration:

Accommodations/Modifications:

Cross-Curricular Integration:

Unit Instruction Plan/Lesson Sequence

Unit:	Focus for Learning:									
Introduction										
Lesson 2:										
Lesson 3:										
Lesson 4:										
Lesson 5:										
Lesson 6:										
Lesson 7:										
Lesson 8:										
Culminating Task										

Chapter 3

Teaching the Learning Brain

"The brain is intimately involved and connected with everything that educators and students do at school. Any disconnect is a recipe for frustration and potential disaster. Brain-based education is best understood in three words: engagement, strategies, and principles derived from an understanding of the brain."
—Eric P. Jensen

My Thoughts

- What have you heard about brain research and its implications for education? How have you reacted to this information—acceptance? scepticism? Why have you reacted in this manner?

- In what ways do you think about "engagement" and "strategies" as you plan your FSL classes?

In this chapter, we will discuss:

- How the Brain Learns

- Five Principles of Brain-Based Learning

  ° Principle 1: Each Brain Is Unique

  ° Principle 2: Emotions Impact Learning

  ° Principle 3: Time for Processing New Learning

  ° Principle 4: Time for Reflection

  ° Principle 5: Developing Higher-Order Thinking Skills

Brain research helps us understand how we learn. It used to be believed that the brain was more or less wired by adulthood, but we now know that the brain changes and adapts throughout life. Brain research has shown that learning is a continuous process as the brain

For a more in-depth overview of brain physiology, see the From the Research section on pp. 80–81 of this chapter.

adapts and changes in response to environmental stimuli. The brain's capacity to adapt to its environment is called plasticity.

How can brain research help us in the second-language classroom? Brain research shines new light on current FSL instructional practices, clarifying why these approaches work and suggesting ways for making them even more effective. In this chapter, you will learn what brain research has to say about the importance of a welcoming yet stimulating environment; of repetition and practice; and of varying instructional approaches, activities, and tasks to provide variety, stimulation, and challenge.

How the Brain Learns

Throughout our lives, our brain continues to make connections among cells. We take data in through our senses, store that data in the appropriate brain regions, and later, when we retrieve it, we reactivate and thus strengthen the neural connections where it is stored, making it easier to re-access the input the next time. The human brain has a remarkable capacity for finding connections and making patterns from all kinds of different data. Finding patterns is, in fact, how we construct meaning. The human brain evolved in response to the challenge of paying attention to clues from the natural world in order to survive. Early humans had to find patterns in many different types of input, all of it relevant to their immediate environments. (Lowery, 2001) They relied on prior knowledge and experience to make sense of the input. The brain that we have inherited from our evolutionary history has given us these characteristics:

- When we want to find out something, we use a variety of techniques: we explore and we use trial and error if we do not know.

- We make connections to what we already know or have experienced; we make hypotheses and predictions.

- We think about what we have observed; we gather data and make mental notes, e.g., we find similarities, we synthesize new with previously learned knowledge. (Lowery, 2001)

When we take in new information (input) through our senses, the input is stored in different brain regions. For example, visual and auditory data are stored in separate places. The brain makes connections between the cells of the various storage regions. The information is then organized according to the systems and subsystems constructed by those cellular connections.

The brain does not store information as a photographic image or as a recording; it has no play-back button. When the connections between different storage areas are activated, the brain reassembles the pieces into meaningful patterns. These reassembled patterns are the memory of the input. How well we remember the object, experience, or new information is determined by the quality of the original input.

Learning occurs when new brain connections are formed. Brain connections are more likely to be created in enriched learning environments with varied experiences and stimuli. These new connections are not necessarily permanent. In order to become part of the permanent storage system, they have to be re-activated on a regular basis through repetition, practice, rehearsal, review, and reflection. (Lowery, 2001)

Key to Success

Knowing that students' intellectual and emotional development influence the ways in which they participate in learning activities

Figure 3.1: New brain connections can only become part of the permanent storage system through regular repetition, practice, rehearsal, review, and reflection.

Brain research gives us a new understanding of how to think about intelligence: people who have "well-connected" brains can more readily solve problems, adapt to new situations, and learn new information and skills.

Making Sense of the Environment

Learning how the brain finds patterns in input and thus creates connections can shed light on how students make sense of and create meaning from their school and extracurricular experience. How today's students create meaning is in some ways very different from how previous generations of students did. In the past, learning meant that students had to master content knowledge in order to reproduce it on written tests. They were not encouraged to be responsible for their own learning. Now educational theories stress teaching students how to learn in order to adapt to the larger world rather than for the final test.

We can align what we know of how education has changed with what the findings of current brain research tell us by considering the following insights.

- Enriched environments (novelty, stimulation) are crucial.

- Learning must be connected to other subjects and areas of thought; it must be capable of being attached to some previous neural connection.

- Learning must be relevant and meaningful.

How Has Education Changed?			
Learning must be...	· novel, enriched	· connected	· relevant
Students must...	· adapt to and use new technologies	· learn how to use metacognitive strategies	· learn relevant content and real-life skills
Teachers must...	· use more integrated approaches to curricula	· help students learn how to learn	· teach to a community of learners

From the Research
The following is a brief and simplified overview of brain physiology: In the 1960s neuroscientist Paul MacLean hypothesized that the human brain evolved as three brains in one. He called this model of brain evolution the Triune Brain Theory. The three brain areas are the reptilian system, the limbic system, and the cerebral cortex. Each brain area is specialized by function to some degree, but all are interdependent.

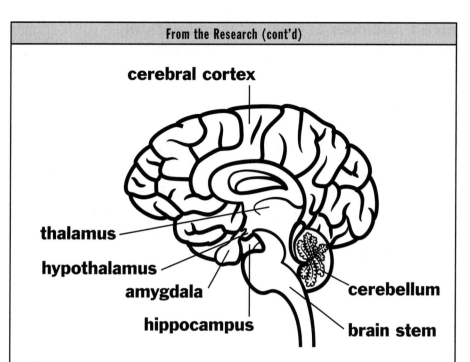

cerebral cortex

thalamus

hypothalamus

amygdala

hippocampus

cerebellum

brain stem

Figure 3.2: Cross-section of the human brain

The reptilian brain, the lowest and oldest region of the brain, consists of the brain stem and the cerebellum. This region is associated with movement, digestion, reproduction, breathing, and the fight-or-flight response.

The limbic system is the second brain or region to evolve. The limbic system includes the amygdala, the hypothalamus, the hippocampus, and the thalamus.

The **amygdala** directs how we associate and respond to events that stimulate feelings such as fear, pity, anger, or outrage. The amygdala can stop, calm, and assess a situation and help us respond accordingly.

In stressful situations, the **hypothalamus** stimulates the pituitary gland to release a hormone called cortisol. An increase in cortisol leads to depression, anxiety, and memory deficits. This explains why we do not learn well under stress.

The **hippocampus** converts information into memory recall or long-term memory. It selects which memories are to be stored, perhaps by attaching an emotion marker to some events to make them easier to recall. The hippocampus is the brain region responsible for new learning and new memory formation.

The **thalamus** relays information from other brain regions to the cerebral cortex. The thalamus is the brain's filing system; it is the final destination in the limbic system before the appropriate information is directed to the cerebral cortex.

The cerebral cortex, the most recent brain region to evolve, constitutes five-sixths of the human brain. It contains two specialized regions, one dedicated to voluntary movement and one to processing sensory information. The cortex allows us to see ahead and plan for the future. Higher-order thinking (judgment, reason, long-term planning) takes place here.

Five Principles of Brain-Based Learning

There are five principles that should guide how you develop your instructional practices in the second-language classroom.

> **Principle 1:** Each learner has a unique brain with a unique learning style.
>
> **Principle 2:** Learning is an interactive, social activity that is most successful in positive and supportive environments.
>
> **Principle 3:** Each learner needs time to process new learning. The learning process involves finding patterns in new input and then having many opportunities to practise in different formats.
>
> **Principle 4:** Each learner needs time to reflect on new learning.
>
> **Principle 5:** Each learner needs opportunities to develop higher-order thinking skills (e.g., learning how to think critically, synthesize, and transfer learning creatively to new contexts).

Principle 1: Each Brain is Unique

The brain is continually capable of learning when exposed to new experiences and stimuli due to brain plasticity.

Learning is not only a natural function of the brain, but it is also essential to the brain's development. We are all profoundly shaped by our personal environment and experiences. As a result, every brain is wired differently. Because the brain is more adept at some activities and has more neuron paths for those activities, the best way to improve perceived difficulties in learning is to teach to a student's strengths. Zull explains that, "information enters the brain through existing networks of neurons... so it is these existing networks, this prior knowledge, that are the substrate for constructing new understanding. We learn by attaching the new to the old. This modifies the old, sometimes beyond recognition, but we are always building on what has gone before." (Zull, 2004) Such awareness is central to instructional activities that enable students to access prior knowledge and make connections between the familiar and the new.

No two human brains are exactly alike; each student has a unique learning profile. Identifying the learning preferences of your students will help you appeal to the many different types of students in your classes, in your choice of activities and in your lesson planning. Understanding that individual students might have unique difficulties with certain concepts and differentiating your instructional practices to suit their learning styles are also part of acknowledging that each brain is unique. Current brain-based research points to the need for considering differentiated instructional strategies as a guiding set of principles in teaching.

Each individual is a unique combination of intelligences: verbal/linguistic, logical/mathematical, visual/spatial, bodily/kinesthetic, musical/rhythmic, interpersonal, intrapersonal, analytical, practical, or creative. (For more information on student profiles and preferences, multiple intelligences, and the Triarchic Theory of Intelligence, see Chapter 4.) How do your students learn best? Are there auditory or visual learners among your students?

Students also differ in when and how quickly they mature. Student age is not always the best way to judge readiness to learn. Considering a student's readiness to learn will help you plan appropriate activities. Brain research has demonstrated that students have different learning styles at different ages. What is appropriate for older elementary or secondary students might not be effective for younger elementary students and vice versa.

Although it is true that each brain is unique, there are broad similarities in brain development at different ages. Because of its plasticity, the brain changes throughout life, but it changes most dramatically up until late adolescence and early adulthood. It used to be believed that human brain wiring was complete by approximately the age of three and that the brain was mature by approximately 12. But recent brain research has shown that the brain continues to develop throughout the teen years and even into the early 20s. (Giedd, Blumenthal, Jeffries, et al, 1999)

Children's and adolescents' brains are different from adult brains in two key ways that have implications for educators.

1. The frontal lobes continue to develop throughout adolescence, but are not fully mature until early adulthood. The frontal lobes are the site of impulse control, reasoning, and long-range planning. (Giedd, Jeffries, et al, 1999)

2. Children and adolescents process emotional clues differently from adults. (National Institute of Mental Health)

To teach to student strengths, teachers need to identify
- student learning profiles and preferences;
- student readiness for learning;
- student interests, motivation, and engagement.

Teaching the Learning Brain

Although we can help students learn how to control impulsivity, make plans, and learn emotional self-control, it is important to remember that these skills are dependent on brain development, and cannot be induced—they will occur naturally in due time.

What I Am Thinking Now

- Picture the students in your class. In what ways are they alike in their learning behaviours? different in these behaviours? In which types of activities are your students most comfortable or adept?

- How does an understanding of the uniqueness of brain development help you as you plan instruction and work with your students?

Principle 2: Emotions Impact Learning

The emotion and thinking areas of the brain are connected. When learners engage in activities that are emotionally and intellectually relevant and challenging, the resulting progress becomes its own reward. Engage learners by

- emphasizing the social aspect of the learning environment;

- giving them choice;

- reducing stress;

- giving them opportunities to collaborate.

Emphasizing the Social Aspect of Learning

Brain research shows that personal relationships are vital to a healthy brain. The human brain is designed for learning in social contexts, with teachers and other students. Creating a safe environment is important so that students have positive emotions about school and so learn more effectively. Emotions can either enhance learning or inhibit it; when students feel positive about their success, they will be motivated to new heights, but if they feel threatened emotionally, learning might deteriorate or even stop.

From the Research

One of the differences between the young brain and the adult brain is the way in which children and adults process emotions. Using fMRI scans (functional magnetic resonance imagining), researchers studied brain activity in a group of young people between the ages of 11 and 17 as they were looking at photos of people with fearful faces. The scans revealed that the teens' amygdalas were activated as they looked at the photos. (The amygdala is the area where fight-or-flight and fear reactions are activated.) The youngest children in the study often misread the emotions, while the older subjects were more likely to correctly identify the expressions. By contrast, the scans of adults who viewed the same photos showed that their frontal lobes were activated. The frontal lobes are the seat of reason and judgment, which suggests that adults are better able to interpret emotional clues and are not as likely to react in fearful, instinctive ways.

(Yurgelan-Todd, 2002)

Choices can be provided to students but controlled by the teacher. For example, providing two or three ways in which to complete an assignment gives students choice, but allows the teacher to guide the choices made.

Giving Students Choice

Relevance is especially important in L2 learning. Students are rarely motivated to learn grammar and vocabulary relating to themes and topics that they would not discuss in their own lives in their first language. The National Core French Study authors recognized this reality and started the trend toward integrating opportunities for relevant communication through the domains of experience.

Wherever possible, encourage students to personalize the topics that they choose to learn about. Alternatively, students might prefer to make choices in the way that they express their understanding of the new learning, e.g., by doing an oral presentation, by writing up a report, by creating an artistic representation (an illustrated poster, big book, website), or by doing a role-play or dramatization.

Reducing Stress

Because the frontal lobes are still not fully developed in the young, students often react impulsively and fearfully to situations that adults would not find stressful. As the research on adolescent brains revealed, their fight-or-flight centres are in control of how they interpret certain kinds of body language. When we are depressed or anxious, the levels of a chemical called cortisol increase in the brain. Prolonged higher levels of cortisol have been correlated to memory deficits. When students are anxious, their ability both to take in and to retain new learning is impeded.

Many students are nervous and self-conscious about speaking aloud in French, or revealing that they have not understood an oral

Consider the stage of brain development of your students when trying to gauge their reaction to possible stressful situations. Their reaction might differ from yours due to their stage of brain development.

Teaching the Learning Brain **85**

message. Reassure them that hesitating, making mistakes, and needing time to process oral communication are necessary in order for their brains to learn and retain learning. To do this, students have to trust the teacher and their classmates not to react critically. Ensuring that students are at the appropriate level for an activity will help them feel comfortable communicating in the classroom with their classmates. In order for students to get the most out of L2 learning, they should feel accepted by the teacher and classmates.

Connecting with students emotionally from the start will engage them successfully in meaningful learning. Make time at the beginning of every school year or term for ice-breaker activities. Use students' names as soon as possible and make oral communication part of your daily routine by having them greet each other by name or introduce themselves to each other. (Students do not have to know that they are teaching you their names while they practise their conversational skills!)

Collaborating with Others

In terms of the findings from current brain research about the impact of emotions on learning, group or partner work can lead to more emotional engagement for students and therefore successful learning.

Working with a partner or in a group is also especially useful in L2 learning because it provides a strong oral communication focus for group members and partners. It also allows students to break up tasks or activities into more manageable subtasks and share the work.

To clarify group roles and responsibilities and ensure successful collaboration, either assign the roles or invite students to choose them. Depending on the task, they could be group leaders, note-takers, researchers, presenters of the group's findings, or in charge of liaising with other groups, and so on.

In the 1920s and early 1930s, Russian psychologist Lev Vygotsky advanced theories of childhood development that have profoundly influenced many educators. Vygotsky emphasized the social aspect of learning. He believed that children develop cognitively by interacting socially with adults and peers. Learning occurs through hearing, seeing, and using language with others. During the early stages of cognitive development, children depend on the help of a teacher or peer, but as they develop more experience with the new learning, they are able to use their own language to understand recently learned concepts and to direct their own learning. Vygotsky referred to this stage of learning as internalization.

He called what children can learn without support the "level of actual development" and what they learn with the help of a teacher or a more capable peer the "level of potential development." (The actual level of development is often captured by tests, but test results reveal only a point in time in the child's development, and not the child's potential for development.) Vygotsky was interested in measuring and encouraging the child's potential for growth over time.

Vygotsky tested his ideas in the classroom. He found that a group of students of the same age and ability level were able to complete the same problem-solving tasks when working independently. But when some group members received help and worked collaboratively, they were able to progress to more challenging tasks beyond the level of their classmates who were not receiving help and were still working independently.

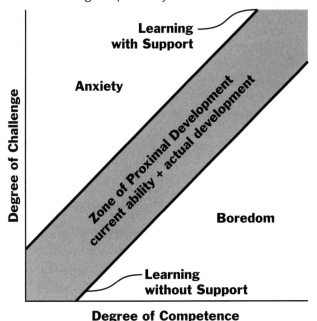

Figure 3.3: Vygotsky's Zone of Proximal Development

See Chapter 2 for information on the Gradual Release of Responsibility model.

How would you compare Vygotsky's Zone of Proximal Development to the Gradual Release of Responsibility model?

Vygotsky theorized that there is a gap between actual and potential development, which he called the "zone of proximal development" (ZPD). Later educators, influenced by the concept of a ZPD, advanced the notion that teachers and more capable peers step into this gap whenever they model learning and provide scaffolding so that students can progress from actual to potential development. Teaching students within the ZPD means having them do activities that are somewhat, but not too far beyond, their current actual development with scaffolding or in cooperation with others.

(Vygotsky, 1986)

Teacher Tip

For collaborative work to be successful, students must have a bank of group and partner language, which they should review before the task. The collaborative language will vary, depending on the grade level and type of task, but generally speaking, students will require language to talk about the following:

Materials

- *Des ciseaux, une gomme à effacer, du papier*
- *Des livres, des affiches, des publicités*
- *L'Internet, un ordinateur, etc.*

Group Roles and Responsibilities

- *Qui est ... (le reporteur, le secrétaire, le présentateur)?*
- *Qui va écrire ... prendre des notes ... présenter ... expliquer à la classe ...?*
- *Moi, je vais prendre des notes, etc.*
- *Moi, je suis le / le reporteur.*
- *C'est Jason qui va / doit ...*

Task Steps

- *Quel est le but?*
- *Quelles sont les étapes de notre ...?*
- *Est-ce que tout le monde comprend les étapes?*
- *Premièrement, on va / doit ... puis ... et enfin ...*
- *Quel est le thème / le sujet?*
- *De quoi est-ce qu'on va parler?*

Opinions

- *À mon avis ...*
- *Je suis d'accord avec ... / Je ne suis pas d'accord avec ...*
- *Je pense que ...*
- *C'est vrai, mais ...*
- *J'aime ... Je n'aime pas ... parce que ...*
- *Je préfère ...*
- *C'est mon / ma .... préféré(e) parce que ...*

Group Behaviour

- *Merci!*
- *C'est une bonne idée.*
- *Bon travail!*
- *Est-ce que je peux emprunter... s'il te plaît?*
- *Simon, peux-tu prendre des notes, s'il te plaît?*

Asking for Help

- *Peux-tu m'aider? Pouvez-vous m'aider, madame?*
- *Je ne comprends pas les directives...*
- *Peux-tu / Pouvez-vous / Peut-on m'expliquer...?*
- *Comment dit-on en français... Comment est-ce qu'on fait...?*
- *Qu'est-ce que cela veut dire?*
- *Où est-ce que je peux trouver...?*

Here are some suggestions for encouraging students to participate in French during group work.

- Keep group work activities short. For early elementary learners, think in terms of two-minute activities, with a maximum limit of five minutes.
- Choose one aspect or step of a project to be done as group work, not necessarily all steps.
- Choose simple, familiar, routine activities (e.g., always have students do entrance and exit passes in groups; do brief ice-breaking conversations about the weather, school activities, etc.).
- Encourage students to think of group work as team work. They should all have a stake in accomplishing the task. Consider that adding a competitive element might also be motivating. Some of the suggestions below could incorporate competition.
- Establish a "time's up!" signal with students so that they know that they will have to accomplish everything within a set number of minutes. This helps them stay on task.
- Challenge students to monitor their use of French and English on a tally sheet. Have a group member note instances of French speaking and give merit points, or alternatively all instances of English speaking and give demerit points, as in a competition. (To prevent cheating, you could have monitors switch groups.) Then invite groups to compete against each other.
- Scaffold or model by giving students a written framework, similar to a script, for carrying out group work. Encourage them to approach it as if they were acting out a scene. If they are uncomfortable with oral communication, the script can provide enough support and can be adapted for other tasks. As they become more comfortable, you can decrease the amount of scripted interaction and provide only sentence starters.

- What strategies have you used to ensure that students carry out group work successfully? What do you do to help students develop more responsibility for their behaviour in group activities?

- How would you use the suggestions for a bank of group- and partner-language with your students? What expressions would you add to this resource?

Principle 3: Time for Processing New Learning

All learners need time to process new learning. We do not progress from a stage of not knowing to knowing without many intermediate steps. We all start at a stage of not knowing, to noticing the new information or idea, to knowing (and being able to do) with help from someone else, and finally to knowing (and being able to do) independently. The steps in the process of passive recognition to active knowledge are the following:

1. The learner might notice the new information, but usually only when it is explicitly pointed out.

2. The learner can recognize the new information again, but cannot reproduce it.

3. The learner recognizes it, but needs help or a model before being able to reproduce it.

4. After practice, the learner can both recognize new learning and reproduce it.

For more information on Gradual Release of Responsibility, see Chapter 2.

Repetition, novelty, and spiralling are key concepts to move learners from passive recognition to active production. These concepts are evident in the "Gradual Release of Responsibility" model for instruction. In this model, instruction is designed to build learners' understanding through observing a competent presentation (teacher modelling or I do it), practising the skill or strategy with the teacher's guidance (we do it), and applying the skill or strategy independently (you do it).

Figure 3.4: Providing time for processing new learning allows students to internalize the new material and experience success.

Learning to Recognize and Find Patterns

The human brain has an innate need to search for meaning. When the brain encounters new information, it responds by trying to find a pattern that matches information that is already stored in its networks of neurons. This new information has found a previous experience or prior knowledge to which it can attach itself. (Wolfe, 2001) However, when there is no match, the brain soon tires and stops processing the information. Because activating prior knowledge prepares the mind to accept and retain new information, encourage learners to remind themselves of what they already know.

In developing resources and instructional materials for the L2 classroom, ensure that they are pattern-rich. Students have to be able to hear and see and practise using the new information as often as possible, and have many opportunities to make connections between the learning in different but related contexts. When they are reminded of what they already know from prior learning and experiences, they are recognizing patterns and forming new neural connections.

There are three aspects to consider when developing instructional materials. They are as follows:

1. developing a bank of linguistic knowledge (vocabulary, grammar, and idioms);

2. making connections to familiar, relevant themes or cross-curricular connections;

3. making connections to L1 skills and strategies to facilitate L2 learning.

Repetition through Spiralling

How do you connect to prior experience and knowledge to create attention-engaging and stimulating activities in the L2 classroom? Students often do not have extensive prior knowledge of vocabulary and linguistic structures. Over time, create a bank of learning for them to draw from by spiralling vocabulary and language structures in your lessons.

Spiralling is the frequent and systematic re-use of linguistic structures and vocabulary. Since you are re-introducing learning, the learning itself is familiar—so students are calling on prior knowledge—but within different formats and contexts, so an element of novelty is introduced. For example, no matter what the theme or topic, incorporate activities based on a previously learned structure (e.g., a verb tense, the interrogative form, adverbs or adjectives) that use vocabulary related to the topic. These spiralling activities could be brief daily warm-up activities.

Develop or choose resources that are strongly thematic in nature so that students have many opportunities to see, hear, and use thematically related language over an extended period of time. Then look for opportunities to re-use this now familiar thematic vocabulary in as many other contexts as possible.

Teacher Tip

Food, clothing, sport, music, and movie preferences are popular topics with students and are often covered in commercial programs as a result of the National Core French Study's influence. Ask students to speculate about preferences for fictional characters or even imagine how real-life people (movie stars, musicians, athletes) might respond to questions about personal preferences in an interview.

Using numbers for budgeting and pricing is also a popular and relevant topic, so consider incorporating a budgeting activity in whatever topic your students are learning. For example, if you are learning about travelling, ask them to plan a trip budget. (The budget does not have to be realistic!) If you are discussing the latest electronic equipment, ask them to compare the prices of two makes of computers or video games. Every time you spiral back to numbers, remind them of other budgets they have created.

Invite students to participate in daily conversational routines (e.g., making small talk about oneself, the weather, school activities, holidays, etc.). Start every day by asking volunteers how they are and gradually give students a wide

---

bank of options for replying to this question, beyond the usual responses (*ça va bien / mal.*). Encourage students to be precise about describing their emotions, and then remind them to use these expressions in conversation or in writing when they are describing a fictional character.

Develop a bank of idioms that allow students to be more expressive and experience a "hip" factor in speaking French. These can be as basic as one-word interjections (*Génial! Sensass! Zut ! Comment?*) or short sentences (*C'est ennuyant, Ça m'énerve, J'aime ça!*). Encourage students to use such models as often as possible. This is also a less threatening way of encouraging shy or risk-averse students to speak.

Using Concept Maps

Concept maps help learners access prior knowledge or develop their understanding of new knowledge visually. Concept maps are also aids for making patterns of meaning clear to students. They are visual pattern detectors.

A concept map is an arrangement of key words and concepts on a specific subject or topic. Relationships between a central topic and subtopic are made apparent through the use of lines that connect them, showing their interrelation. Key words are often placed in a central circle or circles and the details or examples are connected to these key words with lines.

Concept mapping is a process used by students to represent visually what they know about a given topic. Concept maps also help students link new information to existing knowledge and make connections among ideas. Begin with a central idea or topic, from which students can branch out to incorporate new subtopics. Prepare a list of key expressions on a topic and share them with partners or groups. Have students categorize related expressions and link them to key ideas. There are no right or wrong concept maps; they are a great starting point for discussion.

Concept maps perform a variety of functions. They can be used for a variety of purposes. For example, when you are accessing prior knowledge, use concept maps for

- brainstorming ideas;

- jumping-off points for discussion;

- the first steps of a project.

When students are at a preliminary stage of a project or activity and finding patterns, use concept maps to help them

- organize information;

- find patterns, similarities;

- compare and contrast;

- describe ideas, concepts, objects;

- sequence stories, events, timelines;

- plan.

The spider map helps students describe something or someone. It is made up of one central circle with branches leading to other smaller circles. Students write the name of whatever is being described in the central circle, and then add descriptors in the outlying circles. (See BLM 3.1.) Vertical and horizontal bar graphs provide simple ways of organizing information gathered during collaborative group work. Venn diagrams are useful for comparing and contrasting elements and for finding similarities. (See BLM 3.2.)

A Y chart is a graphic organizer that requires students to generate and group ideas around three considerations: what a particular topic/ situation "looks like," "sounds like," and "feels like." Its purpose is to encourage students to think critically and to identify, sort, and classify information under the three categories in order to create a group decision. This strategy removes the influence of a dominant voice in a group, and everyone's point of view is measured equally. (See BLM 3.3.)

Teacher Tip

Graphic organizers and concept maps are valuable instructional tools that come in all shapes. They are flexible and endless in application. They show order and development of a student's thought processes. When selecting a graphic organizer for use, consider the purpose of its use. Some ideal graphic organizers for specific purposes are

1. Brainstorming purposes

   Une étoile (use to list facts, definitions, attributes, or examples related to a single topic)

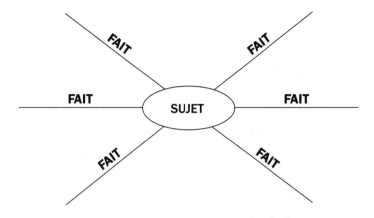

2. Comparing and contrasting purposes

   Le tableau T (use to examine two or more objects, ideas, people, etc. in order to note similarities and/or differences, likes and dislikes, advantages and disadvantages)

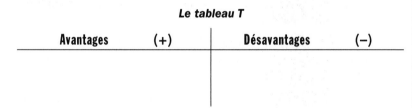

3. Sequencing purposes

   Liste en gradins (use when prioritizing elements from most important to least important; relative position or standing; a series of things or persons; or an orderly arrangement from first to last)

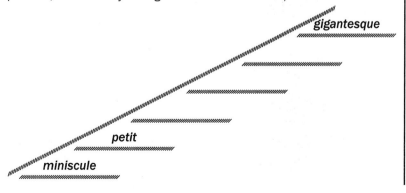

Ligne du temps (use for student to retell a story in sequence—both words and illustrations are acceptable)

Ligne du temps pour:

┌─ COMMENCEMENT

Titre: _____

Auteur: _____

└─ FIN

4. Analyzing purposes

Tableau action / réaction (used to describe and expand on a central idea or a thing. *Questions-clés: Quelle est l'idée centrale? Quelles sont les conséquences que provoque l'événement?*

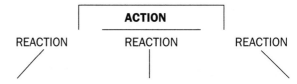

ACTION

REACTION   REACTION   REACTION

Tableau avant / après (use to begin an activity, to activate prior learning, and at the end to allow student to reflect on the learning)

5. Visualizing purposes

Carte de l'histoire (use to help students recall or form mental images or pictures). Consider using the "map" of the Hundred Acres Wood from Winnie the Pooh as your model.

Une esquisse (use to form a mental image or to make perceptible to the mind or imagination)

Dessine trois incidents importants / amusants / mémorables pour toi que tu as remarqués dans l'histoire. Choisis quelque chose au début, au milieu, et à la fin de l'histoire.

Au début de l'histoire...	*Au milieu de l'histoire...*	*A la fin de l'histoire...*

Strategies for Adding Variety and Novelty

Students respond well to novel and challenging learning opportunities. Adding elements of the unexpected will allow you to engage students in the process of self-awareness and discovery that will ensure a commitment to life-long learning. Changing things now and then creates a new and exciting environment.

Teacher Tip

- Change group/team members
- Change partners
- Change seating arrangements (if possible)
- Change daily routines
- Change format of entrance and exit passes
- Ask students to predict the beginning of a fictional piece (play, story) instead of the end
- Have students suggest alternative endings to fiction
- Allow students to be the French teacher for a class or a specified time period during class
- Play a game
- Ask students to perform role-plays
- Create and perform chants to illustrate language points
- Use strategies such as visualization

Varying Methods of Student Response

Questions are important tools that teachers use to add variety and novelty and extend students' learning. Different forms of response enable students to interact with their peers, encourage risk-taking, and provide varied opportunities for you to observe their performance. Here are some ways to invite student response.

- Take some time to think about your answer to this question. When you feel ready, share it with a partner. *(Réfléchissez à votre réponse. Quand vous êtes prêts, discutez de la réponse avec un ou une partenaire.)*

- Please do not raise your hands to answer; share your answers with your group members. *(Ne levez pas la main pour répondre. Discutez de vos réponses avec les membres du groupe.)*

- Thumbs up if you agree, thumbs down if you disagree with this statement. (*Levez la main si vous êtes d'accord. Ne levez pas la main si vous n'êtes pas d'accord.*)

- Think about your answer to this question, then share it with a partner, and finally write your answer down and hand it in. (*Réfléchissez à votre réponse. Discutez de la réponse avec un ou une partenaire; écrivez la réponse sur une feuille de papier. Donnez-moi la feuille avant de partir.*)

A student who feels more appropriately prepared and supported to participate is likely to be more confident and motivated to respond. Because the brain needs novelty and does not react well to stress, varying question and response styles is one way of ensuring productivity and improving student performance.

Teachers who plan classes using a variety of question and response techniques, teaching methods, and learning activities can generally find a way to motivate most students. A classroom with lots of variety is an enriched environment, which is something the brain loves.

What I Am Thinking Now

Question and answer activities can be effective in providing opportunities for your students to express themselves in French. The give and take that students experience in these exchanges with you, with a partner, or in small groups contributes to a communicative environment in the classroom—one that helps build students' confidence in using French.

- If possible, video or audio record one of your lessons in which your purpose is to engage the students in conversation. Observe the way in which you used questions: Did you vary the types of questions? How many questions elicited "yes or no" replies? What opportunities did the students have to use the questions you modelled? Did you give students enough time to respond?

- Novelty can be an effective attention-grabber as students try to make sense of what is happening in the lesson. What are some of the ways in which you use novelty to support your students' learning?

Visualizing and Using Visuals

Visual literacy is the ability to understand non-linguistic visual forms such as photos, art, and graphic symbols. Like literacy, there are levels of different abilities in being visually literate. Beginning readers learn to recognize the symbols of the alphabet, then put them together to form words, then join words together to form sentences and longer meaningful units such as paragraphs. Over time and with the teacher's help, students learn to make sense of what they read and go beyond decoding. In visual literacy, students first learn to recognize the subject matter of photos and art, and to identify graphic signs and symbols and associate them with meanings. Beginners learn to notice details in visuals, but it takes time and practice to make inferences from the visual to help understand its meaning or how it enhances the meaning of the text (written or oral).

Photographs, drawings, posters, and other visual representations can play a vital role in supporting a student's early exposure to second-language learning. As students learn to read and write, they do so with the help of the images and photographs they see. Using a skill that they have already developed in L1 for L2 is an effective way to encourage students to express themselves. Take advantage of the fact that today's students are ever more familiar and comfortable with visual literacy, because it plays an important role in technology and media such as the Internet. Icons, symbols, and signs are pervasive and powerful forms of visual communication in these media.

Techniques for teaching visual literacy include teaching students how to use visuals to enhance their reading comprehension, for example, drawing inferences from art when reading fiction, using titles, subtitles, and captions to infer subject matter, using graphic information in charts and pie graphs, and skimming speech and thought bubbles to infer plot details and make predictions in fiction.

Another technique often used is visualization. Before students read a passage, they are asked to visualize the scene. For example, before students read a selection about an ill-fated camping trip, they are asked to imagine the sights, sounds, and smells of walking in a forest. The teacher's script introduces vocabulary and concepts that will be explored at greater length within the text. As the teacher describes the scene, students must imagine each element. The teacher pauses to give them time to do this, and asks about words or concepts that might have been difficult to visualize.

As students read the text, the teacher pauses to ask students to visualize key words and to identify words that evoke powerful images. Visualizing before and during the reading helps students understand better, remember what they have read better, and identify places or words in the text that they are having difficulty understanding.

Using Visuals for Brainstorming

Visual synectics is an approach to brainstorming that takes seemingly unrelated images and topics and has students make analogies between the images and topics under discussion.

A simple but effective technique for brainstorming is called visual synectics. In visual synectics, a diverse selection of unrelated visuals is used to create analogies for issues or problems under discussion. It is especially helpful in generating ideas and unblocking creative impulses. The technique is useful when students need to develop ideas about a topic and are having trouble getting started. The teacher can choose three or four photos or illustrations unrelated to the topic and provide a starter sentence to generate discussion. For example, if the class is discussing families, find three unrelated photos showing activities (e.g., sports, food, and a landscape scene) and ask students to free-associate connections between the sentences and the photos. You might wish to model a sentence about your family: *Les membres de ma famille ressemblent à cette photo du bateau à voile sur la mer. Mes parents sont très aventureux.* Or a simpler example might be: *Ma famille aime le sport.*

Incorporating Music

For all ages of learners, information presented in song format aids in the recall of that information. Music can activate the emotional and creative side of the learner. It provides the brain with more opportunities to link to a wider number of prior experiences because it is activating experiences on multiple levels.

Some students might enjoy putting the main ideas of a unit into a musical form. Music can also be used to set the mood of the classroom. Consider playing music while students work in groups or write in their journals.

Practice Leads to Production

Learning is neither automatic nor immediate; according to the research, we need to be exposed to a new word between 6 to 16 times before we can integrate it within our knowledge networks and use it. (Zahar et al, 2001) As well, the new learning needs to be frequently repeated and spiralled in order to be truly assimilated. A key concept cannot be introduced, practised, and then not re-introduced for some time. Without repetition and practice, the neural networks that stored that knowledge will have disappeared.

The following chart suggests possible practice and repetition activities and aligns them with the stages from passive recognition to active production.

Recognition to Production	
Stage	**Practice Activities**
Noticing	Show visuals (flashcards, illustrations, posters, flipcharts, etc.); Play chants and songs; Draw students' attention to... *Avez-vous remarqué...?* *Connaissez-vous...?*; Use read-alouds to engage students' attention to an element in the text.
Recognizing	Elicit responses through: Matching activities, True/False, Red-card/Green-card checks, Multiple-choice questions, Drawing, Acting through gestures, Bingo-type games, Fill-in-the-blanks or cloze activities, Choral reading.
Production with Scaffolding	Perform dialogues or Q & A interviews following a template; Sing chants and songs; Make up Q & A games (*Qui suis-je?*, Trivial Pursuit, etc.); Answer simple questions; Create a storyboard.
Independent Production	Prepare and perform a dialogue or interview following a model; Make changes to or create a new song or chant; Answer more complex questions or respond to a visual in sentences; Develop a skit based on a storyboard and perform it.

Although practice is vital to success, in order to be worthwhile, it has to be *efficient* practice. Efficient, worthwhile practice must be

- frequent, regular, and consistent;

- distributed over time rather than done in one brief time period;

"It is easier to recall song lyrics than conversation because a song's beat, melody, and harmony assist the brain in carrying semantic information." (Jenson, 2001)

Teaching the Learning Brain **101**

- focused, with clearly stated purpose and goals;

- broken down into manageable parts or steps;

- reinforced with immediate, frequent, and constructive feedback from the teacher or from peers.

Although practice must occur frequently over a period of time, the purpose of practice is lost if the practice is not at the appropriate level for the learner. Make sure that you are teaching within the appropriate zone for the individual and that the learning is broken down into manageable steps.

What I Am Thinking Now

Time to process new learning is an essential aspect of brain-based learning, particularly for students acquiring a new language. The Gradual Release of Responsibility model provides a framework for organizing instruction that ensures students will have time and varied opportunities to practise the new language.

- To what extent is the Gradual Release of Responsibility model used in your school, for example, in the English language arts program or other areas of the curriculum?

- What activities do you use to model L2 for your students? Do you think you provide enough models and/or sufficient time for students to observe and respond to the models?

Effective L2 instruction combines structure and variety. Structure is needed to build student competence as well as confidence and variety is needed to sustain motivation and interest.

- With a colleague, examine a selection of lesson plans to determine how effectively structure and variety are balanced.

- Consider one or two lessons in depth, taking note of student responses that you had not anticipated when you developed the lesson. How did you address these unexpected responses? Do you think the lessons needed more structure, more variety, or a better combination of the two?

Principle 4: Time for Reflection

"Reflection is thinking—about what you've done, what you've tried to do, and how you feel about what you've done. When you encourage students to think and talk about their own learning, you are providing them with valuable insights. You are also giving students opportunities to extend their understanding of their own learning. While student reflection is not a complicated process, time and practice are essential in making it a positive learning habit." (Davies et al, 1992)

It is important to allow time for students to pause and consider what they learn in order for that learning to matter to the brain. (Jensen, 1998) Activities that involve speaking, drawing, writing, and thinking reflectively every day consolidate new learning. For example, consider building into your daily routines brief activities that allow students to review recent learning at the beginning of the class or repeat it at the end for consolidation.

Teacher Tip

Making quick review time at the beginning or end of a class is a matter of creating and implementing a variety of different routines. Journal writing is an excellent way of incorporating opportunities for review. Make it a habit to have students answer a question in their journals about their learning. Provide prompts based on the current learning objectives.

For example, does the new learning relate to

- a language point (vocabulary, structure, or idiom)
- the theme of the learning period
- the story or DVD being read or viewed
- learning or consolidating a skill or strategy
- speaking in French during group work
- taking responsibility for an element of a group task
- identifying a purpose for speaking/listening/reading/writing
- identifying cognates and familiar words
- identifying the main idea
- identifying a useful strategy and reflecting on why it works

To include novelty in these review and reflection periods, try a variety of approaches, e.g., student journals, whole-class conversations, and entrance and exit passes. Entrance and exit passes include sample questions that students have to fill out before class in order to enter and at the end before they leave. (See BLMs 3.4 and 3.5 for examples.)

Another way to help students review and reflect is a brief question-and-answer routine. This can take many forms, some of them based on L1 practices.

- Remind students of prior learning by asking a brief question about the theme or content of the reading, listening, or viewing selection. Eventually, as students practise this routine, ask for volunteers to suggest the opening question. (The opening question could be based on their answers to the exit pass.)

- Ask students to write a sentence or question using the new vocabulary or structure.
- Extend the above activity to include an oral component by asking volunteers to share their sentences or to write a question based on recently learned material and ask a partner to answer it. For example, if you are reading a story, ask the class to consider one important question that they would ask a character in the story, and to prepare that question as part of their entrance pass.
- Create, or ask students to create, chants for review and consolidation.

Constructive Feedback

Providing students with timely, ongoing, and constructive feedback helps them reflect on their learning. Recognizing students' personal investment in their work with constructive comments helps build their self-confidence. Feedback reduces uncertainty and provides important information for students to expand their understanding and move forward in their learning.

Feedback is a powerful tool because, as Jensen explains, "our whole brain is self-referencing. It decides what to do based on what has just been done." (Jensen, 2001) Learners need time to associate new information with previous knowledge and form neural connections, which are the storage areas of long-term memory.

In order to be meaningful, feedback must be constructive and specific. Some simple guidelines will ensure that feedback leads to improvement.

1. Address observable behaviours.

2. Use specific examples and give precise, rather than general, praise.

3. Focus on areas of strength as well as supporting areas that need improvement.

Making Feedback Meaningful	
1. Address observable behaviours. For example, during oral communication activities or group work, does the student:	• make an effort to speak or consistently speak in French? • focus and pay attention (e.g., to instructions, to other classmates, during listening activities)? • behave considerately and respectfully (e.g., by paying attention to others, not interrupting, demonstrating interest in others by asking questions)?

Making Feedback Meaningful	
2. Use specific examples to illustrate a point; make feedback precise rather than general. For example, comment on:	• how well the activity or task criteria was carried out. • why the work was well done, why you liked it or were impressed by it. • the pronunciation, intonation, and expressiveness during oral work. • the organization, clarity of the ideas, etc. • the good behaviour, explaining why you appreciate it.
3. Focus on areas of strength as well as supporting areas that need improvement. For example, consider these questions:	• In which skill area does the student do well? not so well? • What are the signs that the student is having trouble in a skill area? In listening and speaking, does the student have trouble producing or understanding a particular sound (e.g., distinguishing vowels from nasalized vowels, distinguishing between "ou" and "u" vowels, distinguishing between "un" and "une", "le", "la"; recognizing familiar words when they appear in a context with liaison)? • In reading and writing, does the student have trouble with certain language structures? Are the problems in writing signs that the student is also having difficulty distinguishing certain sounds?

What I Am Thinking Now

Helping your students reflect on their learning and express what they have learned is a core feature of effective instruction in all subject areas. Reflection is also a critical factor for teachers, whether they do it privately or as they participate in professional learning activities.

• In what ways do you think the suggestions for fostering student reflection can be used to help teachers reflect on their instruction?

• If you were to work with an instructional coach, what kinds of constructive feedback would you seek?

Principle 5: Developing Higher-Order Thinking Skills

When students have developed denser neural networks as a result of practice and repetition, the next step is to use the new learning in a way that involves the cerebral cortex. This means asking the student to think about the new learning in ways that go beyond repetition and comprehension questions. One tool for considering the development of higher-order thinking skills is Bloom's Taxonomy.

Bloom's Taxonomy
defines three domains
of learning:

· Cognitive domain—
  mental skills

· Affective domain—
  emotional growth

· Psychomotor
  domain—physical
  skills

Bloom's Taxonomy

Benjamin Bloom was a psychologist who worked with a group of educators over a number of years to devise a taxonomy, or system of classification, of cognitive skills and objectives. Bloom wanted to create a systematic way of organizing and talking about how to devise curricula that would lead students from lower-order to higher-order thinking. In brain science terms, he wanted to encourage students to use the cerebral cortex, where new learning is analyzed, evaluated, and synthesized, and new meanings are created.

Bloom conceived of thinking as cumulative and hierarchical, i.e., one skill builds on the previous and leads to the next skill, and each skill is more complex than the preceding one. Bloom's Taxonomy includes three domains: the Cognitive Domain, the Affective Domain, and the Psychomotor Domain. He wanted to encourage a more holistic approach to teaching and instructional design in which the three domains would be integrated.

Five principles of
brain-based learning to
guide L2 instructional
practices:

1. Each brain is unique.

2. Emotions impact
   learning.

3. New learning
   requires time to
   process.

4. New learning
   requires time for
   reflection.

5. Learners need
   opportunities to
   develop higher-order
   thinking skills.

From the Research

The Affective Domain concerns skills in dealing with one's personal emotions and in relating empathetically to others. Objectives in the Affective Domain involve personal awareness and ability to grow emotionally and to understand the emotional basis of attitudes. The five levels in the Affective Domain, from lowest to highest, are

1. Receiving: Learning is passive and involves paying attention only.

2. Responding: Learning involves participation and reacting in some way to new data.

3. Valuing: Learning involves assigning value to the new data.

4. Organizing: Learning involves combining different values, data, and ideas in new ways or according to previously learned patterns. Learners now compare information, make connections, and build on what they have learned.

5. Characterizing: Learners have so thoroughly internalized the new learning (attitude, belief, emotion) that it influences or changes their actions, behaviour, or point of view.

The Psychomotor Domain involves physical, manual abilities and hand-eye coordination. Bloom and his colleagues did not define subcategories for skills in this domain. In terms of our students, however, it is useful to think of their abilities to manipulate pens and pencils and to assess if certain students have weaker motor skills that would slow down their writing. For these students, the use of a computer for word processing might be more appropriate.

In 2001, Lorin Anderson, a former student of Bloom's, published a revised taxonomy in order to align it with new thinking in pedagogy and education. The revised taxonomy differs from the original one in the form of the classification terms (they are now verbs rather than nouns) and the order and names of the higher-level objectives. Anderson chose verbs to better emphasize the active nature of learning.

Bloom's 1956 Cognitive Objectives	Anderson's 2001 Cognitive Objectives
Evaluation	Creating
Synthesis	Evaluating
Analysis	Analyzing
Application	Applying
Comprehension	Understanding
Knowledge	Remembering

The subcategory Knowledge was renamed Remembering, because Knowledge is a product of thinking rather than the action. Remembering is the skill that learners need to develop in order to have Knowledge.

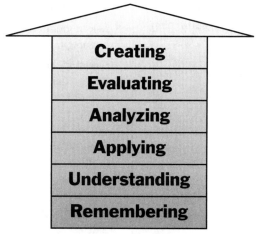

Figure 3.5: New Cognitive Objectives published by Lorin Anderson in 2001 based on Bloom's Taxonomy of 1956

Many educators had debated aspects of the taxonomy over the years. For example, many disagreed with the placement of Evaluation at the top of the hierarchy, and argued either that Synthesis was a parallel skill or that it was the most challenging skill. Not all educators agreed that the skills should be cumulative and hierarchical, and they proposed that Evaluation, Synthesis, and Analysis are interconnected and should be represented as parallel to each other at the top of a pyramid.

In responding to these discussions of the original taxonomy, Anderson and his colleagues interpreted Synthesis as creative in nature (which the original classification descriptor already suggested), changed the descriptor, and placed it at the top of the hierarchy.

Each objective in the Cognitive Domain can be described with a set of action and skill verbs. The following table shows typical descriptors and suggests French verbs that you can use when you create questions, activities, and tasks.

Revised Bloom's Taxonomy for L2 Learning	
Objective	**Implementation Strategy**
Remembering make a list, repeat, remember, name, identify, retell, summarize; *(dresser une liste, répéter, rappeler, nommer, identifier, indiquer, raconter, faire un sommaire)*	· Ask questions about prior knowledge and experiences. Use W 5 questions, including "How?": *Qui, Quoi / Qu'est-ce que, Où, Quand, Pourquoi, Comment?* · Ask students to summarize previous learning in their own words.
Understanding rank or place in order, organize, plan, describe in your own words, discuss, give examples *(mettre en ordre, organiser, planifier, décrire dans ses propres mots, discuter, expliquer, choisir, donner des exemples)*	· Ask students to explain ideas. · Ask students to give examples to support their ideas. · Ask students to rank steps, ideas, information, or events in a story in order of occurrence or importance.
Applying demonstrate, role-play, illustrate, draw, write, use, ask questions of (another person) or about (new information) *(démontrer, jouer le rôle de, illustrer, dessiner, écrire, utiliser, poser une question à / au sujet de)*	· Ask students to use the learning in another way. · Ask students to transform the learning into a drawing, a school website post or newsletter item, a skit. · Ask students to create questions and answers from the learning and interview a partner.

Revised Bloom's Taxonomy for L2 Learning	
Analyzing examine, compare, contrast, find differences, find similarities *(examiner, comparer, contraster, distinguer, trouver des différences / ressemblances)*	• Ask students to examine and make comparisons. • Ask students if they can explain the differences they find.
Evaluating give reasons, justify (an answer, interpretation), recommend and explain why *(donner des raisons, justifier (une réponse, une idée), recommander et expliquer pourquoi)*	• Ask students to give reasons and justify an argument. • Ask students to recommend something (food, music, movie, video game, etc.) to a partner and explain why.
Creating make, create, design, develop, write, propose *(faire, fabriquer, construire, créer, développer, préparer, écrire, proposer)*	• Ask students to create, build, make something new, or suggest a new idea or interpretation.

What I Am Thinking Now

The previous section identifies the five principles of learning related to what we know about how the brain functions. In summary, these principles focus on individuality, social interaction, emotional factors, time for processing and practice, time for reflection, and development of higher-order thinking skills.

- What do you think makes these factors especially important in helping students achieve success in learning French?

- What have you noticed about individual characteristics of your students that facilitate their learning? that affect their learning adversely?

- How can you use these ideas about brain-based principles of learning in your planning?

Summary

Our capacity for learning does not end at any particular age. The human brain, because of its plasticity, has the ability to adapt to new experiences and stimuli. Our students are not blank slates; they are active learners who are engaged by experiential, interactive, and social activities. They thrive in secure, caring environments. As educators, we can optimize activities that stimulate growth and new experiences, require complex thinking skills, and encourage transfer of that learning to real-world applications. As Zull explains, "neuroscience has shown us two key things that lead to change in networks of neurons. The first one of these is simply practice. Neurons that fire a lot tend to form more connections and strengthen new connections… The other thing that helps neuron networks get stronger and become larger and more complex is emotion." (Zull, 2003)

What are the implications of understanding brain physiology for teaching?

- Take advantage of the brain's plasticity: its capacity to adapt to novel experiences and stimuli.

- Challenge students to grow more neural pathways.

- Help students avoid automatic, unthinking, unreflective responses.

- Avoid stressful situations where students will act impulsively.

Curriculum should be delivered clearly, in a collaborative way, and within a sound and healthy environment. Your natural enthusiasm, modelling, and coaching strategies all serve as important signals about the value of what is being learned. Learning is enhanced by complex, active, hands-on, multi-sensory experiences, and achievable challenges. Students will feel connected to learning when they perceive choices in work that are mindful of learning styles, readiness levels, and interests. They will be motivated to learn and will, as a result, retain more of the learning.

My Choices

Advocates of brain-based learning present compelling arguments for teachers to become more aware of how the brain functions and of ways in which to structure instructional activities that keep students engaged.

- What ideas would you share with colleagues about brain-based learning? How do you think your colleagues will respond to these ideas?

- What are the implications of the "ever-learning brain" for you as you think about your students and plan instruction for them?

La toile d'araignée

Nom : _____ Classe : _____ Date : _____

Remplis les bulles pour indiquer les liens entre tes idées.

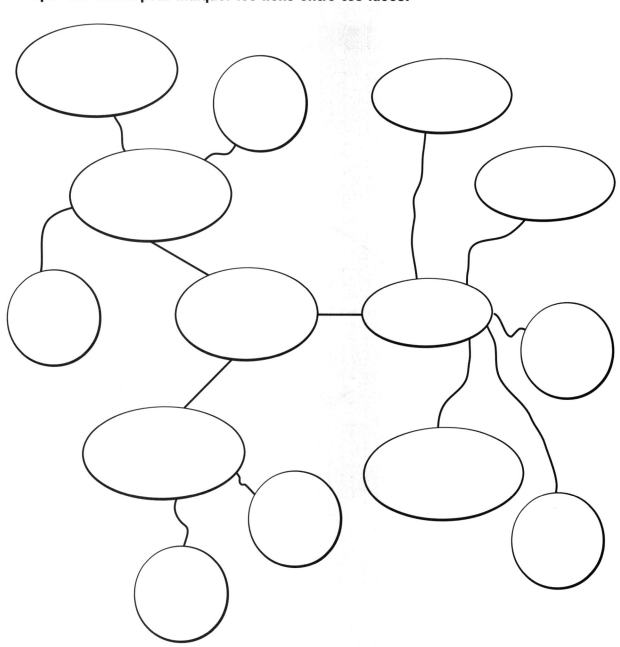

Diagramme de Venn

Nom : _____ Classe : _____ Date : _____

Indique les différences des objets ou personnes que tu compares. Au milieu du diagramme, indique les similarités. Donne un titre a chaque cercle qui clarifie ce que tu compares.

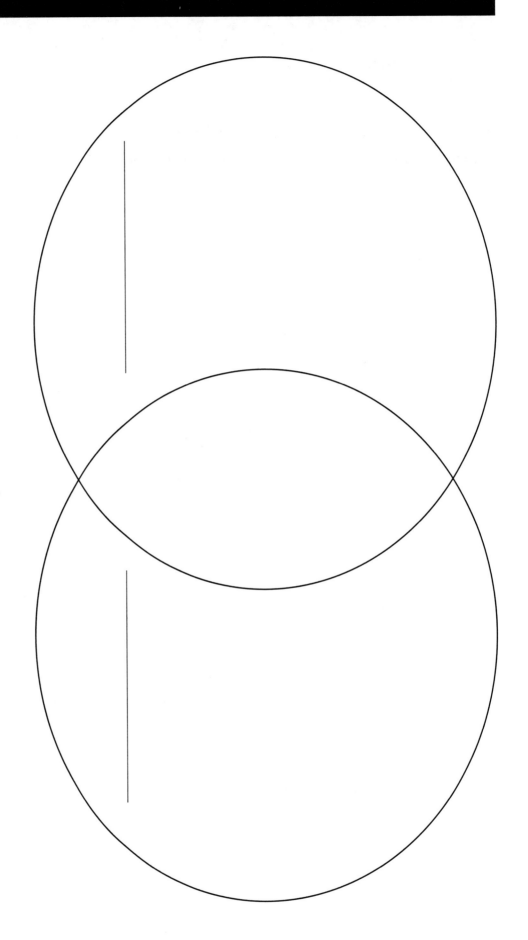

Tableau en Y

Nom : _____ Classe : _____ Date : _____

En groupe, discutez bien le sujet du jour et ajoutez vos réactions sous les trois catégories, « Je me sens », « Je vois », et « J'entends ».

Sujet : _____

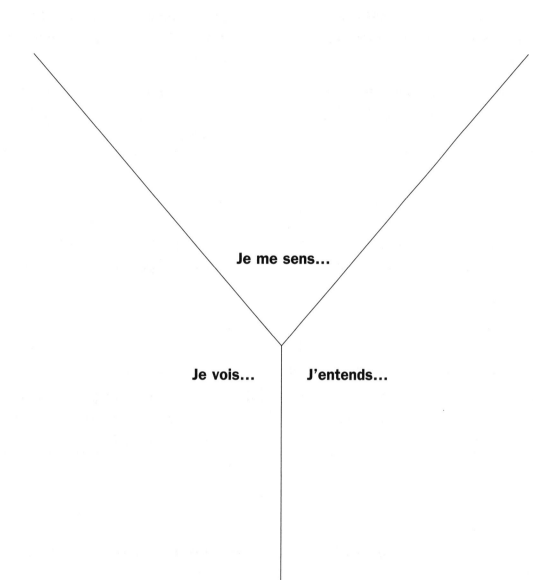

Je me sens...

Je vois...   J'entends...

Billet d'entrée

Nom : _____

Classe : _____

Date : _____

En groupe, discutez des questions suivantes. Puis, écris ou dessine tes réponses.

1. Est-ce que tu peux identifier deux expressions de la classe de français d'hier ?

2. Est-ce que tu peux penser à quelque chose de spécial qui s'est passé hier pendant la classe ?

3. Est-ce que tu peux penser à une chose que tu veux partager avec d'autres élèves ?

Maintenant, choisis une réponse à partager avec ton groupe.

Écoute les réponses des autres et ajoute une réponse que tu aimes à ta liste.

Finalement, chaque groupe choisit une réponse à partager avec la classe.

Billet d'entrée

Nom : _____

Classe : _____

Date : _____

En groupe, discutez des questions suivantes. Puis, écris ou dessine tes réponses.

1. Est-ce que tu peux identifier deux expressions de la classe de français d'hier ?

2. Est-ce que tu peux penser à quelque chose de spécial qui s'est passé hier pendant la classe ?

3. Est-ce que tu peux penser à une chose que tu veux partager avec d'autres élèves ?

Maintenant, choisis une réponse à partager avec ton groupe.

Écoute les réponses des autres et ajoute une réponse que tu aimes à ta liste.

Finalement, chaque groupe choisit une réponse à partager avec la classe.

Billet de sortie

Nom : _____

Classe : _____

Date : _____

Quand je me rappelle la classe d'hier,

je vois...

j'entends...

je pense à...

Pose une dernière question à ton enseignant ou ta enseignante avant la fin de la classe.

Écris ta question :

_____

_____

Billet de sortie

Nom : _____

Classe : _____

Date : _____

Quand je me rappelle la classe d'hier,

je vois...

j'entends...

je pense à...

Pose une dernière question à ton enseignant ou ta enseignante avant la fin de la classe.

Écris ta question :

_____

_____

Chapter 4

Facilitating Differentiated Instruction

"If the child is not learning the way you are teaching, try teaching the way the child learns."
—*Rita Dunn*

My Thoughts

- What was your initial reaction to this quotation?

- What practical considerations come to mind as you think about "try teaching the way the child learns"?

- What challenges do you encounter when trying to adapt your teaching to the needs of individual students in your classes?

In this chapter, we will discuss:

- Differentiated Instruction

- Five Principles of Differentiation

  ° Principle 1: Supportive and risk-free learning environment
  ° Principle 2: Quality curriculum
  ° Principle 3: Respectful work
  ° Principle 4: Flexible grouping
  ° Principle 5: Ongoing diagnostic assessments

- A Framework for Differentiated Learning

Differentiated Instruction

Differentiated instruction is an approach to learning and teaching that acknowledges and honours students as individuals. Students differ in their experiences, interests, learning styles, and attitudes toward learning; these differences determine what and how they learn.

Differentiated instructional practices should provide:

- multiple opportunities for students to process information;

- skills to interpret ideas;

- tools to express and apply what is learned;

- strategies to sustain and expand learning.

One task or one approach rarely meets the needs of all students. Differentiated practices require educators to plan and articulate learning outcomes in response to the learner's needs.

A differentiated instructional framework:

- respects students' learning interests, readiness, and profiles;

- creates a safe and inclusive environment in which to learn;

- values students' prior learning;

- addresses students' need for novelty;

- promotes learning through student interaction and collaboration;

- offers students opportunities to make choices whenever appropriate;

- allows students to engage in higher-level thinking.

There are many interpretations about what constitutes a differentiated instructional framework. Many researchers have outlined what differentiated instruction is but not what it is not. (Gregory and Chapman, 2002; Tomlinson 2003)

Having confidence in your professional capacity to identify student learning needs enables you to make timely and appropriate instructional decisions.

Differentiation is...	Differentiation is not...
aligning instructional practice with students' need to ensure that all students have equal access to the same learning. It is a proactive and not a reactive response to the needs of all learners.	about teachers attending to the needs of one student over another.

Differentiation is...	Differentiation is not...
a purposeful alignment of task and objectives. The nature of the work is equitable and adjusted based on students' readiness, interests, and/ or learning profiles. It is the quality and not the quantity of work assigned that guides educators to differentiated practice.	structuring activities for students without learning goals in mind, which often results in more work for some and less for others.
using flexible grouping. Students move through stages of learning at their own pace and need to interact with peers in a variety of ways. Grouping is a dynamic process.	a way of providing homogeneous grouping.
using appropriate scaffolding of instruction (e.g., conferencing, coaching, and modelling). In diminishing support as the students learn, they become more self-reliant and continue to develop the skills or knowledge on their own.	streaming students.
monitoring student progress with ongoing diagnostic assessments. Students require numerous opportunities for practice and frequent, precise feedback.	assigning grades.
having high expectations for all students. Learners feel rewarded when faced with appropriately demanding tasks and rise to the challenge. Challenging work is respectful of each student's ability and potential to learn.	having lower expectations.

What I Am Thinking Now

Differentiation has also been described in Chapter 2. This observation about differentiation appeared in one of the reflection activities in that chapter: Differentiating instruction is likely easier to describe than it is to implement.

- Do you think the observation is justified? Why? Why not?

- What new insights about differentiation have you gained from reading about "what it is" and "what it is not"?

- In what ways do those insights reflect what you do as you implement differentiated activities with your students?

"There is no one 'right way' to create an effectively differentiated classroom; teachers craft responsive learning places in ways that are a good match for their teaching styles, as well as for learners' needs." (Tomlinson, 1999) However, because teachers respond to student needs, Tomlinson, among others, proposes that the following five principles guide our planning.

Five Principles of Differentiation

Principle 1: Supportive and risk-free learning environment

Principle 2: Quality curriculum

Principle 3: Respectful work

Principle 4: Flexible grouping

Principle 5: Ongoing diagnostic assessments

Principle 1: Supportive and Risk-Free Learning Environment

Pivotal to the concept of differentiated instruction is the organization of classrooms as caring and inclusive communities for learning. It is important to create a climate where students "know that they belong … and that they are responsible for their own learning, as well as their own behaviour." (Gregory and Chapman, 2002) Such classrooms are healthy communities of learners that provide students with opportunities for meaningful participation within a safe and nurturing learning environment. It is here that students feel a sense of belonging and identification, and share a common sense of purpose with their peers.

Make students feel comfortable by using their names, welcoming them at the classroom door, by modelling respect, patience, and attentive listening, and by using inclusive language. A small group project called *Ma salle de classe préférée* (See BLM 4.1.) will help them to think about what a classroom community of learners looks like, sounds like, and feels like. This is an effective way for students to let you know what they consider the best environment in which to learn.

Begin and end each class with a short warm-up activity to help students recall and consolidate new learning. Entrance and exit passes are particularly effective as they are brief and require minimal language skills. Students can draw or write their answers while working with a partner or in a small group. As often as possible, provide choices for their answers. (See BLMs 4.2, 4.3, and 4.4.)

CASE STUDY	Differentiating Instruction

«*Bonjour tout le monde !*»
The itinerant French teacher walked into the Grade 7 classroom and warmly greeted her students. Smiling, she moved among the desks that were arranged in pairs and spoke briefly with each student.

«*Bonjour, Trang. Comment ça va aujourd'hui ?*»

«*Bonjour, Mme Lemieux. Ça va très bien aujourd'hui ! Merci.*»

«*Et toi, Ashley, ça va ?*»

«*Non madame,*» Ashley shook her head,

«*Ça va mal.*»

«*Tu es malade ?*»

«*Oui.*»

The children were familiar with the routine that Mme Lemieux used to begin each lesson and most listened attentively as the teacher and students engaged in their brief exchanges. Stacey, who had recently transferred from a school in which FSL was not offered, looked uncomfortable as the teacher approached.

«*Bonjour, Stacey. Ça va bien ou ça va mal ?*» asked Mme Lemieux as she made facial expressions to help clarify the meanings of the expressions for the girl.

With a hint of newfound confidence, Stacey replied, «Ça va bien. Merci.»

The students and their teacher had been working on the topic. During the introduction Mme Lemieux had asked the children to complete a K.W.L. (What I Know, What I Want to Know, What I Learned) chart. It was evident that the children were familiar with the names of many school supplies and remembered the names of most subjects, but they were interested in knowing the names of places in the school.

"We never know how to ask to go somewhere," said Todd, "or how to say where someone is."

Initially Mme Lemieux had used a computer slide show of digital photos taken around the school to present the vocabulary to the students. A variety of teacher-led, student-led, and whole-class activities reinforced their learning. Today she challenged the class to participate in a "Quick Write."

«Travaillez avec un ou une partenaire. Vous pouvez travailler avec l'élève à côté de vous. Dressez une liste des noms des salles et des endroits de l'école. Décrivez les directives pour marcher de votre salle de classe à un endroit de votre choix.»

The students welcomed the opportunity to collaborate with their peers. Mme Lemieux noticed Stacey and her partner animatedly discussing their work. After the class had shared responses, their teacher asked them how they could demonstrate what they had learned.

«On peut créer des cartes de l'école,» Erin suggested.

Stacey ventured, «Je peux créer des affiches pour des salles de l'école.»

«Bon. C'est à vous de décider le format de votre projet final. Ce qui est important est que vous démontriez ce que vous avez appris. Vous pouvez créer des cartes, des affiches, offrir des tours de l'école en français. C'est à vous de décider. Allez-y!»

What I Am Thinking Now

- In what ways does the case study illustrate principles of differentiated instruction?

- What would a visitor to your classroom notice that indicates how you differentiate instruction?

Principle 2: Quality Curriculum

Good instruction occurs in classrooms where students have access to quality curriculum. Effective planning involves identifying the essential knowledge and skills inherent in the second-language curriculum and then planning accordingly. Proceed with a clear picture of where you would like students to be with respect to reading, writing, speaking, listening, viewing, and representing at the end of a learning cycle. Identify the language structures that will be necessary for students to obtain those objectives.

Principle 3: Respectful Work

It is by acknowledging the commonalities and differences of all students that you can honour each student's uniqueness. When students, as active learners, are involved in decision making, they are free to explore relevant and engaging learning opportunities at their own readiness levels. Respectful work accepts and celebrates students' variances, is solidly focused on curriculum guidelines, and is deliberately designed to support growth in learning.

Principle 4: Flexible Grouping

In a differentiated classroom, students work in teacher-led and student-led groups, depending on the learning goals of the activity and your instructional needs.

Whole-class instruction helps build common experiences and provides a shared foundation for further exploration, problem solving, and skill development.

Small-group instruction provides opportunities to work with smaller groups of students who share common needs and/or interests.

Students must also be given time to work alone in teacher-directed activities to refine their own thoughts. By working independently, students are given opportunities to problem solve, reflect, and consolidate new learning.

In student-led groups, students control the group dynamics and maintain both control and a voice in setting the learning agenda. Student-led groups encourage students to take responsibility for their own learning. Group success depends on individual contribution. By sharing ideas and reinterpreting instructions to help one another, students discover that learning is mutually shared and communally valuable.

Collaborative learning can occur informally in smaller groups or more formally when the task involves problem solving or a research project.

Consider creating formal learning teams for long-term projects, where students can provide each other with direction, answers, encouragement, and help. Learning teams also inform absent members about work missed.

Principle 5: Ongoing Diagnostic Assessments

Assessment tools help teachers understand where students are in the learning cycle and map their progress. Ongoing assessment of student learning is primarily diagnostic and formative in nature. As Guskey explains, "To become an integral part of the instructional process, assessments cannot be a one-shot, do-or-die experience for students. Instead, assessments must be part of an ongoing effort to help students learn." (Guskey, 2003)

There are many ways to assess student learning, including tests, entrance and exit passes, self- and peer-assessments (See BLMs 4.5 and 4.6.), short oral or written student or teacher reflections (See BLM 4.7.), concept maps, and teacher-student conferences.

A full exploration of assessment of, for, and as learning can be found in Chapter 5.

Teacher Tip

Journal logs are excellent pre-assessment and post-assessment tools. They help educators determine entry points (the students' level of knowledge, understanding, and skills) and can inform instruction to best guide student learning. In the early years of L2 instruction, journal entries can be very simple. Students will not only rely on sentence starters, but likely on a bank of vocabulary and expressions provided by the teacher. Illustrations can also be used by students to express their thoughts and ideas. Some journal log starter sentences are given below.

Je veux poser la question suivante à mon enseignant(e).

Je veux inclure l'étude de _____ dans mon école.

Une chose que je veux apprendre demain…

J'aime beaucoup quand la classe…

Je désire un peu plus d'information à propos de…

Un lien entre ma vie et ce que j'ai appris aujourd'hui est…

Frequent assessments propel students forward from their current level of proficiency while providing them with the next steps in the learning process.

The previous section describes various aspects of the five principles of differentiation—supportive and risk-free environment; quality curriculum; respectful work; flexible grouping; and ongoing diagnostic assessments.

- Which of these principles presents the greatest challenge for you to implement in your classroom? How have you attempted to address that challenge in the past? What new ideas do you now have to deal with this challenge?

- Take one of the differentiation principles and consider ways in which you can implement the principle. You might want to think through two perspectives—(1) what I can achieve on my own; and (2) what I need help with and where I can get that help.

- As you read the previous section, which activity jumped off the page and made you want to try it immediately with your students? Talk with a colleague about the activity and why you are so enthused about it.

A Framework for Differentiated Learning

As you use the above five principles to guide your planning, consider what and how to differentiate instruction.

What	How
Content	Readiness
Process	Interests
Product	Learning Profile
Learning Environment	

Content is the material that students use in order to gain knowledge and learn. Consider content through what students should know, understand, and be able to do (K.U.D.—Knowledge, Understanding, and Doing).

Process describes how students use skills and strategies to make sense of their learning. To help students access the process of an activity, consider:

- Format of delivery, e.g., themes, learning centres, technology, etc.

- Different grouping

- Teaching strategies and appropriate scaffolding supports

Product is the means through which students demonstrate and extend what they have learned. Ensure that students have a clear understanding of the learning goals and are provided with choice and more than one mode of expression to demonstrate, transfer, or apply what they have learned.

In the FSL class, typical products that are suitable to the subject matter and the skills that students are learning are:

- writing and performing skits, role-plays;

- conducting oral interviews and surveys;

- creating and performing dialogues with a partner;

- creating and performing raps;

- writing reviews, posters, flyers, ads, PowerPoint presentations, websites;

- researching and writing presentations;

- giving oral presentations.

The learning environment should be as rich as possible, with visuals and resources, and should allow for student and teacher movement for Total Physical Response or collaborative group activities.

Teacher Tip

If you are an itinerant teacher, collaborating with homeroom teachers is key. Consider consulting the homeroom teacher to arrange for bulletin board space for Word Walls, posters, etc. Create, or have your students create, a heading for the space and ask that it be reserved for French. If no space is available, then laminate visuals or put them on stiffer paper that can be rolled up for portability. Post visuals on the blackboard with re-usable sticky gum.

Ask for a bookcase or a corner of the classroom library where you can place a few key resources such as dictionaries. Many elementary classrooms have space for books for Language Arts. Ask if you can leave copies of French books as well. You might want to remind your L1 colleagues that students will be using the same strategies in reading French books as they do in English.

Re-arranging desks for activities is time-consuming, so consider using the existing arrangement and having students move around to form different groups.

What I Am Thinking Now

Content, instructional process, product, and classroom environment are elements to be considered in planning for differentiated instruction of WHAT students are expected to learn.

- How would you rank these topics in order of difficulty (easiest to most difficult) to implement? What factors did you consider in making this ranking? Share your observations with a colleague. Talk about the reasons for the similarities or differences in your observations.

- Suppose you have to explain these aspects of differentiated instruction to your students' parents or caregivers. Create a graphic that illustrates how these factors are connected and why each is important in teaching French.

- Think back to some of your thoughts as you read about creating optimal learning environments in Chapter 1. What new insights have you gained as you read to this point in Chapter 4?

Readiness is the entry point where students find themselves relative to a particular piece of knowledge, understanding, or skill. Learning opportunities based on a student's readiness level will ensure that students continue to learn and progress at an appropriate degree of challenge.

Tools to access prior learning (a learner's awareness of individual strengths and weaknesses, experiences, and knowledge) are useful in determining student readiness, for example:

- diagnostic assessments including pre-tests

- interviews

- self-assessments

- extended name tag activities

- entrance and exit passes

- graphic organizers like a K.W.L. chart

When students are at varying stages of readiness, tiered instruction allows you to make adjustments for different learners while keeping the same K.U.D. outcomes at all tiers. Almost any classroom activity or task can be tiered. Two or three tiers are usually best for implementation.

Be careful that students do not identify themselves as less able when they are doing a tiered assignment. Design tiered activities so that they are slightly above the level of the learner so that students can build from where they are.

Tiered Instruction

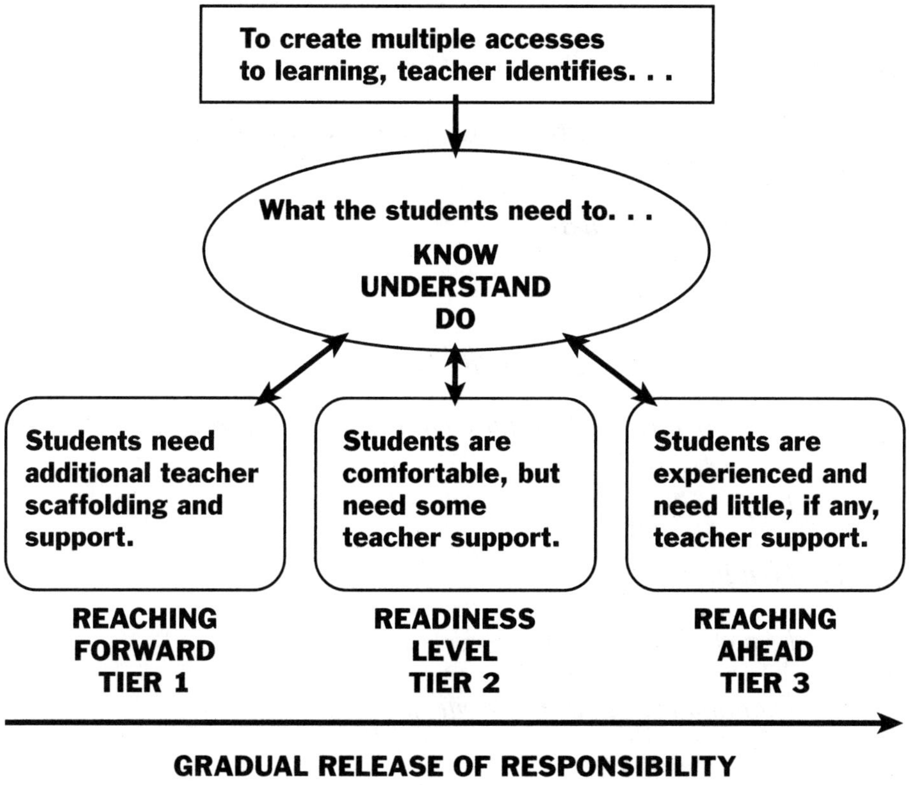

Figure 4.1: Tiered Instruction

In the following example of a tiered activity, students perform the same scenario (helping a new student get acclimatized), with the same outcomes, but in different variations with different levels of support. (See BLM 4.8.) In the first tier, partners are supported with a framework of questions and sentence starters for replying. In the second tier, students are given suggestions only for questions to ask the new student. In the third tier, students are given the option of replying with minimal responses.

In all tiers, students receive the role-play instructions:

> *Il y a un(e) nouvel(le) élève dans ta classe. Ton enseignant(e) te demande de présenter cette personne à tes camarades. D'abord, tu vas parler à l'élève. Tu vas lui poser des questions au sujet de sa vie et de ce qui l'intéresse.*

Tier 1

Each partner receives either sample questions or the corresponding sentence starters:

1. *Comment t'appelles-tu?*

2. *Où habites-tu?*

3. *D'où viens-tu? (Quelle ville? Quelle école?)*

4. *Qu'est-ce que tu aimes faire dans ton temps libre? etc.*

1. *Je m'appelle...*

2. *J'habite à...*

3. *Le nom de mon ancienne école est ...*

4. *Dans mon temps libre, j'aime ...*

Tier 2

Here, the first student conducting the interview receives suggestions for questions in addition to the role-play instructions. The student must supply the questions in full. The second student receives no sentence starters.

> *Demande à cette personne d'où il ou elle vient, de quelle ville, de quelle école, ce qu'il ou elle aime faire, ses intérêts, etc.*

Tier 3

In the third tier, the first student receives suggestions, with the added instruction to prod for full-sentence answers. The trick is that the second student has been instructed to reply only minimally, so Student #1 will have to dig for answers.

*Demande à cette personne d'où il ou elle vient,
de quelle ville, de quelle école, ce qu'il ou elle
aime faire, ses intérêts, etc. Continue à poser des
questions. Demande à l'élève de répondre par des
phrases complètes.*

Élève numéro 2

*Réponds aux questions de ton ou ta partenaire, mais
cette fois dis simplement oui, non, peut-être, je ne
sais pas, je ne suis pas cette fois-ci sûr(e)...*

Teacher Tip

As a tiered activity, try using the cubing game as a way of offering several
different perspectives on an activity. In this activity, choose a topic or theme
based on your students' interests and find objects associated with the topic.
Using the cube template (see BLM 4.9 for template), make several six-sided
cubes. Write a brief question on each side of the six sides of the cube (or
fewer, if you wish). The questions invite students to consider objects that they
will draw from a bag from many different perspectives, using different thinking
processes (Describe, Compare, Make connections, Analyze, Apply, Justify).
Possible cube questions are listed within the script below.

Voici un sac qui contient des objets. Choisissez un objet.

- *Décrivez l'objet. De quelle couleur est l'objet ? Est-il grand ou petit ?*

- *Choisissez un autre objet du sac. Comparez les deux objets.*

- *Trouvez des liens ! Est-ce que l'objet vous fait penser à quelque chose ? À une
  personne que vous connaissez ?*

- *Analysez l'objet ! De quels matériaux est-ce que l'objet est fabriqué ? D'où vient
  cet objet ? À quoi sert cet objet ?*

- *Utilisez l'objet ! Comment est-ce qu'on utilise l'objet ?*

- *Pour ou contre ? Voulez-vous garder cet objet, oui ou non ?*

Interest

High student interest occurs when students have opportunities to do
relevant activities, collaborate with peers, and make their own decisions. Tasks and activities should always be relevant in some way to the
lives of students; that means, whether they relate to their personal experiences and preferences or whether the activity highlights acquiring a
useful skill or content knowledge.

One tool for piquing student interest and differentiating activities for learners is the R.A.F.T. (Role, Audience, Format, Topic) activity. (Buehl, 2001; Tomlinson and McTighe, 2006)

According to Tomlinson and McTighe, "A R.A.F.T. assignment asks a student to assume a particular role, for a specified audience, in a certain format, in regard to a topic that causes the student to think at a high level about an essential idea in a unit of study. By varying the R.A.F.T. elements, teachers can address differences in student readiness, interest, and learning profile."(Tomlinson and McTighe, 2006)

A useful way for adapting the R.A.F.T. tool to the second-language classroom is to add a fifth category, S, for strong verb/*super verbe*. The verb characterizes the purpose or describes the tone of the work, e.g., *expliquer, démontrer, convaincre,* or *persuader.*

R.A.F.T.S. is useful in many ways: as a pre-writing strategy, as a way that students can demonstrate their learning or apply their knowledge at the end of a learning cycle. Once you have modelled a R.A.F.T.S. strategy, students can use BLM 4.10 to create their own R.A.F.T.S. assignment.

CASE STUDY	Use of Technology to Engage Students

Mike was what many teachers might recognize as fairly typical of an underachieving Grade 8 student. Drifting through his final months of elementary school, he was a perennial behavioural concern who was rarely motivated to show his teachers the abilities many felt that he had. Social acceptance came more easily to him than academic success, and French was low on his list of priorities.

His interest was piqued, however, by the "diaporama" assignment Monsieur Séris presented to the class part way through the winter. Mike learned that not only would he be able to work closely with three of his friends, he would also get to inject some humour into their ideas for sentences and photos. On top of that, he would be using a digital camera (either at home or at school, his group's choice) to take photos of his friends and manipulating the various computer programs necessary to put the slideshow together.

The idea for the assignment had all started with one of those eureka moments that teachers enjoy from time to time, very often when they least expect it. Having spent much of the past few weeks extolling the delights of comparative and superlative sentences to his Grade 8 FSL class, Monsieur Séris wondered how his students could showcase their new language in a meaningful, original, and exciting way. Various ideas came and went before he hit upon a project that he felt sure to capture their imagination—a multi-media slideshow. Working in groups of four, the students would collaborate to come up with a series of connected statements using the comparative and the superlative, which they would then illustrate with digital photos and edit into a slideshow. Students were told that the sentences need not be factual but should be created and illustrated as imaginatively as possible. For instance, the sentence « Christina est plus sportive que Ryan. » could lead to a photo of two students, one slouching in an armchair, remote control in hand, devouring a slice of pizza, the other limbering up in full sports star regalia. Captions, background music, and an audio track for the sentences to be read aloud, could all be added, and the use of props would be strongly encouraged. Students would complete the R.A.F.T.S. project form and identify which strong verb would be their focus. Eureka, thought Monsieur Séris!

Little did Mike know it, but it was a eureka moment for him, too. Whereas he would normally spend his group-work time either entertaining his friends or fading into the background, on this occasion he very quickly assumed a leadership role within his group. His ideas for the photos were usually imaginative, sometimes hilarious, and always met with approval by the rest of the group. He was extremely comfortable creating and editing the slideshow on the computer and soon became the "go-to" guy when other groups needed some help.

Needless to say, Monsieur Séris was delighted with the work of the class at all stages of the assignment and with the transformation in Mike's attitude in particular. What he had not anticipated, however, was the longevity of Mike's improvement. Long after the conclusion of the "diaporama" assignment, it was still far easier to engage Mike in the French class than it ever had been before. Technology became the key to Mike's success.

What I Am Thinking Now

Understanding our students and the various ways in which they participate and learn in school activities is perhaps one of the most intriguing aspects of teaching. Observing students in the range of daily activities in school provides valuable insights into how to differentiate instruction.

- What are some things that you always notice about your students the first time you meet them? Are your first impressions usually reliable? How do your impressions change over time? How might Monsieur Séris, from the case study, answer this question?

- Talk with a colleague about your use of "tiered instruction." What makes this approach easy to implement? difficult to implement?

- Examine your methods of collecting and recording information about your students' performance and interests. In what ways would another teacher find this material useful?

Learning Profile

A learning profile is a description of how a student learns. Some students prefer working alone, while others prefer collaboration. Some students approach topics analytically, while others prefer creative approaches. Researchers have described learning styles such as the visual, auditory, and kinaesthetic (VAK); Multiple Intelligences; and the Triarchic Theory of Intelligence.

It takes time to determine individual student learning profiles; as well, tests such as the Multiple Intelligence tests are best administered by professionals trained for that purpose. However, it is feasible to use the ideas from these researchers to inform instructional practice in order to vary materials, content, and approach. (See BLM 4.11.)

Teacher Tip

If possible, either share information with the homeroom teacher or request information from the homeroom teacher about the kind of learner your students might be. Individual learning profiles and styles will be constant across related disciplines, especially in Language Arts and FSL.

We all have a spectrum of abilities and aptitudes, although in varying degrees. Incorporating learning-style and multiple intelligence strategies that are best suited to a particular activity will help improve students' abilities in all areas.

Visual learners learn best through seeing or reading. To teach visual learners most effectively, encourage students to use these strategies:

- Note-taking

- Colour-coding notes and other information with highlighters and sticky notes

- Using graphic organizers

- Learning from audiovisual (TV, DVD, webcast) formats

- Reading text in a variety of formats (books, posters, Internet)

- Using classroom visuals (Word Walls, posters)

Auditory learners learn best through hearing. To teach auditory learners most effectively, encourage students to use these strategies:

- Reread texts aloud in class

- Repeat information

- Take turns reading aloud with a partner

- Play activities in which they have to come up with expressions or adjectives to describe a story or character

Kinesthetic learners learn best by touching, doing, and moving. To teach kinesthetic learners most effectively, encourage students to use these strategies:

- Associate physical actions and gestures with learning (e.g., acting out vocabulary)

- Do warm-ups and daily routines

- Make and explain physical representations (e.g., models) of learning

- Show other students how to do an activity

- Perform role-plays

Multiple Intelligences

Theories of intelligences are varied and complex. It has been said that education changed when Harvard professor of education Dr. Howard Gardner added an "s" to the word "intelligence." Many of today's top researchers (including Gardner, Sternberg, Perkins, and others) agree that a single view of intelligence in light of current brain-based research is no longer realistic or acceptable.

Howard Gardner's theory of multiple intelligences is a way of understanding how students can learn using a variety of different abilities and skills. Gardner maintains that although these intelligences are distinct from one another, we all possess some degree of each of them.

Researchers agree that the brain needs novelty, and numerous opportunities to practise learning new material. The brain likes challenge, but it must be a challenge that it is well prepared to receive in a learning environment that is risk-free and inclusive. It is critical to the learning process that learners are able to make associations between new learning and prior learning. Perhaps the most critical information that has come from brain-based research concerns the brain's plasticity. The brain does not stop learning and given the proper circumstances and stimulation, it will continue to learn throughout an individual's lifetime.

Howard Gardner's multiple intelligences theory is a way for students to demonstrate cognitive ability. Second-language teachers have had great success integrating Howard Gardner's intelligence profiles in lesson planning.

1. **Verbal/Linguistic**: This intelligence describes a student's capacity to think using words. Students who possess this type of intelligence in a dominant way often display an auditory learning style. Verbal/linguistic learners use language to understand and express complex ideas. Generally, they are articulate speakers. Their repertoire of skills includes critical listening abilities and specialized speaking skills that allow them to be engaging storytellers, humorists, and debaters.

2. **Logical/Mathematical**: Students with this type of intelligence are able to think conceptually, and easily make connections between pieces of information. They reason in a logical and often linear fashion and investigate issues in a scientific or deductive fashion. They are deeply curious about the world around them and as a result they like to experiment and explore. They have strong problem-solving skills and are adept at classifying and categorizing information.

3. **Visual/Spatial**: A person who displays visual/spatial intelligence has a visual learning style. This intelligence describes the learner's ability to perceive the visual first and foremost. These learners think in pictures and create mental

images and mind maps to retain information. They are proficient readers and writers. Generally, they understand charts, graphs, and maps with ease.

4. **Bodily/Kinesthetic**: This intelligence explains a person's ability to demonstrate fine and gross motor control. Normally, their learning style is tactile/kinesthetic as well. These learners can perform tasks that require physical precision as they possess a good sense of balance and well-defined eye-hand coordination. They express themselves best through movement. They will remember and process information and new knowledge by interacting with the space around them. They like using their hands to create and build.

5. **Musical/Rhythmic**: Students display this intelligence in their appreciation of music. They are sensitive to tone, melody, and rhythm. These learners have the capacity to make connections in the environment and to create imaginative and expressive performances. They easily remember melodies and will recall information by associating learning to the structure and rhythm of music.

6. **Interpersonal**: Students who are empathic and show an ability to relate and understand other people in the class have interpersonal intelligence. These learners can interact effectively with others as they try to see things from their point of view. They are able, as a consequence, to sense feelings and understand intentions and desires of others. They encourage cooperation among their peers and are great organizers. They use both verbal and non-verbal expression to communicate with others.

7. **Intrapersonal**: Students with this kind of intelligence have the ability to self-reflect. These learners understand the self as a learner and are able to use this information to regulate their life. They are aware of their strengths and weaknesses and understand the role that they play in relation to others.

Intelligence	Description	Instructional strategy
Verbal/Linguistic	• Learning through written and spoken language • Strong at auditory learning • Articulate speakers	Learners can: • tell stories • explain and teach others • debate
Logical/Mathematical	• Learning through thinking conceptually in logical ways • Making connections between pieces of information • Enjoy experimenting and exploring	Learners can: • analyze information texts • present material in the form of problem to be solved • classify and prioritize information and tasks
Visual/Spatial	• Learning through visual means • Interpreting data through charts, graphs, maps, pictures • Learning by imagining objects in space	Learners can: • visualize what they are reading/learning (through images and/or in space) • use charts, graphs, maps, illustrations
Bodily/Kinesthetic	• Ability to do tasks requiring physical skill • Good balance and hand-eye coordination	Learners can: • do physical gestures and mime • build models • make illustrations
Musical/Rhythmic	• Sensitivity to tone, melody, and rhythm	Learners can: • use chants, raps, songs, and poetry as aids to learning
Interpersonal	• Ability to see things from others' points of view • Adept at reading non-verbal body language • Good at group dynamics	Learners can: • work in groups • devise or choose effective group roles
Intrapersonal	• Ability to reflect on personal strengths and weaknesses, on strategies for learning	Learners can: • use metacognitive strategies by reflecting on how and why strategies for learning work

Over the years, Gardner has added to this list of intelligences. He has described naturalist, existential, and spiritual intelligence types. The above intelligences, however, work best for considering students' skills and abilities and aligning instructional practices and activities with them.

The Triarchic Theory of Intelligence

Sternberg offers an additional way for educators to perceive learning profiles and intelligences in students. In his theory of triarchic intelligence, Sternberg defines intelligence as "your skill in achieving whatever it is you want to attain in your life within your sociocultural context by capitalizing on your strengths and compensating for, or correcting, your weaknesses." (Interview, 2004) The Sternberg's Triarchic Theory of Intelligence does not depend on a cognitive scale of information or intelligence test, but rather on a person's ability to adapt to the environment.

Sternberg's Triarchic Theory of (Successful) Intelligence contends that intelligent behaviour arises from a balance between analytical, creative, and practical abilities, and that these abilities function collectively to allow individuals to achieve success within particular sociocultural contexts. (Sternberg, 1988, 1997, 1999) Analytical abilities enable the individual to evaluate, analyze, compare, and contrast information. Creative abilities generate invention, discovery, and other creative endeavours. Practical abilities tie everything together by allowing individuals to apply what they have learned in the appropriate setting.

To be successful in life, the individual must make the best use of his or her analytical, creative, and practical strengths, while at the same time compensating for weaknesses in any of these areas. This might involve working on improving weak areas to become better adapted to the needs of a particular environment, or choosing to work in an environment that values the individual's particular strengths. For example, a person with highly developed analytical and practical abilities, but with less well-developed creative abilities, might choose to work in a field that values technical expertise but does not require a great deal of imaginative thinking. Conversely, if the chosen career does value creative abilities, the individual can use his or her analytical strengths to come up with strategies for improving this weakness.

Thus, a central feature of the Sternberg's Triarchic Theory of Intelligence is adaptability, both within the individual and within the individual's sociocultural context. (Cianciolo and Sternberg, 2004)

Activities that involve the same themes, vocabulary, and language structure can be adapted to incorporate the three intelligences. For example, if the theme involves current technologies (e.g., cell phones, computers), you might adapt an oral or written presentation on the same theme in three different ways:

Analytical	Creative	Practical
Debate cell phone/Internet use in schools. Should students be allowed to use cell phones/surf the Internet while in school? Why or why not?	Describe the cell phone/Internet of the twenty-third century. Will we still be using cell phone technology/Internet?	If you could talk to a cell phone/laptop manufacturer, what improvements would you suggest? What other tasks or functions would you suggest?

Sternberg believes that it is critical to focus instruction on all three of these intelligences by deliberately balancing activities to incorporate all of these skills. The necessity for the students to be aware of their own intelligence preferences cannot be underestimated. It is only when we know how we learn best that we all become better learners.

These ideas support and help further define differentiated instruction. Planning with these abilities and intelligences in mind can diversify and expand your instructional strategies to meet the needs of a greater number of learners.

What I Am Thinking Now

· What did you learn about your own learning style as you read this section? In what ways do you think your learning style affects how you teach?

· Think back to your first-impression observations of your students. Did those impressions take into account any factors that relate to learning profiles? How do you think your understanding of learning profiles will affect your initial impressions of your students in the future?

· In what ways do you think you can incorporate information about learning profiles in your observations of your students?

· What impact do you think the learning profiles of individual teachers have on collegial efforts at school? Talk with your colleagues about this matter.

Summary

Chapman and King (2005) invite educators to develop an acrostic to describe their differentiated classroom. The following acrostic summarizes the main points of this chapter.

Differentiate

- **D**etermine students' Knowledge, Understanding, and what they can Do (K.U.D.).

- **I**dentify your students' needs with multiple assessment tools before, during, and after learning.

- **F**ocus on knowing the student.

- **F**lexible grouping will allow students access to the same classroom curriculum on the basis of their strengths.

- **E**ngage students in activities that are of interest to them and appropriate to the ways in which they learn.

- **R**espond to students' readiness, interests, and learning profile.

- **E**ncourage risk-taking and provide opportunities for student choice.

- **N**urture students' need for a safe and inclusive environment.

- **T**arget the learners' needs and use strategies and activities to teach them all.

- **I**nstill a love and a joy of learning in your students.

- **A**ctivate their prior learning before introducing new concepts.

- **T**ailor classes with student-focused activities.

- **E**nhance your students' learning experiences by matching student intelligences to instruction and assessment.

My Choices

Differentiating instruction is about making choices—choices that affect both you and your students.

What factor did you encounter in this chapter that had the most impact on your thinking about your students? about your teaching practices?

Much of the discussion about differentiating instruction centres on accommodating students' needs—and that is an important consideration. But teachers are also individuals. What do you think should be done in professional learning to accommodate teachers' individual learning styles and interests?

Notre salle de classe préférée

Noms : _____ Classe : _____ Date : _____

Partie A

En groupe, considérez les actions des élèves et l'enseignant ou l'enseignante dans votre salle de classe. Associez des mots qui décrient ces actions dans votre salle de classe. Soyez spécifique.

Dans notre salle de classe, les gens...

a. écoutent

_____

_____

b. parlent

_____

_____

c. chantent

_____

_____

d. rient

_____

_____

e. travaillent

_____

_____

f. lisent

_____

_____

g. font des devoirs

_____

_____

Partie B

Complétez le tableau.

Dans notre salle de classe préférée...

Je vois des camarades qui...	J'entends des camarades qui...	Moi, je fais...

Partie C

Défi !

Regroupez avec deux élèves différents et partagez vos listes de la Partie A.

Mimez les actions dans votre liste et demandez aux autres élèves de deviner l'action.

Passe d'entrée

Nom : _____

Classe : _____

Date : _____

Bonjour et bienvenue à ta classe de français !

Pense à notre leçon de français d'hier et écris ou dessine des réponses.

3 choses que j'ai bien comprises hier…

2 choses que je veux améliorer…

1 chose que je vais faire aujourd'hui…

Passe d'entrée

Nom : _____

Classe : _____

Date : _____

Bonjour et bienvenue à ta classe de français !

Pense à notre leçon de français d'hier et écris ou dessine des réponses.

3 choses que j'ai bien comprises hier…

2 choses que je veux améliorer…

1 chose que je vais faire aujourd'hui…

Passe de sortie (1)

Nom : _____

Classe : _____

Date : _____

Avant de partir...

Pense à notre leçon de français d'hier et écris ou dessine des réponses.

3 choses faciles à comprendre...

2 choses difficiles à comprendre...

1 chose qui va m'aider...

Passe de sortie (1)

Nom : _____

Classe : _____

Date : _____

Avant de partir...

Pense à notre leçon de français d'hier et écris ou dessine des réponses.

3 choses faciles à comprendre...

2 choses difficiles à comprendre...

1 chose qui va m'aider...

Passe de sortie (2)

Nom : _____ Classe : _____ Date : _____

Réponds à la phrase suivante. Tu peux écrire, dessiner, ou décrire ta réponse à un ou une partenaire.

Ce soir, pendant le souper, je vais raconter à ma famille qu'aujourd'hui j'ai...

Écris ta réponse :

_____

_____

Dessine ta réponse :

Prends des notes pour décrire ta réponse à un ou une partenaire :

_____   _____

_____   _____

Passe sortie (2)

Nom : _____ Classe : _____ Date : _____

Réponds à la phrase suivante. Tu peux écrire, dessiner, ou décrire ta réponse à un ou une partenaire.

Ce soir, pendant le souper, je vais raconter à ma famille qu'aujourd'hui j'ai...

Écris ta réponse :

_____

_____

Dessine ta réponse :

Prends des notes pour décrire ta réponse à un ou une partenaire :

_____   _____

_____   _____

Auto-évaluation—Le travail de groupe

Nom : _____ Classe : _____ Date : _____

	Moi	Les autres membres
J'ai participé activement à l'activité.	😐 🙂 🙁	
J'étais concentré sur la tâche.	😐 🙂 🙁	
J'ai encouragé les autres membres.	😐 🙂 🙁	
J'ai organisé mon travail.	😐 🙂 🙁	
J'ai fini à temps.	😐 🙂 🙁	

Qu'est-ce que j'ai fait pour aider mon groupe?

_____

_____

Qu'est-ce que je vais améliorer la prochaine fois?

_____

_____

Auto-évaluation—Mon équipe et moi

Nom : _____ Classe : _____ Date : _____

Evalue ton rendement dans le groupe a l'aide de l'echelle Toujours-Jamais.

1. Je felicite et encourage les autres membres de mon groupe.

◆───────────────────────────◆

TOUJOURS   JAMAIS

2. Je partage mon materiel avec les autres.

◆───────────────────────────◆

TOUJOURS   JAMAIS

3. J'ecoute les autres sans les interrompre.

◆───────────────────────────◆

TOUJOURS   JAMAIS

4. Je m'assure que tout mon groupe comprend bien ce que nous devons faire.

◆───────────────────────────◆

TOUJOURS   JAMAIS

5. J'aide les autres et j'accepte aussi leur aide.

◆───────────────────────────◆

TOUJOURS   JAMAIS

6. J'assume la responsabilité d'encourager le groupe à bien travailler.

◆───────────────────────────◆

TOUJOURS   JAMAIS

Suggestions pour notre prochain travail en groupe :

_____

_____

_____

_____

_____

(Adapté de Clarke, Wideman et Eadie, 1994)

Je comprends la leçon—Réflexion

Au commencement	Pendant la leçon	Â la fin
J'ai compris les instructions du professeur.	J'ai compris les instructions du professeur.	J'ai compris les instructions du professeur.
J'ai suivi les directives.	J'ai suivi les directives.	J'ai suivi les directives.
J'ai bien travaillé seul(e) et avec mes camarades de classe.	J'ai bien travaillé seul(e) et avec mes camarades de classe.	J'ai bien travaillé seul(e) et avec mes camarades de classe.
J'ai compris la leçon.	J'ai compris la leçon.	J'ai compris la leçon.
J'ai accompli le travail requis.	J'ai accompli le travail requis.	J'ai accompli le travail requis.

Tâches en gradins : jeu de rôles

Le nouvel élève de ma classe

Niveau 1 :

L'élève A

La situation
Il y a un nouvel élève dans ta classe. Ton enseignant(e) te demande de présenter le nouvel élève à tes amis. D'abord, tu vas parler à l'élève. Tu vas poser des questions au sujet de sa vie et ses champs d'intérêt.

Voici quelques questions à poser :

1. Comment t'appelles-tu ?

2. Quel âge as-tu ?

3. Où habites-tu ?

4. D'où viens-tu ? (Quelle ville ? Quelle école ?)

5. Qu'est-ce que tu aimes faire dans ton temps libre ?

6. Est-ce que tu aimes faire du sport ? Quel est ton sport préféré ?

7. Est-ce que tu aimes écouter de la musique ? Quelle est ta musique préférée ?

8. Est-ce que tu aimes lire ? Quel est ton livre préféré ?

9. Est-ce que tu aimes regarder des films ? Quel est ton film préféré ?

10. Est-ce que tu aimes jouer à des jeux vidéo ? Quel est ton jeu vidéo préféré ?

L'élève B

Réponds aux questions de l'élève A.

1. Je m'appelle _____ .

2. J'ai _____ ans _____ .

3. J'habite à _____ .

4. Le nom de mon ancienne école est _____

_____ .

5. Mon sport préféré est _____ .

6. J'aime écouter la musique _____ .

7. Ma musique préférée, c'est _____ .

8. J'aime lire. Mon livre préféré, c'est _____

_____ .

9. J'aime regarder des films. Mon film préféré, c'est

_____

10. Non, je n'aime pas jouer à des jeux vidéo.
Oui, j'aime jouer à des jeux vidéo. Mon jeu vidéo préféré, c'est_____ .

Niveau 2 :

L'élève A

La situation
Il y a un nouvel élève dans ta classe. Ton enseignant(e) te demande de présenter le nouvel élève à tes amis. D'abord, tu vas parler à l'élève. Tu vas poser des questions au sujet de sa vie. Par exemple, demande au nouvel élève d'où il vient, de quelle ville, de quelle école, ce qu'il aime faire, ses champs d'intérêt, etc.

L'élève B
Réponds aux questions de l'élève A. Sois polie et enthousiaste !

Niveau 3 :

L'élève A

La situation
Il y a un nouvel élève dans ta classe. Ton enseignant(e) te demande de présenter le nouvel élève à tes amis. D'abord, tu vas parler à l'élève. Tu vas poser des questions au sujet de sa vie. Par exemple, demande au nouvel élève d'où il vient, de quelle ville, de quelle école, ce qu'il aime faire, ses champs d'intérêt, etc. Continue à poser des questions. Demande à ton ami de répondre par des phrases complètes.

L'élève B
Réponds aux questions de l'élève B, mais cette fois dis simplement : oui, non, peut-être, je ne sais pas, je ne suis pas sûr(e) ...

Gabarit d'un cube

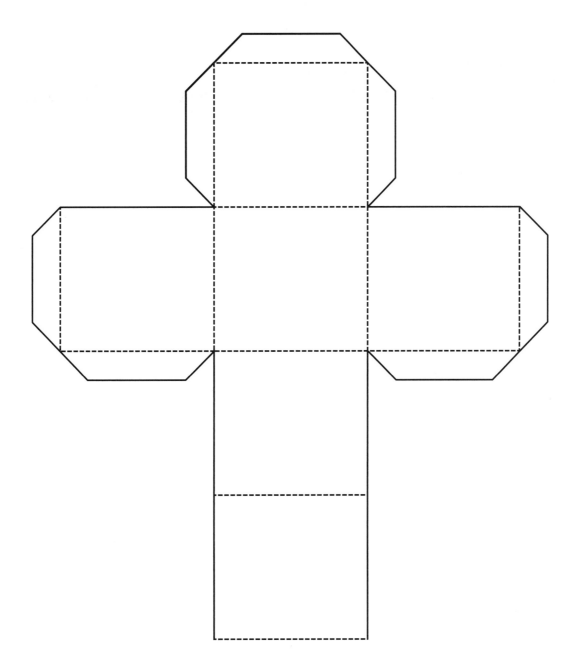

Mon projet de R.A.F.T.S.

Nom : _____ Classe : _____ Date : _____

Titre de mon projet : _____

Rôle	Audience	Forme	Thème	Super verbe
Quel est ton rôle ? Qui es-tu ?	Qui va écouter, regarder, ou lire ton travail ?	Comment vas-tu faire ton travail : présentation orale, écrite, illustrée ?	Quel est le sujet ?	Choisis un verbe qui décrit le but de ton travail : Expliquer Démontrer Convaincre Persuader

Prenons l'autobus ensemble

Noms du groupe : _____

Classe: _____   Date: _____

Le conducteur / La conductrice va décrire des actions. Si tu l'entends parler d'une action que tu aimes, monte dans l'autobus !

Défi : Mime les actions ! Fais des gestes !

Monte dans l'autobus si...

1. tu aimes dessiner
2. tu aimes lire
3. tu aimes regarder les sports à la télé
4. tu aimes courir
5. tu aimes les mathématiques et les sciences
6. tu aimes faire du camping
7. tu aimes écouter de la musique
8. tu as ton propre ordinateur
9. tu as un téléphone cellulaire
10. tu as un chien
11. tu as un chat
12. tu as voyagé en dehors du Canada

Défi : À deux, pensez à deux autres actions. Prenez le rôle du conducteur ou de la conductrice et demandez à vos camarades de monter dans l'autobus si...

_____

_____

_____

Chapter 5

Assessing for Success

"Without continuous assessment, student learning is limited to a one-shot, hit-or-miss event—maybe they get it, maybe they don't."
—McTighe and Emberger, 2005

My Thoughts

- What do you think are some characteristics of continuous assessment? How does continuous assessment apply in your teaching?

- Sometimes "hit-or-miss" events occur inadvertently during lessons. In what ways do your assessment strategies help you deal with student behaviours/responses that you have not anticipated in your lesson planning?

- In what ways do your assessment purposes, methods, and uses vary across reporting periods, for example, at the beginning of the school year? at mid-year? at the end of the year?

In this chapter, we will discuss:

- What Is Assessment?

- BIG Assessment Ideas

- Planning with Assessment in Mind

- Assessing with the Learner in Mind

- Building an Assessment Toolkit

- Creating Communicative Assessment Strategies

- Your FSL Assessment Toolkit

What Is Assessment?

Assessment is a cyclical process involving the gathering of data about student knowledge and skills in order to inform teaching and enhance learning.

A variety of terminology is used to further define assessment. Definitions for and use of the terminology differ significantly across the country. Some jurisdictions use the terminology *assessment* and *evaluation* while in others, the terms *diagnostic, formative,* and *summative* are used; while yet others are beginning to use *assessment FOR learning, assessment OF learning, and assessment AS learning.*

Regardless of the terminology used, the need for assessment is the same. Diagnostic and formative assessments are integral to instruction—these are classroom-centered activities distinct from many summative assessments that (at least traditionally) have often been external to classroom activities. Effective classroom-based assessment takes all three aspects into account to meet the different purposes teachers have for assessing student performance and progress.

Diagnostic, formative, and summative practices are repeated as often as necessary in order for the teacher to gather evidence about student progress before a formal evaluative mark is assigned. (Kristmanson and Cogswell, 2007)

As in many areas of learning, involving students directly in the assessment process will encourage them to take ownership of their own learning. Achievement improves when students understand the purpose of their learning, where they are in relation to it, and the steps needed to achieve their goals.

- *l'évaluation au service de l'apprentissage* (for)
- *l'évaluation de l'apprentissage* (of)
- *l'évaluation en tout qu'apprentissage* (as)

Teacher Tip

When referring to assessment and evaluation in French, note that, in French, *évaluation* is used for both: *évaluation au service de l'apprentissage* and *évaluation de l'apprentissage.*

The following chart summarizes and defines, for the purposes of this book, the most commonly used assessment terms.

Term	Definition
Assessment	Gathering data about student knowledge and/or skills, either through informal methods, such as observation, or formal methods, such as testing.
Evaluation	Making judgments about student-demonstrated knowledge and/or skills.
Diagnostic Assessment	Assessment to find out where a student is in relation to material or a skill, and to determine appropriate starting points for instruction.
Formative Assessment	Assessment that occurs during the learning process and provides feedback to both students and teachers to help improve learning.
Assessment FOR Learning	Assessment designed primarily to promote learning and determine students' next steps. Designed to improve on students' most recent best work, through descriptive feedback, not marks.
Assessment AS Learning	Assessment that emphasizes self-reflection and metacognition. Students learn to reflect on how they learn and how to use learning strategies effectively, both during and after the assessment activity.
Assessment OF Learning	Assessment to determine student achievement at a given point in time (e.g., grades, marks) intended for parents, students, school, and board administration. Usually assessment provides a snapshot of student progress and indicates if he/she is ready to move forward.
Summative Assessment	Assessment that occurs at the end of a significant period of learning and summarizes student achievement of that learning.

(Adapted from Cooper, 2007)

Links can be made between the various terminologies.

Equivalent Terminology	
Diagnostic Assessment	**Assessment FOR Learning**
Formative Assessment	**Assessment FOR Learning** **Assessment AS Learning**
Summative Assessment	**Assessment OF Learning**

BIG Assessment Ideas

In *Talk About Assessment*, Damian Cooper lists eight assessment principles to consider during planning.

1. Assessment serves different purposes at different times: it can be used to find out what students already know and can do; it can be used to help students improve their learning; or it can be used to let students and their parents know how much they have learned within a prescribed period of time.

2. Assessment must be planned and purposeful.

3. Assessment must include oral, performance, and written tasks, and be flexible in order to improve learning for all students.

4. Assessment and instruction are inseparable because effective assessment informs learning.

5. For assessment to be helpful to students, it must inform them in words, not numerical scores or letter grades, about what they have done well, what they have done poorly, and what they need to do next in order to improve.

6. Assessment is a collaborative process that is most effective when it involves self-, peer, and teacher assessment.

7. Performance standards are an essential component of effective assessment.

Consult the CD-ROM for a short video segment on the development of a unit of study using the unit planning sheet (See BLMs 2.3, 2.4, and 2.5.)

8. Grading and reporting student achievement are caring, sensitive processes that require teachers' professional judgment.

(Cooper, 2007)

Planning with Assessment in Mind

Our assessment practices have a direct impact on student success. This is why it is so important to consider which assessment methods are available for use and in what situations they are most appropriate. There are three fundamental questions to ask each time you do assessment FOR and AS:

1. What is the purpose of the assessment?

2. How will I gather appropriate assessment data?

3. How will I use this data to inform instruction and improve student achievement?

(Sparks, 1999)

Assessment Question	Assessment Type	Assessment Step	Assessment Tools
1. What is the purpose of the assessment?	FOR	During this step: • Determine what to assess • Set criteria against which student outcomes will be assessed • Ensure that students understand the purpose of assessment activity	Refer to curricula information, outcomes, expectations, as necessary
2. How will I gather appropriate assessment data?	FOR AS OF	During this step, choose appropriate information-gathering strategies: • Focused observations • Questioning • Conferencing • Self-assessment • Peer assessment	Learning logs Checklists Rubrics Journals Entrance and exit passes Portfolios
3. How will I use this data to inform instruction and improve student achievement?	FOR AS OF	At this step: • Provide students with accurate feedback • Provide students/parents/guardians with ideas for support • Differentiate instruction as necessary • Provide scaffolding	For Assessment AS Learning: Reflection tools, e.g., strategy checklists For Assessment of Learning: Rubrics

Backward design is the term for creating a lesson, activity, or unit of learning by starting with the end result in mind: the student learning outcomes. Planning assessment is an integral part of the backward design process and requires knowing the goal.

Share the goals and outcomes to be achieved and the assessment instruments to be used with students. Review curriculum expectations if necessary. Identify the K.U.D. (what students should know, understand, and be able to do as a result of their learning), within the context of student and teacher goals, learning profiles, and interests.

Before planning a unit, ask yourself the following three questions:

Curriculum: What do I expect students to know and be able to do at the end of this unit, term, or year?

Assessment: How will I determine whether they have learned these things?

At this point, consider what evidence would make it possible for students to demonstrate not only that they have learned, but also that they have understood the material.

Instruction: What series of lessons will be most effective in enabling students to demonstrate they have learned these things?

The emphasis is on an inquiry-based approach to learning as students work through a variety of learning experiences to slowly uncover the content.

(Cooper, 2007)

Setting the Goal

- What should the end result be? What should students be able to do?
- Consider the nature of the goals
- Review curriculum expectations/outcomes
- Consider student interests

Measuring Attainment of the Goal

- How will student achievement be determined/assessed?
- What assessment strategies and tools will be helpful?

Instructing with the Goal in Mind

- What are the elements—the knowledge, learning, linguistic and communicative goals, skills—that the unit/lesson/activity should include?
- What pre-activities will be required?
- What resources and materials will be required?

Since units and classes are planned with the end target in mind, so too must assessment be purposefully designed during each stage of instruction. You cannot determine acceptable evidence of learning (assessment FOR, AS, and OF learning) unless you have identified the desired outcome. As a unit of learning progresses, you undoubtedly make decisions, rethink, and try out various strategies and instruction practices to better suit student needs. It is also important to rethink, try out, and reflect on your assessment practices. Assessment is an integral part of a process whose primary role is to facilitate student learning and improve instruction. (See BLMs 5.2, 5.3, and 5.4 to assist in planning assessment.)

CASE STUDY | Implementing Backward Design

Mme Castelli's Grade 7 French class is learning about festivals throughout la Francophonie. Among the festivals the class is learning about, Mme Castelli has decided to concentrate on Mardi Gras because her class will be learning about it in February, and it seems appropriate to cover Mardi Gras in depth when the class will need an excuse to have a party in the middle of winter! The students are reading about Mardi Gras and watching a DVD about the preparations for the Mardi Gras parade.

The resources available to Mme Castelli are reading selections from a non-fiction book, from a website on Mardi Gras, and a DVD clip of the parade. Her students are already familiar with describing and organizing elements such as dances, decorations, and food for general parties from other French class activities. Mme Castelli decides to use the material and the principles of backward design to devise assessable tasks for her students related to the Mardi Gras theme.

Mme Castelli decides that the final project will be a class party and that, in groups, students will be responsible for organizing a different party element. Each group's task will require members to decide on their contribution together, assign roles and responsibilities, make plans, prepare and rehearse as necessary, and orally present to the other groups.

Mme Castelli makes notes based on the three fundamental assessment questions: what to assess, how to gather data, and how to use the data to inform her instructional practice and move students forward in their learning. In addition, she notes resources and how she and the students will use them.

My Unit Planning Notes

1. Students should be able to:
   - Appreciate Francophone culture (curriculum outcome) through learning about Mardi Gras, its history and traditions
   - Research festival customs or traditions (curriculum outcome)
   - Communicate orally about some element of Mardi Gras (curriculum outcome)

2. How will I assess student achievement?
   - Informally assessing partner conversations
   - Choosing one partner conversation for formal assessment
   - Conferencing with groups to ensure that they are on task
   - Each student is responsible for one element in the party/parade planning (making and describing a costume or food item, creating a banner, writing a song) and performing or explaining it orally/describing it in writing

3. Students will need to be able to:
   - Use reading strategies
   - Use viewing and listening strategies
   - Use the following language and expressions in class and pair conversations, during oral presentations:
     - imperative of –er verbs
     - *assister à, décorer, goûter, organiser, participer à, préparer, des babioles, une bannière, cajun, un collier de perles, une fête, un maquillage, la nourriture*

4. What activities will students do to achieve the learning and communicative outcomes?
   - Read information on Mardi Gras history and food in Louisiana
   - Watch DVD about people preparing a Mardi Gras float
   - Create a poster to advertise a Mardi Gras event (using imperative, related vocabulary)
   - Listen to conversations between Mardi Gras participants
   - Discuss Mardi Gras activities with a partner using recorded conversations as models
   - State preferences about activities they would like to participate in
   - Make suggestions about activities or food for Mardi Gras celebrations
   - In groups, organize a Mardi Gras party with at least two of the following elements:
     - song or rap
     - float design
     - costumes
     - props (*babioles*, banners)
     - food
     - other, depending on their interests, to be discussed with teacher

5. What resources do I need for the activities?
   - Group work sheet (for members to fill in their roles, responsibilities)
   - Reinforcement exercises for language structures (imperative)
   - Textbook, magazine article, website, DVD, audio CD listening activities, and *cahier*
   - Share past examples (pictures of oral pres., videos) *<Catch: ED Note Please Check>*

What I Am Thinking Now

Reflect on the Case Study: Implementing Backward Design

- What do you see as the advantages of the backward design approach to lesson planning?

- To what extent do other teachers in your school follow this approach to lesson planning? If backward design is not widely used, how would you initiate a discussion with other teachers about this approach?

Assessing with the Learner in Mind
Involving Students

Engaging students in the assessment process encourages them to take more responsibility for their learning. Invite students to participate in the selection of the various assessment instruments that will be included in a learning cycle. Building trust and giving quality feedback on student achievement is imporant for involving students in the assessment process.

Building Trust and Confidence

In all learning environments, and especially in the FSL classroom, it is essential to establish a culture of trust and collaboration. Make explicit the role that both you and your students play in learning. Share with students ideas about the process of assessment.

Students will come to understand that each assessment tool is just one of many assessment tools used to determine an entry point rather than an end point in their learning experience. Students will feel confident to use all available assessment information provided to redirect their efforts to meet the goals and see themselves as winners in the process of assessment.

Giving Feedback

Assessment tools are effective when students receive timely and specific feedback. This feedback helps them celebrate their successes, focus on where additional practice is required, and retain their learning.

Students demonstrate learning in a variety of ways. This is why it is vital to provide a variety of ways to assess their learning. No single assessment can do it all. Students require opportunities to say, do, and write in order to demonstrate what they have learned. The goal is to provide them with valuable, meaningful feedback regarding their progress and at the same time hone in on one or two areas that require additional time, strategies, and practice so that they can improve.

Given that the primary goal of language learning is the ability to communicate, it is understandable that students might want to "run before they can walk." Students might experience the frustration of not being able to say what they want to say. Encourage them to tolerate some initial incomprehension and appreciate all gains in language competency.

In a learning or assessment situation, your attention should be focused primarily on the message that the student is trying to transmit. The desire to communicate (the message) should therefore take priority over the language and grammar (the form).

Encourage students by assuring them that they will have multiple opportunities to hear, repeat, and practise. Let them know that, in time, they will be able to talk about themselves, their family, and friends. They will be able to ask and answer questions, and share information and events, and they will do so in French.

Figure 5.1: Driving Lessons. It is accepted that driving is a skill that all should learn and, therefore, re-testing is an accepted practice. A paradigm shift is afoot in formal education settings that recognizes that learners follow different paths of achievement and, as a result, multiple opportunities to perform assessment of learning tasks is sometimes a necessary and valuable practice. The emphasis is placed on the achievement of the learning outcome.

"Form carries the message but is never more important than it. This implies that errors in form must be 'tolerated' so long as they do not hamper communication. The teacher slowly encourages refinement of form, first by being a good model and secondly, by intervening in an appropriate manner." (Manitoba *programme d'études*, 2006)

Teacher Tip

To provide meaningful feedback, consider the following tips:

- If a group of students has the same difficulty, provide them with a mini-lesson or review while other students are engaged in an independent task.
- If all or most students in the class are having difficulty with a specific task, analyze an (anonymous) example of student work together.
- Examine anchor papers with the class. Anchors are useful tools associated with specific levels of achievement. Ask students to identify the differences between the above level and below level papers to set a benchmark.
- Allow for regular conferencing time with individuals or small groups. Conferencing, especially at the beginning of a learning cycle, provides students with the immediate, anecdotal, qualitative feedback that they need.

From the Research

Six types of corrective feedback were identified by second-language researchers Roy Lyster and Leila Ranta. (Lyster and Ranta, 1997) As you read the six different types of corrective feedback, think about which ones you use in your teaching practice. Which one method do you think proved to be the most effective?

Explicit correction: Tell students that the statement is incorrect and provide the correct form.

Student: *Je suis faim.* Teacher: *En français, on dit j'ai faim.*

Recast. Provide the correction indirectly through reformulation, but do not explicitly point out the error.

Student: *Je suis faim.* Teacher: *J'ai faim, aussi. Il est presque midi.*

Clarification request. Tell students that you have not understood. Ask students to repeat or reformulate the statement.

Student: *Je suis faim.* Teacher: *Pardon ? Je ne comprends pas.*

Metalinguistic clues. Do not provide the correct form. Instead, ask questions or make comments about how the statement was phrased.

Student: *Je suis faim.* Teacher: *Est-ce qu'on dit je suis ?*

Elicitation. Ask questions or make comments to prompt the correct form, e.g. "Say that again," so that the student is encouraged to give more than a yes or no response.

Student: *Je suis faim.* Teacher: *Essaie encore.*

Repetition. Repeat what the student has said, stressing the error through intonation.

Student: *Je suis faim.* Teacher: *Je suis faim?*

In cases where students responded to the feedback, they could only repeat what the teacher said in explicit correction and recasts, but could self-repair after clarification requests, metalinguistic clues, elicitation, and repetition. Of these four feedback types, metalinguistic clues and elicitation led to the highest rates of student-generated repair.

What I Am Thinking Now

There are distinct differences of opinion on the benefits of error correction in spoken and written language. One school of thought is that if there are errors in writing, then the student is also making them orally. For the student to not make the errors in writing, you have to correct the same error in oral production for awareness of the error to be internalized.

What are your experiences with error correction in the FSL classroom? Have you ever experimented with your approaches to error correction? with what results?

Building an Assessment Toolkit

Figure 5.2: Assessment Toolkit

One of the greatest challenges in teaching lies in discovering how to encourage students to want to learn. When appropriate assessments for learning strategies are incorporated into the second-language classroom, the result is that students want to learn and feel able to learn. The challenge often resides in discovering the strategies that best assess students in such a way that they become more successful learners.

Routine classroom activities provide many opportunities to collect information about students' performance. These activities can be used at various stages in lessons and enable you to develop composite pictures of your students as learners.

An **assessment toolkit** must contain a wide range of **assessment strategies** and tools to be used for the purpose of gauging learner attainment of goals. An **assessment strategy** is the activity that the teacher sets for the student. An **assessment tool** provides feedback to the student, helps teachers make instructional decisions and compiles data for reporting

Assessment strategies can take many shapes, for example:

- games and activities that are catalysts for role-play or dialogues

- songs and rhymes that encourage retention of expressions

- learning logs, journals, entrance and exit passes

Or they can be more formal instruments such as

- graphic organizers to help students organize their thoughts

- performance tasks, end-of-unit tests

When properly used, these strategies facilitate learning, increase trust between you and your students, generate a more positive atmosphere in the class —and sometimes are just plain fun.

Every time you intend to assess, first consider what information the assessment is to reveal and then decide which assessment strategies and tools are most likely to provide the information.

Assessment Strategies: Consider a strategy in the sense of a behaviour—the action a teacher takes to learn more about a learner's performance.

Assessment Tools: Consider a tool in the sense of resources— the instruments that illustrate or record what the behaviours reveal.

Information-Gathering Strategies
· Observing and noting student behaviours, responses, and attitudes in various settings
· Asking questions
· Assigning and reviewing homework
· Conducting interviews
· Engaging students in casual conversations
· Conferencing with students about selected projects/assignments
· Analyzing samples of student work collected over time
· Using learning logs to discuss progress/performance with individual students
· Analyzing products of projects developed individually or with partners
· Engaging students in developing guidelines for self-assessment and peer assessment activities
· Conducting student discussions about how learning occurs and how to monitor individual learning

What to Look for During Observations	
· During lessons...	interest, attention, listening, responses to questions, asking questions, interactions with peers, use of prior knowledge, making connections across topics/lessons
· During independent work...	use of time, focus on task, self-direction
· During partner and/or small group work...	attention to task/topic, turn-taking behaviour, contributions, listening to peers, cooperation with peers, controlling or passive behaviour, spontaneity
· Within student resources (e.g., learning logs, portfolios, journals)...	growth over time, application of strategies or ideas from lessons, evidence of how student monitors/regulates own learning, evidence of pride in own work, evidence of expanding interests and use of learning resources

It is not realistic to even attempt to remember everything that you witness each day as you work with your students. Some simple tools can be used to organize your observations so that you can interpret how to use the material to shape instruction. Some tools such as a rubric, can be developed with the students so that they are aware of the expectations for the tasks they are to complete.

Tools for Interpreting Observed Behaviours

- Checklists for skill and content development
- Checklists for self-assessment
- Checklists for peer assessment
- Scoring guide
- Marking scheme
- Running records
- Rating scales
- Rubrics

Record-keeping tools
- Anecdotal records
- Individual student profiles
- Portfolios: writing samples; records of personal reading; comments about personal interests

Tools for communicating information
- Demonstrations, presentations (to parents, school community)
- Parent-student-teacher conferences
- Report cards

What I Am Thinking Now

- What tips can you offer for collecting information about students in ways that are timely and efficient?

- In what ways have you used checklists or rubrics with your students? How did these tools help students improve their performance?

Further information is provided below on certain strategies and tools most useful in the second-language learning environment.

Graphic Organizers

Graphic organizers are visual representations that provide non-linguistic ways for assessing students' ability to listen, explain, and relate information. A well-constructed graphic organizer can help students

- identify key information

- include relevant details

- compare and constrast

- show cause and effect

- use information for an assigned purpose

- show understanding of key ideas

- classify objects, animals, places, movies, foods, etc.

- use classroom resources (e.g., dictionaries, other books, magazines, websites) for solving problems

- use strategies to discover the meaning of unfamiliar expressions

- articulate next steps

Portfolios

Portfolios come in different types and are used for different purposes. There are three main types of portfolios: a **working portfolio** that travels with a student from grade to grade demonstrating work for a subject area; a **showcase portfolio** that demonstrates the best work; and an **assessment portfolio** that features the work that demonstrates achievement of learning goals. These could be combined into one portfolio.

Portfolio assessment reveals student progress over time and can be a very useful strategy for engaging learners in metacognition. (See BLMs 5.5, 5.6, and 5.7.)

As you assess work for inclusion in the portfolio, look for work that

- includes a variety of learning (best pieces, pieces that show specific learning strengths, others that need improvement, etc.)

- demonstrates the student's role in constructing understanding

- shows reflection and goal-setting

- includes self- and peer assessments to demonstrate students sharing and commenting on each other's work

- demonstrates your role in promoting, assisting, and developing understanding

- suggests next steps

Look at the time taken to prepare and select porfolio pieces as added-value in the FSL classroom. Students' ability to reflect on the merits of their selections will benefit future learning and make that learning more efficient.

Teacher Tip

Portfolio use is sometimes viewed as onerous for teachers. So consider the following tips for streamlining the process:

- Work with the homeroom teacher to have your FSL students add their French portfolio selections to their homeroom portfolios. Teachers have described that the perceived value of the French work is increased in the mind of parents when it is presented alongside the English work, particularly if the portfolio includes samples from other disciplines.
- Integrate portfolio use into your instructional routine. Remember that the time spent on selection of portfolio pieces and reflection on those pieces is valuable learning for the students.
- Begin with a small group at first and as your comfort level rises, increase the number of students using portfolios. Apply the principles of Gradual Release of Responsibility to your teaching as well as students' learning.

Portfolios can be useful tools for communication with parents and teachers of the next grade level.

- Make sure that portfolios move with students to the next grade and their next school.
- The materials within a portfolio can often bridge the information divide that can sometimes exist between schools, thus improving relations among teachers and providing diagnostic information for the next teacher.

From the Research

Teachers have used portfolios to personalize and foster learning with students for decades. Research in Europe resulted in the development of a new structure for the typical learner's portfolio.

European Language Portfolios (ELPs) are a strategy used by language learners to record their progress and reflect on their learning of language(s). The Council of Europe underwent a two-year development and pilot process in order to create and standardize the European Language Portfolio. The European Language Portfolio was launched Europe-wide in 2001 with the intent of increasing plurilingualism and pluriculturalism.

Performance Tasks

Performance tasks or culminating tasks are opportunities for students to demonstrate their abilities to synthesize and apply their learning. They often complete the end of a unit of learning where the goals for the tasks were outlined at the beginning of the unit.

When you are assessing students' understanding of key information against established criteria in a variety of creative representations, in the process look for

- recognition of key expressions

- correct sequencing of steps

- confidence in approaching tasks

- logical predictions

- commitment to the task

- willingness to take risks

- explanations of the clues and strategies used

- suggestions for next steps

In the product, look for the

- use of an increasing number of high-frequency words and expressions

- use of key information

Outlining learner outcomes from the outset of a performance task often achieves buy-in from students. It provides students with the big picture of the task and allows them to focus their efforts to attain the outlined goals.

Peer and Self-assessment

Participating in peer and self-assessment helps students comprehend the standards of quality work as they learn to apply those standards to themselves and to others. Participation improves their critical thinking skills, allowing them to become more independent, flexible and open to adjusting the quality of their work.

During self-assessment, students review what they have done in a learning cycle and make decisions about their accomplishments. Self-assessments can occur in various ways, but because self-assessment

Familiarity with routines allows students to peer and self-assess quickly and purposefully. Time dedicated in the beginning to establish routines will permit greater independence on the part of the students later in the school year.

requires practice and guidance in the beginning, self-assessment questionnaires offer a simple way for students to reflect on their performance, strengths, and weaknesses. As students become aware of the ways in which they learn best, self-assessments become critical learning tools. (See BLMs 5.8, 5.9, 5.10, and 5.11.)

Peer assessment reflects the work produced by a group of students working co-operatively on a particular task. (See BLM 5.12 for suggested guidelines for ensuring fair and positive results from peer assessment.) Encourage students to help each other. This co-operative and social skill is invaluable in the FSL classroom.

Learning logs are simple and straightforward descriptions of student learning. Students make entries in their logs about the tasks that they have accomplished, the observations that they have made in the process, the steps that they have undertaken, the questions that they have had, etc. It is necessary in an L2 classroom to provide sentence starters, a bank of words, and suggested topics to students.

Journals Reflection is an important self-assessment tool. A journal is a personal record of a student's learning experiences. It can be used to explore the development of ideas, analyze ways of thinking, increase understanding, and allow for self-development or growth. Because reflective journals explore learning from a personal perspective, they will reflect a student's learning preferences and can contain words, photographs, graphs, charts, images, drawings, and other types of materials. In L2 journal writing, it will likely be helpful to provide sentence starters and often a topic with related useful vocabulary or expressions.

Observation Checklists

Use checklists to note daily observations of communicative interactions. These instruments enable you to check off observable behaviours at various moments. They provide objective criteria to be used systematically to monitor student progress. They can also be used to assess the extent to which specific concepts or skills have been acquired through either a numeric or a descriptive rating scale for individual or group assessments. (See BLM 5.13.)

Checklists can also be useful to students for reflection purposes or in ensuring the completion of tasks for assessment.

- How much latitude do you have in determining the assessment procedures you can use with your students? What effect do school or district regulations have on the ways in which you assess your students and report their progress?

- How do you communicate with your students about assessment activities? What techniques do you use to help them learn to assess their own performance?

- How do your assessment practices help your students appreciate that mistakes help move learning forward?

Anecdotal Data Sheet

Anecdotal observations are used for gathering assessment information about students. The most useful information to record in the early stages of assessment concerns quality of work, work habits, and prior knowledge. Anecdotal data sheets do not typically include numerical marks because the purpose of collecting information is to inform instruction or to communicate information to students or parents. (See BLM 5.14.)

Although you will be observing students individually, at the end of an assessment session, it might be helpful to consolidate your observations of all class members in order to identify shared areas of concern.

The following are suggestions of the kinds of behaviours and prior knowledge that would be appropriate and useful to observe in an FSL classroom. Observe and note evidence that students

Consult the CD-ROM for a short video segment on How to Gather and Organize Anecdotal Observations for assessment to inform instruction.

- listen actively and follow instructions;

- choose the appropriate expression to communicate an idea from those they have had multiple opportunities to practise;

- approximate French pronunciation;

- take risks in order to speak in French;

- support and encourage each other.

An anecdotal data sheet might include space for writing notes about a student's prior knowledge or notes on the next instructional steps under these categories: Skills, Attitudes, Prior Knowledge or Experiences, Notes.

Name: Alyssa Peterson				
Date	**Focus**	**Strengths**	**Immediate Needs**	**Next Steps**
September 27	Diagnostic test	Listening, speaking, reading • works best in groups • articulate and creative • artistic and musical	Writing: • punctuation • −er verbs in the plural	• small-group writing activity • mini-lesson with Cathy and others with the same need • analyze anchor papers
October 25	Halloween story draft	• followed checklist criteria • excellent illustrations convey story mood, reveal character details • neat, focused on task	• verbs; −er verbs in the plural	• learning group • analyze small writing pieces as a whole class, then in small groups • four corners oral activity • pair-writing activity • peer assessment with Daniel

(Adapted from Cooper, 2007)

Using anecdotal observation sheets throughout the course of a term or learning period is useful in capturing data about student progress and performance that is not always, or easily, captured on final tasks and tests. A template for keeping anecdotal information over a period of time is useful for the purposes of review.

Teacher Tip

When observing a small group of students on a given day, use adhesive notes to capture anecdotal observations. Add a name and date to each post-it note and place the five or six adhesive notes on your clipboard. After recording your observations, attach the adhesive notes to students' individual anecdotal record sheets. This will prevent you from possibly losing a student's cumulative record, particularly if you are an itinerant teacher travelling from room to room in a school.

Direction Cards

A direction card clarifies the steps and procedures needed to perform a performance or culminating task. To help students practise planning and making predictions, determine together the necessary steps of a task. As students complete a step, they place a check mark beside it. Direction cards provide students with direction in the completion of a multifaceted task. The cards can serve as a guide to the task criteria and can later be used by the teacher as a tool to assess student accomplishment of the learning goals. (See BLM 5.15 for an example.)

Rubrics

A rubric is a set of scoring criteria for assessing student work and for providing feedback. Rubrics should be used to assess complex tasks involving a variety of skills in a qualitative rather than quantitative way. Because they outline the task expectations, rubrics are useful guideposts for students. A well-designed rubric shows students the elements of a good performance.

Ideally, the fewer rubrics you have to manage the better, not only for you but for students as well. Creating general rubrics for certain tasks (e.g., oral projects such as a presentation, an interview, and written projects such as a book or movie review, story, research project, etc.) will help students internalize the standards for which they should be aiming.

Devising a Rubric

Rubrics consist of three elements: criteria, scoring scales, and indicators. The criteria are the overarching achievement standards that reflect the essential learnings of the task. The scoring scale can be specific to the task or can be mandated by your province or school board or district. Indicators are the descriptors for each scale.

To devise a rubric, follow these steps:

1. Choose the task to be assessed.

2. Consult relevant curriculum or jurisdiction documents.

Consider Can do... statements as a foundation of your rubric scoring scale to inform the rubric indicators. The statements were developed by the Association of Language Testers of Europe (ALTE). The statements are positive reflections of students' performance in the target language. Visit the ALTE website for more information.

3. Consider the criteria necessary for accomplishing the task. (If you have samples of similar work from previous years, it is helpful to review them in order to develop both the criteria and the indicators.) Limit the criteria to between four and six elements. Rubrics can include criteria for skill assessment and for such tasks as developing, organizing, and presenting ideas (either orally or in writing). Below are some suggested general criteria. (You might want to review Bloom's Taxonomy for suggestions as well. See Chapter 3.)

   - Subject Content
   - Use of Language/Applying Language
   - Organization of Ideas
   - Problem Solving/Making Comparisons
   - Analyzing
   - Creativity
   - Use of Secondary Sources/Research

4. Decide on your scoring scale. For example:
   Limited/Adequate/Proficient/Excellent
   Needs Improvement/Acceptable/Above Acceptable/Excellent
   Levels 1–4

5. Now write the indicators. It is helpful to use a previous year's sample work as a base from which to develop all the indicators. For example, start by thinking about what an acceptable performance might look like (what in the scoring scale would be called Proficient, Good, Acceptable, or Level 3). Consider what the elements of that level of performance are for each criterion. Then develop the indicators for the other scales with reference to that indicator. For example:

Criteria	Limited	Adequate	Proficient	Excellent
Subject Content	• Gives *incomplete* information and *no* general ideas on topic. • Gives *irrelevant* or *incorrect* information. • Demonstrates *little* knowledge of content, *does not* engage reader's interest.	• Gives *some* facts and *some* general ideas on topic. • Gives *some* general information on topic. • Demonstrates *some* knowledge of content, somewhat engaging.	• Gives *detailed* facts but *only general* ideas on topic. • Gives *new, but not detailed*, information. • Demonstrates *enough* knowledge of content to engage reader.	• Gives *detailed* facts and *specific* ideas on topic. • Gives *new, detailed* information on topic. • Demonstrates *thorough* knowledge of content, *easily* engages reader's interest.
Organization of Ideas			• Ideas are *organized*, *coherent*, and *generally easy* to follow. • Introduction *explains* topic. • Conclusion *sums up* findings. • Introduction, middle, and conclusion follow logically.	
Use of Secondary Sources			• Uses *relevant* research sources from more than one source. • Student has been *able to* synthesize/ analyze material from those sources.	
Use of Language			• Writer is *able to* use vocabulary relevant to the theme accurately. • Writer has used *some* language features to engage reader's interest.	

6. Now write the indicators for the other levels, ensuring that the degree of improvement in performance across the levels is consistent. Note the parallels (the boldfaced text) among the four levels in the way that the criterion is being described.

7. Review the completed rubric, considering the following:

   a) Does the rubric reflect provincial or jurisdictional standards?

   b) Does the set of indicators for each criterion deal with the same features and elements across all levels?

   c) Are the degrees of improvement across all levels for each criterion appropriate (for the grade level) and logical (for the task)?

   d) Does the rubric reflect the richness and complexity of the task or does it measure elements that would be better assessed quantitatively?

If the answer to any of the above questions is no, then the rubric will need to be revised.

(Adapted from Cooper, 2007)

CASE STUDY	Planning with Assessment in Mind

John rolled the die and moved his game piece. « *Quatre! Un, deux, trois, quatre. C'est une table. La table est dans la salle à manger.* »

Small groups of students in Monsieur Beaulieu's Grade 6 French class were scattered around the room, playing board games that they had created for a learning unit entitled *Ma maison*.

While planning the unit, Monsieur Beaulieu had carefully targeted several learner outcomes for the students to achieve. On the first day of the unit, he gave the students checklists to put in their *cahiers*.

« *À la fin de l'unité qu'est-ce que tu seras capable de faire?* » asked the teacher.

« *Décrire les types de maison et identifier les différentes salles,* » replied Jessie.

"Use *le, la, l', les, un, une,* and *des* correctly with the names of furniture and household items," answered Mark.

Kim added, « *Utiliser 'la lampe est dans le salon' comme modèle.* »

« *Ah, regarde!* » called out Taylor as she pointed to the unit checklist. « *Créer des jeux de société, Monsieur Beaulieu?* Board games? »

The students and their teacher moved eagerly into the first lessons of the unit. Monsieur Beaulieu presented pictures of homes, rooms, and furniture. He then engaged the students in a variety of activities to help them become familiar with the vocabulary and structures. During this initial learning period, the teacher gathered information about the students' progress by making observations and using questioning techniques. He used the information to provide focused feedback to each student and to reteach concepts when necessary. He also encouraged the students to look back at their checklists and place check marks beside outcomes as they were achieved.

When Monsieur Beaulieu determined that his students were ready to begin the final project that would be used to assess their learning, he showed the students a rubric that provided clear and detailed outcomes for the games they would create and the language they were expected to use while playing the games. The students developed their plans, met with their teacher, and began working.

Finally, the big day arrived when everyone would get to play the games. Monsieur Beaulieu explained to the students that they would be assessing their peers. «*Compléter une grille de rendement pour chaque jeu que tu joues. Je vais aussi compléter les grilles. Les grilles de rendement vont vous donner des résultats à vous et à vos parents, sur la façon dont vous avez réussi la tâche. Alors, amusez-vous bien!*»

The classroom was a buzz with excitement that day as the students demonstrated their newly learned skills while playing their very own board games!

What I Am Thinking Now

- From this case study, what conclusions can you draw about the classroom environment? the teacher, Monsieur Beaulieu? the students?

- What do you think are some of the specifics Monsieur Beaulieu was looking for as he observed the students during the initial learning period? (See BLM 5.16 for tips on coaching students toward success.)

Creating Communicative Assessment Strategies

Assessing communication is at the heart of FSL planning. When you create your own assessment strategies, consider these principles:

- Determine the communicative intent: What is the purpose of the assessment strategy? How does it match the students' development? What do you and the student need to know about his/her progress?

- What is the communicative context of the piece? Is it production based (oral or written) or is it receptive in nature (listening or reading)? What is its format?

- What are the linguistic and vocabulary elements students will need to succeed?

- How does it relate to whatever you and your students are currently learning about? Have students seen the task modelled? Have they had opportunities to practise?

The following examples are given to demonstrate the features of communicative assessment pieces and show how you might develop your own. Remember that these activities would be part of your larger unit and long-range planning.

Assessing Communicative Learning Strategies

Assess communicative strategies using checklists at all stages of the learning process—before, during, and after an activity. Student reflections on their abilities to use different strategies will enable them to better internalize the strategies and transfer the use of the strategies to other activities and situations.

Assessing Listening Skills—Reception

Find or create labelled photos or illustrations of a topic that students are learning about currently, for example, *ma famille, ma maison, mon école, mes amis, ma voiture,* etc. Show the visuals to students; choose one but do not tell students which one; and describe it. Ask them to identify the photo you are describing. Depending on the ability level of the students, you can ask that they identify merely by gesturing, or by producing a simple sentence (e.g., *C'est le frère*).

For more advanced students, provide a descriptive clue based on the game "I spy."

> Q: *Dans cette photo, je vois quelqu'un qui porte un chandail rouge. Peux-tu identifier cette personne?*
>
> R: *C'est le frère qui porte un chandail rouge.*

An effective way to assess listening is to have students respond to a description of actions by acting out the directions. For example, for elementary students, ask them to perform a set of actions based on typical classroom routines: *Assieds-toi sur la chaise. Montre-moi ton pupitre. Enlève ton crayon. Va au tableau. Écris la date au tableau,* etc.

The script could also be based on a « *Simon dit* » type game, e.g., *Touche les épaules, saute sur place.*

For more advanced students, create a script in which they have to follow a route through the school either physically or on paper, e.g., *Tourne à gauche. Descends l'escalier. Puis tourne à droite. Marche tout le long du corridor. Arrête-toi à la porte de la troisème salle de classe à gauche. Quel est le numéro de cette salle ?*

These types of listening assessments also work effectively if students respond by drawing what the script describes, e.g., a person or object, or a map showing a route through a real space (the school, neighbourhood) or an imaginary route based on a story your class is reading.

Students' listening skills can also be assessed by providing short recorded messages (school, class, or community announcements, weather report, news broadcast) and creating questions in a variety of formats (cloze passages, multiple choice, matching sentences, true/false questions). Although the response part of the assessment could be written, the activity calls upon students to use their listening skills.

Assessing Reading Skills—Reception

Assess student reading for information skills by providing or creating a brief reading passage in a familiar format (a magazine ad, school newspaper, classified ad, social network personal description, poster advertising an event, e-mail or text message, cafeteria menu, etc.) and provide questions in a variety of formats (cloze passages, multiple choice, matching sentences, true/false questions).

Students can be assessed for their ability to make inferences and supply information from reading passages. For example, create reading passages on current themes and ask students to identify the subject of the passage based on clues given in the text.

> *J'aime les animaux! J'aime aller au zoo. Mon animal préféré est un mammifère. Il a quatre jambes. Il a une queue. Il est brun. Il peut survivre sans eau pendant plusieurs semaines. Quel est mon animal préféré?*
>
> **a)** *C'est un cheval.*
>
> **b)** *C'est une chèvre.*
>
> **c)** *C'est un chameau.*

In the following example, students have to read one side of a dialogue and infer the appropriate responses of the second speaker by choosing A or B.

> *Deux amis se rencontrent à l'école*
>
> Christine : *Bonjour, Roger. Qu'est-ce qu'il y a? Tu as l'air triste.*
>
> **a)** *Roger: Oui, Christine. Je ne peux pas être membre de l'équipe de soccer. Je suis trop petit.*
>
> **b)** *Roger: Au contraire—je suis heureux! J'ai gagné le cent mètres.*
>
> Christine: *Dommage! Tu es un athlète formidable. Tu as gagné beaucoup de trophées.*
>
> **a)** *Roger: Ça m'est égal. Je n'aime pas le soccer.*
>
> **b)** *Roger : Merci, mais je veux pratiquer un sport d'équipe cette année.*
>
> Christine : *Oh, je comprends. L'équipe d'athlétisme a un nouvel uniforme. Il est beau, n'est-ce pas?*
>
> **a)** *Roger : Oui, tu as raison. C'est un bel uniforme.*
>
> **b)** *Roger : Non, je n'aime pas cette couleur.*
>
> Christine : *Un bel uniforme pour un beau garçon.*
>
> **a)** *Roger : Je vais rentrer chez moi pour regarder le match de tennis à la télé.*
>
> **b)** *Roger : Je vais impressionner toutes les filles dans cet uniforme!*

Assessing Speaking Skills—Production

Interacting in a conversation is the most challenging form of communication. To help scaffold students so that they attain this level of communication, provide simpler tasks where they can practise. For example, ask them to leave a voice-mail message for a friend or parent about after-school plans. You will likely need to provide a model for students to use or create a cloze passage that they complete orally.

> *Allô, Cécile. C'est Danielle. Lise et moi allons au cinéma ce soir pour regarder le nouveau film de Batman. Nous allons au Starciné à 19h 30. Le film commence à 20h. Veux-tu nous accompagner? Rappelle-moi sur mon céllulaire, 555 1120, si tu veux nous accompagner.*

An effective way of assessing students' oral communication is to conduct an oral interview, preferably recorded so that you can listen to it more than once. Devise open-ended interview questions about such topics as the student's family, interests, friends, sports, favourite books, movies, music, foods, etc.

During the conversation, consider these elements for assessment. Can the student

- respond to and use greetings?

- provide personal information?

- describe (self, house, friends, etc.)?

- describe a sequence of events?

- justify opinions?

- speak in connected sentences?

- ask simple questions?

When you are preparing interview questions, avoid the ones that call for yes/no answers. Frame your questions so that they will elicit elaboration when the student answers. For example, instead of asking "Do you have a favourite book/movie/sport, etc.?, say "Describe your favourite... ." Instead of asking "Do you have a brother/sister/pet?", say "Describe your family. Who are your family members?"

Use situation cards to help students develop dialogues in which partners ask and answer questions. Each partner should have a card with questions and answers to prepare.

> *Décris à ton ou ta partenaire ton film préféré. Ton ou ta partenaire va te poser des questions sur :*
>
> **a)** *l'action du film*
>
> **b)** *les acteurs*
>
> **c)** *le genre du film (est-ce un film policier, un drame, une comédie, un film de suspense)*
>
> **d)** *ton opinion du film (Est-ce que tu l'as aimé ou non ? Donne tes raisons pourquoi tu aimes le film.)*

Partners can be assessed simultaneously as they interview each other.

Assessing Writing Skills—Production

In the elementary levels, FSL students will need models and scaffolds before they can attempt writing tasks. Some suggestions for different types of writing tasks are to

- Ask students to prepare a lost and found item notice based on the theme or topic that they are learning about (e.g., for an item of clothing, school supplies, sports equipment, pet). They should use the parameters that they are familiar with for describing the item, e.g., describing its colour, size, use, age, where they last saw the item or pet, etc.

- Ask students to complete open-ended sentences about a favourite movie, book, video game, song or singer, movie actor, etc.

> *Quelle est ton opinion….*
>
> *J'ai aimé / J'aime…*
>
> *Je n'ai pas aimé / Je n'aime pas… parce que…*
>
> *C'est mon _____ préféré parce que…*
>
> *J'aime / Je déteste ce personnage parce que….*
>
> *Une dernière observation….*

For some students or for beginner FSL students, this could be the writing task. For more advanced students, providing open-ended sentence starters scaffolds the writing task in which they write a connected paragraph. For example:

Give students a written dialogue between two people with some response lines missing and ask them to complete it. The dialogue could be a familiar situation to all students (e.g., two friends discussing the school team's last game, trying out for a team or for a talent show, a recent field trip or an interview for a part-time or summer job) or it could be one based on a story they are reading or on historical characters they are learning about (two voyageurs talking about their preparations for a trip), etc.

Many more communicative activities are explored in Section 2: Literacy Development Strategies. Depending on your planning and assessment needs, the activities can be used as assessment strategies.

Your FSL Assessment Toolkit

Now that you have explored the principles of assessment and types of assessment strategies and tools, reflect on your own assessment toolkit. Refer to the table, How Balanced Is My Assessment Toolkit? Then complete the grid below to see which strategies and tools are currently in your assessment toolkit and which you might want to implement. You might have others that you are currently using that you might wish to add to your list.

How Balanced Is My Assessment Toolkit?		
Assessment Mode and Strategy	**Assessment Purpose**	**Assessment Tool**
Oral Communication Conference Informal discussion Oral questioning/defence Structured talk with peer	provide feedback on work assess skills (e.g., reading) assess depth of understanding assess depth of understanding	Anecdotal record

Performance Assessments
Skills demonstration
 	
Design project
Inquiry/investigation
Media product
Simulation
 	
Presentation
Role-play
	assess level of performance of
	   skills
	
	assess application of knowledge
	   and skills
	assess understanding
	assess understanding and
	   communication skills
		Checklist/rubric/rating scale
		Checklist/rubric
		Checklist/rubric

Written Assessments **Quizzes/Tests** Selected response Short answer Extended response **Graphic Organizers** Mind map Word web **Extended Writing** Article Brochure Report Review Journal Portfolio	assess knowledge assess knowledge assess knowledge and understanding assess understanding assess understanding assess depth of understanding assess communication skills assess metacognition	Scoring guide Scoring guide Marking scheme Rubric Rubric Rubric/checklist Rubric/checklist

Some assessment strategies and tools that I use to assist my students in becoming independent and confident learners:	Yes	No	Not yet
1. Pre-assessment / diagnostic testing			
2. Informal observations			
3. Focused observation forms			
4. Anecdotal reports			
5. Rubrics			
6. Checklists			
7. Rating Scales			
8. Graphic Organizers			
9. Exemplars (examples of strong work and work needing improvement))			
10. Feedback (constructive, precise)			
11. Metacognative activities (reflection)			
12. Focused revision			
13. Portfolios			
14. Self-assessment			
15. Peer-assessment			
16. Teacher-student conferencing			
17. Learning Logs (reflective journals)			
18. Grades (scored form of work)			
19. Parent-teacher-student conferencing			
20. Other			

For listening, speaking, reading, and writing use paper or electronic means.

Now ask yourself these questions about each strategy and tool:

- How do they promote student learning?

- How do they respond to individual needs?

- How can I adjust these tools to correspond to the needs of individuals and the class?

- In what ways do the assessment tools that I use reflect a sufficient sample of learning?

- In what ways are these tools valid measures of what I intend to assess?

- In what ways are these tools reliable measures of what I intend to assess?

- In what ways are these tools manageable for me in terms of my workload?

(Cooper, 2007)

Summary

Ongoing assessment of student performance provides the insights that guide teachers' planning for effective instruction. Assessment activities serve both teachers and students. Students can be involved in various aspects of assessment—this participation builds their understanding of how they are progressing, where they are encountering challenges, and what they can do to improve their performance. Such involvement alleviates the trepidation students often experience when they know that their performance, particularly their oral expression, is being evaluated. Assessments in FSL instruction are designed to help students recognize their accomplishments—this is what I can talk about, this is what I understand from the read-aloud selection, these are the words/ expressions that I can use in conversation. Effective assessment practices draw upon many resources, all of which are integral to what takes place in daily lessons where students are engaged in the full range of activities that support acquiring a new language. Teachers who possess a repertoire of assessment tools have the resources they need to design effective lessons that lead their students to success.

My Choices

This chapter offers a wealth of assessment strategies and tools that you can use to examine your assessment practices. Think back to what you read and how you responded to the activities within the chapter.

· What additional insights about assessment have you gained from working with the resources in this chapter? What impact do you think these insights have had and will continue to have on your practice?

· What similarities do you find in the assessment resources offered here and those that are in general use in the school where you teach? Which assessment practices are common across subject areas in the school? Do you think it is important for teachers to have shared understandings about the nature and purposes of assessment even though they teach different subjects? Why or why not?

· If you had the opportunity to participate in planning a professional learning program about assessment, what topics would you include?

· "When the cook tastes the soup, that's formative; when the guests taste the soup, that's summative." (Robert Stake). What do you think of this quotation as a metaphor for assessment in school? Share the quotation with your colleagues.

Comprendre des concepts-clés

Nom : _____   Classe : _____

Unité : _____   Date : _____

Ton professeur va te donner une série de concepts-clés que tu vas voir dans la nouvelle unité. Inscris chaque concepts-clé au centre d'un soleil. Puis, ajoute, sur les rayons de chaque soleil, les informations que tu connais déjà au sujet de ces concepts-clés.

Long-Range Assessment Plan

Planner:

Subject/Grade:

Units/Strands/Domains and Big Ideas/Essential Skills

Units/Strands/Domains:	Units/Strands/Domains:	Units/Strands/Domains:	Units/Strands/Domains:
Big Ideas/Essential Skills:	Big Ideas/Essential Skills:	Big Ideas/Essential Skills:	Big Ideas/Essential Skills:

→ → → →

Culminating Tasks

Title/Description:	Title/Description:	Title/Description:	Title/Description:

↔ ↔ ↔ ↔

↑

(continued)

Long-Range Assessment Plan (cont'd)

Enabling and/or Other Assessment Tasks

Title/Description:	Title/Description:	Title/Description:
Title/Description:	Title/Description:	Title/Description:
Title/Description:	Title/Description:	Title/Description:
Title/Description:	Title/Description:	Title/Description:
Title/Description:	Title/Description:	Title/Description:

Assessment of Learning Summary

Nom : _____ Date : _____

Chapter Goals	

Chapter Task Summary

❑ Problem Solving

❑ Understanding of Concepts

❑ Application of Procedures

❑ Communication

Summary of Anecdotal Records:

REPORT CARD COMMENTS

Strengths:

Areas of Need:

Next Steps:

Summary of Interview(s):

Je réfléchis au contenu de mon portfolio

Fiche de réflexion

Complète cette fiche de réflexion et place-la à côté de chaque travail que tu choisis d'inclure dans ton portfolio.

Nom : _____

Date : _____

Ce travail représente :

❏ Comment je me suis amélioré(e)

❏ Quelque chose d'important que j'ai appris

❏ Quelque chose dans quoi je dois faire plus d'efforts

❏ Quelque chose dans quoi j'ai besoin d'aide pour réussir

❏ Quelque chose dont je suis fier(ère)

❏ Ce que je fais en dehors de l'école

❏ Quelque chose que j'ai bien réussi

1. J'ai choisi d'inclure ce travail parce que :

_____

_____

2. Comment ce travail démontre-t-il ce que j'ai coché plus haut ?

_____

_____

3. D'autres choses importantes que ce travail révèle sur moi :

_____

_____

Fiche de réflexion

Complète cette fiche de réflexion et place-la à côté de chaque travail que tu choisis d'inclure dans ton portfolio.

Nom : _____

Date : _____

Ce travail représente :

❏ Comment je me suis amélioré(e)

❏ Quelque chose d'important que j'ai appris

❏ Quelque chose dans quoi je dois faire plus d'efforts

❏ Quelque chose dans quoi j'ai besoin d'aide pour réussir

❏ Quelque chose dont je suis fier(ère)

❏ Ce que je fais en dehors de l'école

❏ Quelque chose que j'ai bien réussi

1. J'ai choisi d'inclure ce travail parce que :

_____

_____

2. Comment ce travail démontre-t-il ce que j'ai coché plus haut ?

_____

_____

3. D'autres choses importantes que ce travail révèle sur moi :

_____

_____

Le contenu du portfolio

Date	Élément retenu	Choisi par l'enseignant(e)	Choisi par l'élève	Choisi par le parent
1.				
2.				
3.				
4.				

Ma réaction au portfolio

Cher(ère) : _____ Date : _____

Bravo pour la présentation de ton portfolio.

Dans ton portfolio, j'ai apprécié _____

_____

_____

_____

_____

_____

Je pense que _____

_____

_____

_____

_____

_____

J'espère que _____

_____

_____

_____

_____

_____

_____

Signé : _____

Auto-évaluation: J'écoute

Nom : _____ Classe : _____ Date : _____

Lisez cette auto-évaluation avec les élèves et discutez-en. Avec le temps, les élèves pourront remplir la grille sans aide.

	Non	Parfois	Oui
Auto-évaluation : Mes comportements d'écoute	☹	😐	☺
Je regarde la personne qui parle.			
Je réfléchis à ce qu'elle dit.			
Je sais ce qui me distrait quand j'écoute.			
Je peux ignorer les distractions.			
Je sais pourquoi j'écoute. (le but)			
Je pose des questions quand je ne comprends pas.			
Je respecte la personne qui parle.			

J'écoute mieux quand :

_____

_____

_____

_____

_____

_____

Auto-évaluation: Je parle

Nom : _____ Classe : _____ Date : _____

Lisez cette auto-évaluation avec les élèves et discutez-en. Avec le temps, les élèves pourront remplir la grille sans aide.

	Non	Parfois	Oui
Auto-évaluation : Mes comportements de parole	☹	😐	☺
Je regarde la personne à qui je parle.			
Je parle clairement.			
Je parle assez fort, mais pas trop fort.			
J'essaie de ne pas changer de sujet.			
Je sais comment prendre la parole dans une discussion.			
J'envoie un signal à la personne pour qu'elle sache quand j'ai fini de parler.			
Je sais comment interrompre poliment la personne qui parle.			

Autoévaluation: Je comprends

Nom : _____ Classe : _____ Date : _____

Aujourd'hui, j'ai lu _____

Ce texte était facile　　　**juste assez difficile**　　　**difficile**

Je pense cela parce que :

_____

_____

_____

Aujourd'hui, j'ai :	**Oui**	**Non**
1. lu le titre et le nom de l'auteur(e) et regardé la page couverture avant de commencer à lire.		
2. réfléchi à ce que je savais déjà sur le sujet.		
3. fait une prédiction avant de commencer à lire.		
4. utilisé des stratégies pour m'aider à comprendre.		
5. aimé le texte.		

J'ai raconté l'histoire / le texte à _____

Ma prédiction était　　**exacte**　　　**plutôt exacte**　　　**inexacte**
　　　　　　　　　　　　　　　☺　　　　　　　😐　　　　　　　☹

Voici une image que j'ai imaginée pendant ma lecture.

```



```

Je réfléchis à mon travail

Nom : _____ Classe : _____ Date : _____

Quelque chose dont je suis fier(ère) :

Quelque chose que j'ai appris :

Quelque chose qui m'a étonné(e) :

Quelque chose que je veux améliorer :

Quelque chose que j'ai aimé dans le travail d'un autre élève :

Grille d'évaluation par les pairs

Nom : _____ Classe : _____ Date : _____

Évalue le travail des membres de ton équipe. Utilise les symboles suivants pour donner ton appréciation : Très satisfaisant ☺ ; moyennement satisfaisant ☺ ; insatisfaisant ☹

Membres de l'équipe Critères	Nom	Nom	Nom	Nom	Nom
A exprimé clairement ses idées et son opinion					
A respecté les tours de parole					
A écouté attentivement les autres					
A respecté les idées, les opinions, et les suggestions des autres					
A encouragé les autres à participer à la discussion (poser des questions, donner la parole, demander des explications)					
A parlé français durant le travail					
A participé activement à la planification des étapes du travail					
A participé à la division du travail entre les membres de l'équipe					
A respecté les directives et le temps donné					
A complété adéquatement sa partie du travail					
A donné de bons conseils pour améliorer la qualité du travail					
A fait des compromis pour améliorer le travail d'équipe					
A aidé ceux qui avaient de la difficulté ou a demandé de l'aide					

Fiche d'observation

Noms des élèves :	Dates :											
Critères:												
1. L'élève montre de l'intérêt pour le cours. (Fait ses devoirs, participe au cours, essaie de s'améliorer, manifeste de la curiosité, etc.)												
2. L'élève participe aux discussions. (Pose des questions, commente, échange des idées)												
3. L'élève fait des efforts pour parler français.												
4. L'élève prend des risques.												
5. L'élève s'applique aux travaux demandés.												
6. L'élève s'applique à la tâche.												
7. L'élève collabore facilement avec les autres.												
Commentaires												

Échelle d'observation : S : souvent, **P :** parfois, **R :** rarement, **J :** jamais

Fiche anecdotique

Nom : _____

Date : _____

Contexte :

Observations :

Commentaires :

Nom : _____

Date : _____

Contexte :

Observations :

Commentaires :

Nom : _____

Date : _____

Contexte :

Observations :

Commentaires :

Nom : _____

Date : _____

Contexte :

Observations :

Commentaires :

Nom : _____

Date : _____

Contexte :

Observations :

Commentaires :

Nom : _____

Date : _____

Contexte :

Observations :

Commentaires :

Grille d'accompagnement pour interviewer un ou une camarade

Nom : _____ Classe : _____ Date : _____

Section 1 : Mon contenu

Dans mon interview, j'ai une question pour connaître :

❑ Son nom : Il / Elle s'appelle _____

❑ Son âge : Il / Elle a _____

❑ Où il / elle habite : Il / Elle habite _____

Pour compléter mon interview, je choisis quatre choses que j'aimerais savoir sur mon ou ma camarade. Je vais écrire les question et les réponses ci-dessous.

(Voici des idées de sujet : activités préférées / sports / traits de personnalité / famille)

❑ _____

_____

❑ _____

_____

❑ _____

_____

❑ _____

_____

Section 2 : Ma présentation orale

Message

❑ Je dis « bonjour » et je me présente avant de commencer.

❑ Je donne le sujet de ma présentation.

❑ Je présente un dessin ou une photo de mon / ma camarade.

❑ Je fais des phrases simples et claires.

❑ J'utilise un vocabulaire juste et précis.

❑ Ma présentation est bien structurée. (progression logique)

❑ Je dis « merci pour votre attention » à la fin.

Attitude

❑ Je regarde l'auditoire.

❑ Je parle assez fort.

❑ Je parle clairement. (prononciation, articulation)

❑ Je parle assez vite, mais pas trop.

❑ J'utilise des gestes et des mimiques.

❑ Je parle avec enthousiasme. (sourire, intonation de la voix)

Aider les élèves à réussir

Utilisez les questions suivantes pour aider vos élèves à améliorer leur apprentissage. Vous pouvez donner une copie de cette fiche à vos élèves.

Nom : _____ Classe : _____ Tâche : _____

Connaissances et compréhension	Mise en application	Habiletés de réflexion	Communication
· Explique-moi ce que tu dois faire. · Explique-moi ce que tu as fait. · Ne parle pas trop mais je veux comprendre tes pensées. · Ajoute des détails.	· Quelle(s) connaissance(s) vas-tu utiliser pour répondre à cette question / finir cette tâche ? · Comment est-ce que cette activité ressemble à une autre activité que nous avons déjà faite cette année ? · Quelle(s) stratégie(s) vas-tu utiliser pour t'aider ? · Comment est-ce que cette stratégie peut t'aider dans un autre cours ? · Pourquoi est-ce que cette activité est importante en dehors de l'école ?	· Qu'est-ce que tu dois faire ? · Quelles informations importantes vont t'aider à accomplir cette tâche (p. ex., qui, quoi, où, quand, comment, pourquoi) ? · De quelle(s) connaissance(s) as-tu besoin pour accomplir la tâche (p. ex., la situation, les personnages, les événements) ? · Quelles sont les étapes que tu dois suivre pour accomplir cette tâche (p. ex., d'abord, ensuite, à la fin) ? · Est-ce que tu as préparé un plan ? · Qu'est-ce que tu as utilisé pour t'aider à planifier la tâche (p. ex., des stratégies, des diagrammes, tes notes) ? · Justifie ce que tu as fait.	· Fais-moi un compte rendu de tes idées (?) avant de commencer, pendant ton travail, et après avoir fini. · As-tu relu ton travail (p. ex., silencieusement, à haute voix) ? · Est-ce que tu as corrigé les erreurs ? · Est-ce que tu as changé quelque chose d'autre ? Quoi ? Pourquoi ? · Est-ce que ton travail est logique / complet ? · Est-ce qu'un(e) camarade de classe a lu ton travail ? · Qu'est-ce que ton ou ta camarade de classe a dit de ton travail ? · Si c'est une présentation orale, est-ce que tu as pratiqué ton travail devant un miroir ou devant quelqu'un d'autre ?

> **"** Literacy is about more than reading and writing—it is about how we communicate in society... literacy takes many forms: on paper, on the computer screen, on TV, on posters and signs. Those who use literacy take it for granted—but those who cannot use it [or don't know how to use it] are excluded from communication in today's world... literacy is freedom **"**
> —*UNESCO Statement for the United Nations Literacy Decade 2003–2012*

My Thoughts

· This quotation presents an expanded interpretation of the term "literacy." Have you ever thought of literacy in this way? If so, how has this interpretation influenced your teaching practices?

· What do you think this quotation implies for FSL instruction in your school and community?

Section 2

Literacy Development Strategies

Keys to Success

Students' development in language involves inter-related experiences in listening, speaking, reading, and writing. Speaking and listening provide the foundations from which reading and writing develop. FSL instruction focuses on strategies that build students' proficiency and confidence in their second language.

Strategy development is a central concept in this book. In this context, strategy describes deliberate actions that enable students to control and modify their efforts at learning.

Key messages in literacy development strategies include:

- Lesson design is consistent, encompassing three phases—before, during, and after.

- Communication activities, both oral and written, are authentic.

- Explicit, scaffolded strategy instruction helps students recognize that strategies they have learned in L1 classes can be used to support their learning in French.

- Learning another language is an enriching experience.

These are but a few of the factors that are examined in the chapters that make up this section of *Strategies for Success*:

- Chapter 6: Listening Strategies
- Chapter 7: Speaking Strategies
- Chapter 8: Reading Strategies
- Chapter 9: Writing Strategies

Listening Strategies

*"Learn how to listen and you will prosper even from those who
talk badly."*
—Plutarch (A.D. 46–120)

My Thoughts

- What was your initial reaction to this quotation? Relate an incident that you were reminded of when you read the quotation.

- What is the relevance of this quotation for students in your French classes? How could you use the message from this quotation to help your students understand the importance of listening well (and often)?

- If you were to share this quotation with colleagues, what do you think their reactions might be?

In this chapter, we will discuss:

- Listening and Oral Communication

- Interactional and Transactional Listening

- Listening Intention

- Teacher Talk for Developing Listening Strategies and Skills

- Using Listening Strategies

- Developing Listening Activities

- Listening Activities to Motivate Your Students

Listening and Oral Communication

"Speaking and listening are the foundations of literacy development and academic success…". (Trehearne, 2006) Students need multiple opportunities to use language in a variety of contexts involving both listening and speaking. Language is the basis of social interaction, the vehicle for utilizing prior knowledge, sharing personal experiences, critical thinking and problem solving, and reflection and self-monitoring. As teachers, we need to create language-rich classrooms to help our students succeed.

For many years, second-language teaching did not emphasize the importance of listening. We now recognize that listening is critical to all areas of language development. Oral communication cannot occur without effective listening. Listening is not a passive activity, but one during which the listener is actively engaged in analyzing and interpreting messages and meanings.

The ways in which we listen, hear, and process information can be effective, active, and skilful. An effective listener is able to understand relationships across a variety of contexts. An active listener possesses skills to identify and manage the natural barriers to listening. A skillful listener has the ability to receive, interpret, and respond to messages.

Key to Success

Knowing that the four strands of language—listening, speaking, reading, and writing—are inter-related and inter-dependent ensures that you apply a communicative-experiential approach to instruction.

From the Research

Listening plays a critical role in language acquisition, but let us consider specifically some of the stages in the acquisition of a child's first language and how they relate to second-language learning at school.

From birth, infants are surrounded by spoken language with limited expressive capabilities on their part. In the first two months of life, infant vocalizations are primarily expressions of discomfort. By two to four months of age, infants begin to make sounds of pleasure typically while interacting with a caregiver. Infants then move to vocal play at four to seven months and then develop babbling that resembles the pattern of adult speech rhythms. It is around 10 months of age that infants start to utter their first recognizable words.

Vocabulary Expressed	
Age	
13 months (range 8–16)	10 words
17 months (range 10–24)	50 words
24 months	310 words

The above pattern is similar for all typically developing children the world over. Expressive language is slow to emerge; however, experiments reveal that newborns can distinguish speech from non-speech and can distinguish between phonemes. By two months of age, most infants can distinguish speech in their first language from speech in other languages. Experiments focusing on infants' eye gaze demonstrate that infants can indicate understanding of words as early as four to nine months.

What I Am Thinking Now

Reflect on the information shared in the previous From the Research section.

· Think about your students' introduction to FSL at school. How does this compare with the learning of their first language?

· What observations can you make about early language acquisition? What impact might these observations have on your approach to FSL teaching?

Interactional and Transactional Listening

Interactional listening is:

· Social and interpersonal

· Two-way communication

· Based on personal, daily information

Transactional listening is:

· Informational and content driven

· One-way communication

· Requires a high level of listening accuracy

There are two general ways of thinking about types of listening. Richards calls these two types of listening interactional and transactional. (Richards, 1990) Interactional listening is listening within a social context and it is two-way: it involves interaction between at least two participants: a speaker and a listener who alternate roles. The communicative purpose of interactional listening is the exchange of information about daily events that involve both participants, i.e., small talk. In a classroom setting, interactional listening would mean listening to, understanding, and responding to greetings, feelings, and conversations about the date, weather, school week, etc. The context is immediate and relevant to the lives of the students and teacher, and the school.

In the second type of listening, transactional listening, the purpose of communication involves transmitting information. Transactional listening is one-way: it involves listening to content in order to glean information. In transactional listening, the aim is for accuracy in understanding content. Since transactional listening is one-way, there are no opportunities for the listener to ask questions to clarify information. (Vandergrift, 2002) Typical examples of transactional listening in a school setting are a school PA or assembly announcement, and recorded language-listening activities from a variety of media such as radio broadcasts, podcasts, or films.

In order for transactional listening activities to be effective, they must have clearly stated purposes. Research has shown that it is crucial to give students a purpose for listening, but the purpose of transactional-type listening activities might not always be readily apparent to students. In the next section, suggestions for connecting purpose and listening will be presented.

Remember that in order for students to become effective oral communicators, they must learn to become effective listeners.

What I Am Thinking Now

Take some time to envision what happens during your classes, noting activities that involve interactional listening and those that involve transactional listening. What do you observe about the nature of listening activities in your classes? In which aspect of listening instruction do you think you have the most success?

Students sometimes find the effort involved in listening to be overwhelming, especially when they are listening to presentations in another language. What activities have you found to be most effective in getting your students to listen? Where do you concentrate your efforts—helping students with the content? helping them with strategies that make them effective listeners?

What have you learned from observing the listening behaviours of adults that you can use to ensure that your students learn to use listening as an effective tool for learning?

Listening Intention

All listeners make choices about what they will pay attention to. "Listeners do not pay attention to everything; they listen selectively, according to the purpose of the task." (Vandergrift, 2002) As with reading, students have to understand both the "what" and the "how" of listening. They should have a clear understanding of the purpose of the listening. Understanding why they are listening helps motivate them and helps them focus on what to listen for.

In order for students to become effective listeners, they must

- understand the purpose of the listening activity;

- prepare for the activity;

- use listening strategies.

Students need to be prepared before they can participate in a listening activity. Before introducing a listening activity, consider some of the same kinds of questions that you would use to prepare for a reading activity.

- What are students listening for? Is the purpose clear to them?

- Are there key words or expressions that they should listen for?

- Are there contextual clues or information that will help students?

- Can students make predictions about the content or topic of the listening?

- If the listening is accompanied by visuals, are there clues that they can glean from looking at them?

Setting a listening intention during the pre-activity stage allows students to concentrate on specific information. A focused listening goal is important as students will not be able to comprehend everything they hear in a second language.

Listening activities can provoke anxiety in students, but you can reduce their nervousness by reminding them that they do not have to understand every word. As Vandergrift points out "...knowing the purpose for listening...greatly reduces the burden of comprehension since listeners know that they need to listen for something very specific, instead of trying to understand every word." (Vandergrift, 2002) We should encourage our students to "listen for the main idea" just as they have learned to read for the main idea.

An example of an authentic activity that can be adapted to many grades and levels is listening to a weather report.

You can use current weather reports available from the Internet for Francophone regions in Canada or elsewhere. Many commercial programs have units on the weather that include weather reports, or you can prepare and "broadcast" your own.

The purpose for listening will depend on what your students have already learned or are learning. For example:

- Listen for specific information, e.g., highest and lowest expected temperatures

- Listen for vocabulary: *ensoleillé, nuageux, venteux, pluvieux*

- Listen for expressions: *il y a du vent, il fait soleil, il neige, il fait froid / chaud / frais,* etc.

- Listen for activities that the weather might permit: If the weather is fine, people will get outside and participate in outdoor activities such as… etc.

Teacher Talk for Developing Listening Strategies and Skills

Teacher talk in the second-language classroom is the most constant language model provided to students. Teacher talk "fosters the development of oral language skills for school-based social interaction, literacy development, and learning… Teachers' awareness of what language they use and how they use it is critical." (Trehearne, 2006)

English Language Arts teachers and second-language teachers have often used the same techniques to foster learning despite the language difference. A current trend for first-language instruction is the importance of oral communication in developing students' literacy, even when the skill focus is reading and writing. A big new idea for second-language teachers is the connection between listening and reading: "The process of listening is in many ways similar to the process of reading. Both involve comprehension rather than production, and both involve the active construction of meaning." (Gibbons, 2002, p. 102)

One technique for developing well-conceived teacher talk is the think-aloud. Think-aloud activities can effectively combine listening and reading skills and strategies. For example, a teacher comments on the text while reading aloud to the class from a big book, transparency, or reading passage projected from a computer or SMART Board. The eventual goal is for students to read independently, but the first step in that gradual process is for them to listen to the reading. During a shared reading, the teacher comments on the text in a variety of ways by

Consult the CD-ROM for a short video segment on How to Use Think-Alouds in FSL. The emphasis is on development of reading strategies, but the principles used can be transferred to think-alouds emphasizing listening strategies.

- drawing connections between the text and the visuals

- making predictions (what do I think happens next? What does the title tell me about this passage?) *Qu'est-ce qui se passe ensuite dans l'histoire? Qu'est-ce que le titre indique?*

- making connections to prior learning (what do I already know about this subject/story?) *Qu'est-ce que je sais déjà à propos de ce sujet / de cette histoire?*

- making connections to personal experiences (what does this remind me of in my life?) *À quoi est-ce que ce sujet / cette histoire ressemble dans ma vie?*

An effective way to teach the strategies discussed above is to explain them first explicitly and then to model them (often during a shared-reading activity) as a think-aloud. In a think-aloud, the teacher gives a running commentary on the strategies he/she is using. For example, in the following think-aloud, the teacher reads aloud a passage about making New Year's resolutions, reminding students to use the context clues to help them understand.

> *Hmm... Je me demande quel est le sujet de cette histoire. Je regarde le titre de cette histoire* [pointing to the title]. *Ah!* [reading the title slowly, emphasizing the sound relationship to English] *Le titre est Mes résolutions. C'est comme le mot anglais.* [pointing to subtitles and photos] *Je regarde les sous-titres et les images. Ah! Voilà un garçon. Il pense à quelque chose. Il ne parle pas. Comment est-ce que je sais que ce garçon pense? Parce que ses pensées*

sont inscrites dans une bulle de pensée [pointing to the bubbles from the boy's head to the thought bubble]. *À quoi pense-t-il? Il pense à ses résolutions pour le Nouvel An. Moi aussi, je fais des résolutions au Nouvel An. Quels mots est-ce que je connais? Le mot vélo… Sa résolution, c'est de faire de l'exercice physique en faisant du vélo* [miming the action].

Early second-language learners must concentrate on listening primarily for the main idea.

Notice that the successful use of a read-aloud involves pausing to let the meaning sink in, physical gestures such as pointing and miming, repeating new or key words and expressions, and pronouncing new or key words slowly and in syllables to allow students to hear the phonetic similarities between cognates.

For a think-aloud to be successful in the FSL classroom, ensure students are aware of the listening purpose for the activity before beginning. Depending on students' needs, the teacher might also find it useful to provide students with a checklist of the listening strategies that will be useful to them during the think-aloud.

Teacher Tip

Listening is hard, even in a first-language situation. Under the wrong conditions, all listeners can suffer from listener fatigue. Brain research shows that when students are tired, their rate of retention of new concepts and learning drops.

You can prevent listening fatigue by

- chunking a recorded listening activity
- pausing frequently during a read-aloud or explicit teaching of a new concept to monitor student comprehension
- pausing to allow for reflection time or to allow the meaning to sink in
- slowing down
- repeating key concepts or messages by paraphrasing them
- speaking expressively wherever appropriate
- using gestures as you explain ideas and language structures that give students a visual and kinesthetic key for accessing their memory of the learning
- asking students to be physically active (e.g., by miming an action described during listening)
- asking students to respond in very simple or more complex ways as they listen by: head nodding; saying *Oui, je comprends; Oui, c'est ça; Non;* etc.; by paraphrasing key ideas or instructions

---

Listening Strategies

What I Am Thinking Now

"Talk is the central tool of their [teachers'] trade. With it they mediate children's activity and experience, and help them make sense of learning, literacy, life, and themselves." (Johnston, 2004, p. 4)

Reflect on various situations (e.g., classroom routines, informal conversations, small group activities) in which your students are engaged in listening. What expressions do you use to facilitate the students' listening to French and responding to what they have heard? How does your use of language enable the students to learn what is required to listen effectively?

How would you characterize "teacher talk" that fosters students' listening?

Remember that students will need to listen to a passage more than once. A tracking sheet or graphic organizer can provide additional support. (See BLMs 6.1, 6.2, and 6.3.) For example, you could provide a weather chart with missing information. You can also post expressions related to the theme on a Word Wall. Students might need to refer to these in order to complete the listening task.

Using Listening Strategies

As teachers, we want to help our students deal with listening situations not only in the classroom but in the outside world. Students can become skilfull listeners when we encourage them to focus on the process—the how—rather than the product—total comprehension of the content. Teaching students listening strategies and metacognitive strategies to help them improve their listening skills can accomplish that goal. (See BLM 6.4.)

Strategies to Use Before the Listening

When students understand the purpose of the listening activity, the next steps in the process are to acquire background contextual knowledge and access their own prior knowledge. If the listening has accompanying visuals or follows a storyline, ask students to consider what they already know about the topic or story and encourage them to make predictions.

What do I already know about the topic/story…? *Qu'est-ce que je sais déjà au sujet de cette histoire?*

Does it remind me of anything in my life/in our classroom/school? *À quoi est-ce que ce sujet / cette histoire se ressemble dans ma vie? à notre salle de classe? à notre école?*

Do I see any familiar words or cognates (in the accompanying visuals, in the activity title)? *Est-ce que je vois des mots que je connais ou qui ressemblent aux mots anglais?*

Can I make any predictions (about what will happen in the story, about what we will learn as we listen)? *Qu'est-ce que je peux prédire? Qu'est-ce qui va se passer dans l'histoire? Qu'est-ce que je vais apprendre?*

The strategies for this stage are often most effective when they are modelled with teacher talk. For example, in a listening activity in which two people order food at a restaurant, refer to accompanying visuals to identify the location, the two characters, the type of restaurant, etc. You might wish to bring visuals of food items and of a menu. Model possible responses and then ask questions of students.

Qui sont ces deux jeunes?

Où sont-ils? C'est un restaurant? Quel est le nom de ce restaurant?

On peut commander quel genre de cuisine dans ce restaurant?

Regardez. J'ai apporté un menu de mon restaurant préféré.

Moi, j'aime la cuisine chinoise. Je mange souvent à un bon restaurant chinois. Et toi, Claire?

Regardez l'expression de Guy. Est-ce qu'il est content?

Selon vous, quel plat est-ce qu'il va commander?

Two processes are key in becoming a successful listener: top-down and bottom-up. When listeners use strategies based on top-down processes, they are accessing their prior knowledge of the topic, its context, what they know about the format or genre of the listening activity, and making predictions. When listeners use bottom-up strategies, they are relying on their knowledge of the language, i.e., familiar words, cognates, expressions, and sentence structure.

Listening comprehension is never based on only one process; it always involves a seamless integration of top-down and bottom-up strategies. Effective listeners ask themselves top-down questions:

- What do I already know? *Qu'est-ce que je sais déjà?*
- What type of listening is this? *C'est quelle sorte d'activité?*
- How is it related to me or what my class is doing? *Comment est-ce que cette activité a rapport à ma vie ou aux activités de la classe?*
- What's the main idea to listen for? *Quelle est l'idée principale?*
- Can I predict what will be discussed? *Quelles prédictions est-ce que je peux faire?*

Effective listeners ask themselves bottom-up questions:

- Which words and expressions do I know? *Quels mots et quelles expressions est-ce que je connais?*
- Am I expecting to hear them in the listening? *À quoi est-ce que je m'attends dans cette activité?*
- Is there specific information I need to listen for? *Quelles informations importantes est-ce que je dois identifier?*
- What are the key words related to that information? *Quels sont les mots-clés de ce sujet?*

(Vandergrift, 2002. NCLRC, 2003, 2004)

Strategies to Use During the Listening

Effective listeners ask top-down and bottom-up questions to assist in comprehending the listening selection.

Most language learners will need to hear the listening activity more than once. Some useful strategies for students to apply as they listen are:

Listen first for the main idea. *J'identifie l'idée principale.*

Decide what is important to pay attention to and what can be "skimmed." *Je détermine les informations importantes et les informations supplémentaires.*

If the listening is related to a story, listen for clues to the characters' emotions, e.g., intonation. *Si j'écoute une histoire, j'écoute pour identifier les émotions des personnages.*

If the listening is filmed, fiction or non-fiction, watch for physical movements and gestures. *Si j'écoute un film, je regarde les mouvements des personnages.*

Listen for sound effects. *J'écoute les effets sonores.*

Monitor predictions. *Je vérifie mes prédictions.*

Listen for familiar words, cognates, and expressions. *J'écoute pour les mots que je connais, les mots-amis, et les expressions.*

Listen a second time to fine-tune comprehension of details. *J'écoute une deuxième fois pour mieux comprendre les détails.*

It is crucial that students monitor their comprehension at this stage and after the listening. By pausing the recording or DVD from time to time, you will allow students time to think about what they have just heard, ask questions for clarity, and verify their predictions. A prepared BLM or a list in their notebooks will help them place a check mark beside accurate predictions.

Metacognitive Strategies to Use After the Listening

Skilful listeners learn to use metacognitive strategies to reflect on the strategies that helped them. Encourage students to ask themselves which of the Before and During, top-down, and bottom-up strategies were most useful. It is helpful for students to share with the class or groups what they understood from the listening and which strategies were most effective. Encourage students to share their reflections with others and verify their predictions, comparing them with other students'.

Verify predictions. Were they correct? *Je vérifie mes prédictions. Est-ce qu'elles étaient bonnes?*

Which strategies did I use? *Quelles stratégies est-ce que j'ai employées?*

Were they helpful? Which was the most helpful? *Est-ce que ces stratégies étaient utiles? Quelles stratégies étaient les plus utiles?*

Can I explain why certain strategies were helpful? *Est-ce que je peux expliquer pourquoi ces stratégies étaient utiles?*

A prepared checklist will help students identify useful strategies and self-assess.

Asking-for-Help Strategies

A critical skill for students to master in the art of listening is the ability to ask for various kinds of help, depending on whether the listening is one-way or two-way communication. In two-way interactive communication, students will want to ask the other speaker to speak more slowly, more loudly, and to repeat. They might also want clarification about a term or expression, or ask for something to be rephrased. In one-way (transactional) communication, which typically involves some kind of recorded activity, students might ask you to pause and replay the recording. Model asking for help frequently and provide opportunities for regular practice, especially in pairs, so that students acquire them as a part of their repertoire of listening skills.

Teacher Tip

Some useful expressions for asking for help:

Parle plus lentement, s'il te plaît.

Parlez plus lentement, s'il vous plaît, madame.

Je ne comprends pas. Peux-tu répéter?

Pouvez-vous répéter, monsieur?

Qu'est-ce qu'un / une…?

Que signifie…?

Qu'est-ce que cela veut dire?

Est-ce qu'on peut arrêter le DVD / l'enregistrement, madame (ou monsieur)?

Either post the above list of question starters in the classroom or provide students with a copy for their notebooks.

What I Am Thinking Now

In what ways do you help your students appreciate that strategies they use in English Language Arts can be used in their French classes (or vice versa)?

To what extent is there communication among teachers in your school about strategies that students can use across the curriculum? In what ways do you think "teachers' shared knowledge" leads to student success?

Differentiating Instruction for Listening

Consider the following methods for differentiating your instruction for listening activities.

See Chapter 5 for details on facilitating differentiated instruction for your students.

Give different purposes for listening to different students. The purposes will depend on what you already know about your students' learning profiles. For example, some students could listen for details, some for the main idea. Some students could be responsible for listening for information about one character in a storyline. Students can be responsible for listening for key words or expressions.

Giving different students different purposes for listening will lessen listener fatigue. Each student (or group) can be responsible for one element in the weather forecast, e.g., some can listen for the temperature highs and lows, some can identify a key descriptive word, and some a key expression with *il fait*. Many authentic weather forecasts cover more than one region, so different groups could be responsible for different regions.

Mime the actions of the listening activity as a Before activity and have students use prior knowledge to identify them. For example, in a play-by-play commentary of a hockey game, model for students the actions (*lancer, marquer un but, patiner, passer la rondelle*). Retention of knowledge is improved if the learning is introduced with an associated action.

Create a rap or chant on the topic using key vocabulary and have students perform before the activity.

As a technique for differentiating instruction during the activity, encourage students to make the motion when they hear the associated action or topic. (For example, in the hockey commentary example, clear space in the classroom and have students respond to the listening by miming the slap shot and the goal.)

Consider preparing a blackline master with a list of the expressions or words that students can check as they hear them. Ask students to verify their answers.

Students should be encouraged to self-assess their listening skills on a regular basis. (See BLM 5.8.)

Developing Listening Activities

Explicitly define the purpose of listening for students each time they are participating in a listening activity. Students will have greater success in reaching the goal when they know what they are to achieve from the beginning.

As you develop listening activities in your classroom, consider whether the listening activity is interactional (involves interpersonal situations) or transactional (involves the transfer of information). Include both two-way and one-way listening activities in a learning cycle.

For young second-language learners, interpersonal topics or topics on everyday life are often easier to process than information-based topics. As you select listening activities from various media, choose topics that are developmentally appropriate and relevant. Students at all levels are interested in hearing about personally relevant topics and interpreting that information in light of their own interests and experiences.

If you are developing your own listening activities or modifying existing ones to better suit your students' learning styles, the following are guidelines that you might like to consider.

Setting the Purpose for Listening

The ultimate goal of all listening activities is to provide opportunities for success and build confidence. Start with small, clearly defined objectives and build to longer, more complex tasks. Each successfully completed listening activity is part of the scaffolding for the next activity.

Listening activities must be embedded in the context of your students' current topics and related learning (vocabulary, language expressions, structures, themes).

Determine the purpose of the activity. Will students be listening to determine main ideas or specific information? Are they listening for main ideas or details?

Is the listening goal interactional (two-way communication) or transactional (one-way communication)?

Consider the type of response the listening activity will require. Will students place a check mark beside answers from a list, match pieces of information, or match text to visuals? Will their responses lead to a question-and-answer exchange with a partner?

Features of the Listening Activity

The following guidelines can be used both to create your own listening activities and to analyze or adapt existing ones to suit your students' learning profiles and needs.

Is the level of difficulty appropriate? Is there a storyline to follow, with a clear beginning, middle, and end?

What clues to the ideas in the selection do the titles and subtitles convey?

Are ideas in an informational passage presented in a logical sequence? Does the passage have a clearly stated main idea? If the main idea is inferred, what clues will help listeners identify the main idea?

Is there redundant material in the passage? Beginner students need short and to-the-point passages, but more advanced students can benefit from repetition.

Are there visual aids (illustrations, photos, graphic organizers)?

(Adapted from the National Capital Language Resource Centre, 2004)

Considerations for Before, During, and After the Activity

As you develop the surrounding Before, During, and After activities, you might wish to keep in mind these considerations.

Develop questions that prepare students for the listening activity. The questions should help them determine the context and the listening type, and remind them of prior knowledge (thematic and linguistic). Pre-activity questions should help them make predictions and focus on what they have to listen for.

Keep writing (e.g., note-taking, cloze passages) to a minimum during the activity. For the best results, students should concentrate on the listening.

If the follow-up activities involve a written response, read the instructions to students or make sure that they read them before the activity so that their listening will be focused.

Verify the answers with students immediately. If the activity is an interactive partner task, give immediate feedback.

(Adapted from the National Capital Language Resource Centre, 2004)

A model listening activity takes into consideration the before, during, and after needs of students:

- As we discussed in Listening Intention, listening to a weather forecast is an effective activity. Record your own broadcast or visit the Radio-Canada website and listen to a live weather report.

- Describe the format of the listening activity and discuss the purpose, either with simple statements or questions.

  On va écouter la météo (sur Internet, à la radio, à la télé, etc.).

  On va décrire les conditions météorologiques d'aujourd'hui.

  On va écouter les prévisions de la température pour la fin de semaine.

  Quel temps fera-t-il cette fin de semaine ? J'espère qu'il fera beau.

- Then set the context with visuals showing weather conditions (sun, clouds, wind, rain, snow) and bring in the weather page from a newspaper, etc. Remind students of what they already know about describing the weather.

  Comment est-ce qu'on décrit la météo ? Quelles expressions connaissez-vous ? Oui, il fait beau, il fait soleil, etc.

- Help them identify key words or expressions to focus their listening, e.g., *la pluie, la neige, le soleil, le vent, ensoleillé, froid, neigeux, pluvieux, nuageux, venteux,* etc.

Listening Activities to Motivate Your Students

The following activities are useful suggestions to include in lesson plans. The activities will not only be motivating for students and teachers, but also purposeful when part of a well-designed unit of study or lesson plan.

Information Gap Activities

Information gap activities are a specific type of listening and speaking activity. These are most often set up with students in pairs. One student is given part of the information required and the other student is given different information. Neither student has all of the information, so they must communicate with each other to complete the task. The two students then ask questions and listen to the answers in order to create the complete set of information required. These activities are designed to create a situation where students must communicate in order to accomplish the task.

Music

Music can enhance the learning environment in the second-language classroom. Regular repetitions of age-appropriate songs can add a positive dimension to classes. It is helpful for students to learn the expressions and have the opportunity to repeat and practise. In this way, students are listening, repeating, comprehending, and enjoying learning.

Teacher Tip

Most students hear one main language model in their second-language classroom: you, their teacher. It is important to include real listening passages that feature other speakers. Radio and television clips, podcasts, short cartoons, and DVDs can all be used to enhance classroom instruction and motivate students to practise listening.

Short, contextualized listening activities from a variety of media are an excellent way of motivating students to become effective listeners. It is important that the purpose for listening be clear and that it be introduced with pre-activities. As well, it is not advisable to play a full-length cartoon or video.

Listening activities that are accompanied by visuals support learning. Visual learners are especially assisted by images. Brain research tells us that people tend to doze when the lights are dimmed, so leave the lights on!

Cloze Activities

Cloze activities include a transcript of a listening text with blanks for missing words and expressions that students attempt to fill as they listen. Students should be familiar with the missing information. You might wish to provide the missing words and expressions on a sheet, on the board, or on a Word Wall. Before you do a cloze activity, prepare students by

- setting the context, e.g. Is the listening about a current topic?

- asking for predictions about key words and expressions

- playing a song or a rap with the vocabulary to prepare students (Make sure students have a chance to sing the song!)

Play the listening activity several times to allow students time to verify their predictions and answers. Cloze activities are ideal for partner work.

Jigsaw Listening

This co-operative learning technique makes every student responsible for completing and understanding one part of the whole. Students must share their knowledge effectively with the group to complete a listening puzzle.

In a jigsaw activity, members of the base group are numbered 1, 2, 3, 4, etc. Students form new groups according to their number (all number one students in one group, etc.). Each group listens to a different passage several times, noting key information in a chart or graphic organizer. Then students return to their base groups to share that information in order to complete the task.

Note-taking is an essential part of jigsaw listening activities. Providing students with a structure in which to record, jot down, illustrate, or doodle what they need to remember will support their note-taking efforts. There are simple ways for students to organize their work during a jigsaw activity. (See BLM 6.5.)

From the Research
• The more notes that are taken in a variety of ways, the better.
• Verbatim notes are the least effective type of note-taking.
• Notes are works in progress.
• Notes should have a greater purpose. They can be used as learning guides.

(Adapted from Marzano, Pickering, Pollock, MCREL, 2001)

Jigsaw-Listening Example

Provide groups with a simplified map of a town or a diagram of a building or grounds. Their task is to listen to a script of a path, journey, or route and trace that route on the map. Each group listens to a different part of the route or journey. When they have finished their section, they rejoin their base groups and combine what they have learned about the journey to determine the end point of the trip.

For example, a typical task might involve students finding a missing dog by tracing the dog's route on the map. They each listen to a part of the dog's journey. Then, back as a base group, students take turns explaining the part of the route that they traced on the map, based on the section of the passage they heard. Together they will find the dog by putting all the pieces of the journey together.

This activity could be adapted to other characters or situations to suit your students' interests or the current learning theme in your class. Other examples include the following:

- Provide a map of bus routes in your community and create a script describing a passenger's trip to do errands.

- Ask students to create a treasure map. Create a script to show where pirates have hidden the treasure.

- Ask students to draw a large diagram of the school and grounds. Write a script to describe a typical day and path through the school of a new student.

To develop the script for such a listening activity (or for one of the scenarios above), brainstorm answers to the W5 questions (who, what, why, where, when, how).

- Who is the main character taking the trip? Are there any actions that could be used to describe the character (e.g., a dog runs, jumps, barks, sniffs, plays with children, chases after balls, etc.)?

- Why is the main character making the trip?

- Who are the other characters that the main character will meet during the trip?

- Where are the landmarks on the route (e.g., streets, schools, school yards, etc.)?

- What are the obstacles that the character might run into? What are the interesting objects that the character might find?

- How is the character making the trip (by foot, by bicycle, by skateboard)?

Have the class or groups brainstorm answers to these questions and come up with a script. You might wish to ask students to draw the scene first before developing the script, and then use the visuals to accompany the completed listening activity. (The visuals could also be used as the basis of a sequencing and listening activity as described below in Sequencing Games.)

For a challenge, consider having groups of students create their parts of the route in isolation (assuming that they have agreed on a main character and a location such as the school and surrounding neighbourhood known to all) and then put the script together in some logical order.

Sequencing Games

Provide students with photos, illustrations, or other images that depict a story. As they listen to you read the story, they must order the images correctly. This activity can be done individually, in groups, or as a listening centre activity.

Riddles

Using riddles in the classroom involves reading, writing, and listening skills. However, this is an activity that should be attempted only when students are familiar with the vocabulary and expressions connected to a unit. Writing riddles provides additional practice.

Following a model, students write a riddle on a slip of paper and sign it. Put the riddles in a container and ask a student to draw one and read it aloud. After someone guesses, the riddle writer verifies the answer. Depending on students' level of language acquisition, you might wish to read aloud while students listen and guess.

> *Je suis un fruit. Je suis rond. Je pousse en Floride. Je suis une _____.*

> *Je suis un animal. J'habite sur une ferme. J'ai une queue et quatre pattes. J'aime manger des carottes et des pommes. Je suis un _____.*

Matching Games

Provide students with a variety of numbered illustrations or photos. Write a description of each picture and give each description a letter. Students match the number of the picture with the letter of the description. The pictures must be similar in most details. For example, use a variety of pictures of butterflies, ladybugs, cats, dogs, or people (for different physical characteristics, clothes, or professions).

Listening and Drawing Barrier Games

This simple interactive activity provides students with the opportunity to develop speaking and listening (reception/comprehension) skills, as well as appealing to visual learners. Students learn how to give clear instructions and descriptions, listen well, and ask questions for clarification. You might choose to have one person give instructions to a group or whole class. Alternatively, you might wish to have individuals positioned across a barrier from one another or have pairs of students stand back-to-back.

Model the activity first. Then describe something and have students draw what is being described.

Teacher-Led Listening and Drawing Barrier Games: This activity works with many different themes or topics. For example, students can practise describing object positions by drawing a table in the middle of a sheet of paper. Then ask them to follow a list of drawing instructions, for example: draw a chair beside the table on the right; then draw a cat underneath the table. Continue the description of the room while the students draw what they hear. To verify answers, show them a picture of the description.

> *On va dessiner une scène. Dans cette scène, il y a des objets. Je vais vous décrire les objets de la scène, et vous allez dessiner ce que vous entendez.*
>
> *On va commencer. On est dans une salle. [pause to give students time to draw] Dans cette salle, il y a une table ronde. Sous la table, il y a un gros chat. Le chat est blanc. Il a des oreilles noires. [point to your ears] Il a des pattes noires. [mime four paws]*
>
> *Sur la table, il y a un vase. Dans le vase, il y a trois fleurs. Sur la table, il y a aussi un gros gâteau au chocolat. Sur le gâteau, il y a cinq bougies. À côté de la table, il y a une chaise en bois. Il y a quelqu'un qui s'assoit sur la chaise. C'est un… grand chien noir. Le chien regarde le gâteau attentivement… Hmmm… Je me demande ce qui va arriver… C'est à vous de terminer le dessin. Bon! Vous avez terminé vos dessins ? Qu'est-ce que vous avez dessiné ? Montrez-moi vos dessins.*

Student-Shared Listening and Drawing Barrier Games: This paired barrier game activity follows the teacher-led example above and builds on it. This activity involves positioning simple shapes *(un cercle, un triangle, un rectangle, un carré)* in a drawing.

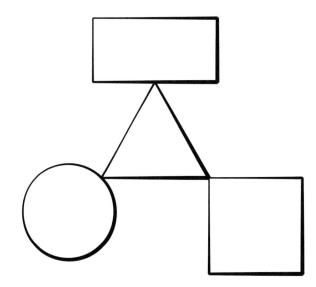

Figure 6.1: Visual created by a student participant in a listening and drawing barrier game

Before you begin, ensure that the key expressions for this activity are posted on a Word Wall. Have students sit in pairs, back-to-back. Distribute a copy of a simple shape picture to one student in each pair. Those students describe the simple shape drawing to their partner who tries to draw it on a piece of paper by listening attentively. The listener asks questions for clarification, if necessary, and then follows the instructions. When the simple drawing has been clearly communicated and completed, students check their work.

An effective way to prepare students to do the activity is to act out the expressions and prepositions through gestures or to model them with objects first.

Voici Robert. Lise, place-toi à gauche de Robert, etc.

Dessine un triangle au centre de la page.

Puis, sur l'angle (top angle) du triangle, dessine un rectangle.

À l'angle gauche du triangle, dessine un cercle. Le cercle touche à l'angle gauche.

À l'angle droit du triangle, dessine un carré. Le carré touche à l'angle droit.

Summary

Listening plays a critical role in language acquisition; it is a key skill that leads to success in oral communication, reading, and writing. At one time, listening was not emphasized in second-language instruction, nor was it given much attention in L1 instruction. However, that situation has changed and listening is now an integral part of instruction in both L1 and L2 classes.

Instructional activities in listening are designed to help students understand two aspects—the "what" or content and the "how" or strategies. For each aspect, teachers can scaffold activities so that students gradually develop effective listening behaviours. Listening activities extend students' knowledge of French—vocabulary, sounds, sentence structures, and cadences. These experiences provide the foundation for ongoing development of oral expression, reading comprehension, and written expression.

Listening is not an easy task, particularly when the presentation is in a language with which students are not conversant. However, well-designed listening lessons present students with supports that enable them to recognize the purposes for listening and how to use strategies that further their ability to understand and communicate in French. These lessons follow a format that is familiar to students from their experiences in L1 listening and reading—before, during, and after listening activities. Throughout these lessons, students have opportunities to learn new ideas, as well as ways in which to become effective listeners.

My Choices

Make a tally of your responses to the teacher listening checklist on the next page. What does the tally reveal about your approach to listening activities?

Talk with colleagues who teach English Language Arts to find out how much attention they give to listening activities and the purposes of those activities. In what ways are the purposes of instruction similar in the English program and the French program?

Share the listening activities from this chapter with your colleagues who teach English Language Arts. Work together on plans to use selected activities concurrently in both English and French classes over a period of several weeks. During the course of using the same activities, consult regularly about your observations of the students' listening behaviours.

It is rather easy to find quotations about listening and these can be fun to use in professional learning sessions. Here are a few to get you started:

"We have two ears and one mouth, so we should listen twice as much as we speak."—Epicetus

"She was…one of those rare people who could invest as much effort in her listening as in her talking."—Dennis LeHane, *Mystic River*

"Are you listening or are you waiting to talk?"—John Travolta's character, Vincent Vega, in *Pulp Fiction*

"If the person you are talking to doesn't appear to be listening, be patient. It may simply be that he has a small piece of fluff in his ear."—Winnie the Pooh

"Women like silent men. They think they are listening."—Marcel Achard

Teacher Checklist			
A listening intention is considered with all listening activities.	YES ☐	NO ☐	SOMETIMES ☐
An authentic reason for listening is provided.	YES ☐	NO ☐	SOMETIMES ☐
One-way and two-way listening activities are both used as part of instruction.	YES ☐	NO ☐	SOMETIMES ☐
Carefully chosen authentic, multimedia listening texts of an appropriate length are included.	YES ☐	NO ☐	SOMETIMES ☐
Students know how to ask for clarification.	YES ☐	NO ☐	SOMETIMES ☐
Listening activities are a regular part of the units of instruction.	YES ☐	NO ☐	SOMETIMES ☐
A Word Wall is posted in the classroom to support student comprehension.	YES ☐	NO ☐	SOMETIMES ☐
Graphic organizers and visual supports are provided for students to assist them with listening activities.	YES ☐	NO ☐	SOMETIMES ☐
A variety of different listening activities are included: interviews, information gaps, surveys, etc.	YES ☐	NO ☐	SOMETIMES ☐
Students regularly listen to appropriate music as part of their second-language experience.	YES ☐	NO ☐	SOMETIMES ☐

Tableau SVAP

Nom : _____

Date : _____

Classe : _____

Sujet : _____

Ce que je sais	Ce que je veux savoir	Ce que j'ai appris	Ce que je veux savoir de plus

La météo d'hier et d'aujourd'hui

Hier

1. Encercle les mots qui décrivent le temps (la météo) d'hier.

Aujourd'hui

2. Écoute et encercle les mots qui décrivent le temps (la météo) d'aujourd'hui.

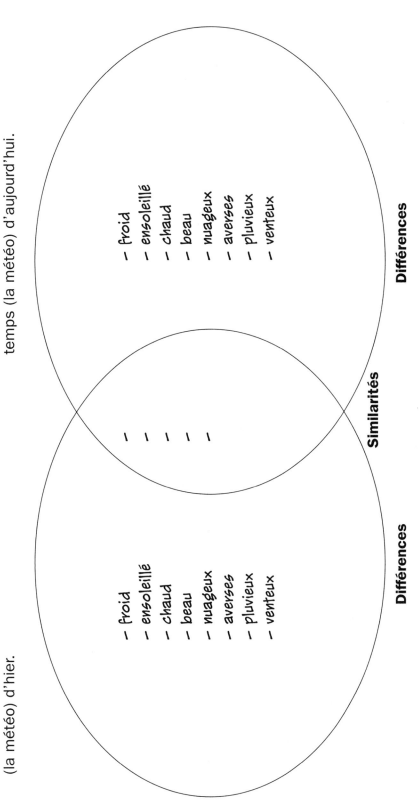

Hier — Différences

- froid
- ensoleillé
- chaud
- beau
- nuageux
- averses
- pluvieux
- venteux

Similarités

Aujourd'hui — Différences

- froid
- ensoleillé
- chaud
- beau
- nuageux
- averses
- pluvieux
- venteux

3. Avec un ou une partenaire, trouve les similarités entre le temps d'hier et celui d'aujourd'hui.

4. Finalement choisissez un, deux, ou trois mots pour prédire le temps de demain. Soyez prêts à partager votre prédiction avec la classe, oralement ou avec un dessin simple.

Tableau de veille météorologique

Nom : _____ Classe : _____ Date : _____

	lundi	mardi	mercredi	jeudi	vendredi
Température (°C)					
Conditions atmosphériques					
Direction du vent					
Précipitations pluie / neige (mm / cm)					

TOI

LES YEUX

ATTENTION EXCLUSIVE

LE CŒUR

L'OREILLE

Ce symbole démontre tous les aspects impliqués pour bien écouter. Ce n'est pas seulement les oreilles qui écoutent; ce sont les yeux, le cœur, toute la personne et son attention exclusive qui signalent l'intérêt à une autre personne.

Est-ce que tu écoutes attentivement?

1. Regarde la personne qui parle

2. Penche-toi en avant

3. Indique ton attention par un signe de tête

4. Donne toute ton attention à la personne qui parle. Ne détourne pas l'attention!

5. Écoute le message jusqu'à la fin sans interruption

6. Pose des questions

Activité en *Jigsaw*

Nom : _____ Classe : _____ Date : _____

Inscris ci-dessous les informations importantes qui correspondent à ta tâche.

N'oublie pas, les membres de ton groupe comptent sur TOI !

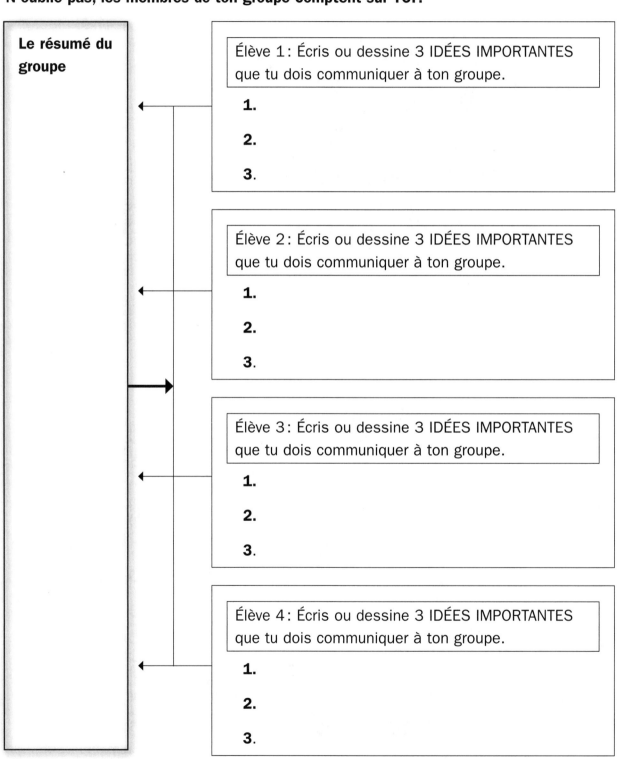

Le résumé du groupe

Élève 1 : Écris ou dessine 3 IDÉES IMPORTANTES que tu dois communiquer à ton groupe.

1.

2.

3.

Élève 2 : Écris ou dessine 3 IDÉES IMPORTANTES que tu dois communiquer à ton groupe.

1.

2.

3.

Élève 3 : Écris ou dessine 3 IDÉES IMPORTANTES que tu dois communiquer à ton groupe.

1.

2.

3.

Élève 4 : Écris ou dessine 3 IDÉES IMPORTANTES que tu dois communiquer à ton groupe.

1.

2.

3.

Chapter 7

Speaking Strategies

Speaking proficiency... is the most difficult and time-consuming dimension of language proficiency to develop and is most often the skill implied when people refer to knowledge of a language or a reason for wanting to learn another language. Indeed, it is speaking that is... the current basis for determining the number of Canadians who are functionally proficient in their second language. This information is based on a "yes" or "no" response to the census question "Do you speak English or French well enough to conduct a conversation?"
—Larry Vandergrift

> **My Thoughts**
> - What reasons do you think your students have for learning French? If you are in a situation where their only reason for taking French is because it is a required subject, what can you do to help them move beyond this limited perspective?
> - How often have you heard people say, "It is a lot easier to read French than it is to use (i.e., "speak") it?" What does this remark tell you about the kind of experiences these individuals might have had in learning French?

In this chapter, we will discuss:

- Key Concepts: Input and Output
- Authentic Communication
- Establishing Communicative Goals
- Creating a French Classroom Environment
- Collaborative Group Work
- Oral Warm-Ups
- Oral Activities to Motivate Your Students
- Oral Presentations

In order to achieve literacy success, students must possess a strong oral language base.

Knowing that the four strands of language—listening, speaking, reading, and writing—are inter-related and inter-dependent ensures that you apply a communicative-experiential approach to instruction.

The ability to communicate orally is the foundation of all other forms of learning. In second-language teaching, we often think of oral communication as the ability to converse on thematic topics in the classroom. But oral communication is more than that—it is the basis for developing skills in other areas, such as reading and writing. Oral communication is the vehicle through which students formulate, discuss, and revise their ideas as they read and write. It is also a vehicle for self-assessment: they can discuss with the teacher and classmates how well they have understood a listening activity, a reading, or an idea, and can analyze and compare the metacognitive strategies they used.

Research shows that in order to achieve literacy success, students must possess a strong oral language base. Students benefit from understanding that their thoughts need to be expressed orally first, and then can be written about later. Teachers of English Language Arts, who traditionally focused on reading and writing, are now realizing the importance of oral communication in teaching literacy strategies to students. "…As late as the 1930s, literacy…was represented by the capacity to read and copy simple passages and to write an occasional short text." (Gibbons, citing Christie's work (1990), 2002, p. 51) Literacy today involves acquiring the proficiency to adopt, adapt, and apply critical thinking skills in an ever-changing world and work context.

Focusing on the key components of a comprehensive literacy program has a positive influence on the development of literacy skills of second-language students. FSL students will not be at the same level of literacy development in their second language as they are in their first language; however, "although students may be linguistically limited, they have a well-developed bank of knowledge and experience on which to draw." (Cogswell and Kristmanson, 2007, p. 27) Students can transfer knowledge of certain concepts such as text structure or genre from the first- to second-language contexts. Careful and deliberate teacher scaffolding and modelling of critical literacy skills are essential for beginning second-language learners with little real-life experience and partial competence in their second language.

Key Concepts: Input and Output

All of the language skills—listening, speaking, reading, and writing—are interrelated. Listening and reading involve input from other sources, while speaking and writing involve output. Before students can successfully produce output, they need practice in dealing with input. Krashen introduced the concept of comprehensible input—linguistic stimuli that are relevant, meaningful, and understandable. Becoming a competent and confident oral communicator is inseparable from becoming an effective listener.

In the second-language classroom, the students' most frequently heard source of input is usually the teacher. As we discussed in Chapter 6, Listening Strategies, students must spend time listening before they will feel confident enough to produce oral output.

The model for teachers and students to follow is the Gradual Release of Responsibility. First, teachers model the language in a variety of ways, e.g., through:

Comprehensible input: Linguistic stimuli that are relevant, meaningful, and understandable.

—as defined by Stephen Krashen

- modelled daily routines

- oral warm-up activities

- shared reading

- read-alouds

- think-alouds

As students listen, gradually involve them by asking simple questions. Provide sentence starters, if necessary.

Bonjour, mes amis! Comment allez-vous? Moi, ça va très bien aujourd'hui. Et toi, Marcus? Ça va?

Moi, j'aime le chocolat. J'aime aussi la pizza. Et toi, Isis? Est-ce que tu aimes le chocolat?

Krashen's work dominated the field in the 1980s and (as Swain points out) had a significant impact on French Immersion programs in Canada. However, alternative theories have been developed since that time.

From the Research

Swain (2005, p. 471) observes "the processes involved in producing language can be quite different than those involved in comprehending language." Teachers are well aware of these differences and the special challenges their students encounter as they attempt to speak French both in and out of class. Acquiring functional proficiency in speaking French is a primary goal of the FSL program. But what are some behaviours that students should acquire as they talk with their peers and respond to the teacher?

According to Swain, three functions can be considered in examining speaking (2005, p. 471). Noticing or triggering language is one function. As students produce the target language, they gradually begin to notice what they do not know how to say precisely to convey the meaning they intend (Swain 2005, p. 474). Such awareness is a vital element in learning because it enables learners to recognize when they need assistance as well as the kind of assistance they need. They might need help with vocabulary, with syntactic patterns, with pronunciation, with emphasis, etc. They become aware of holes and gaps in their use of the target language. As they practise speaking the target language, they become more fluent. Although practice does not always lead to perfection or accuracy, students who have many opportunities to produce language in settings where they can identify gaps will improve their performance over time. The quality of these opportunities is more important than the quantity.

Speaking activities can provide trial runs for students—attempts that enable them to estimate what they want to say or how to say it. Teachers provide invaluable support to students as they make these attempts. By prompting the students, teachers encourage them to talk about what they are having difficulty with and lead them to recognize what they know and what they need to know in order to communicate. Swain explains these activities as the hypothesis-testing function of language output (2005, pp. 476–478).

Using language to reflect on one's own expression as well as that of others (as in listening activities) is the third function of language output (Swain 2005, pp. 478–480). Through conversations and dialogues, students have opportunities to build knowledge about how language works. The communication strategies they learn enable them to talk in ways that can be understood by their listeners. By talking about language and how it works students learn to crystallize their thinking and expression. Think-alouds and guided recalls are particularly effective strategies that help students to understand what constitutes effective communication.

Hypothesis-testing function of language output: Activities where L2 learners talk about what they know and what they need to know in order to communicate. Students need opportunities to estimate what they want to say or how to say it.

—adapted from Swain, 2005

What I Am Thinking Now

- Examine some of your lesson plans and code them according to "input" and "output" activities. What do you notice about the distribution of activities in each of these categories? What do you notice about the consistency or continuity of activities across the two aspects of language use?

- In what ways do you differentiate activities so that all students contribute through talk? What activities do you use to motivate students who are least confident in their ability to speak French?

Authentic Communication

The authors of the National Core French Study, published in the early 1990s, emphasized authentic communication as the foundation for successful FSL programs. Topics that lead to authentic communication have these features:

- they are relevant to students;

- they are highly motivating;

- they are familiar topics that students already know something about.

Typical topics that can lead to authentic communication are personal interests, family, friends, animals, weather, holidays and celebrations, community and school events, travel, physical fitness, and food.

Many commercial FSL programs are based on these topics, but there are also themes and topics that you might wish to develop outside the ones listed above to take advantage of your students' areas of interest and expertise. As students gradually develop confidence and oral competence, they will be better equipped to expand their range to topics of wider interest. At the beginning of each new topic or theme, however, students spend more time listening than they do communicating orally, so developing a bank of activities such as warm-ups about familiar topics will give them the practice they need.

Establishing Communicative Goals

Whatever the topic in your FSL classroom, it is essential to develop goals for communication as well as goals for learning language structures; communicative goals and language goals should be interdependent.

Examples of communicative goals

- introducing oneself or another person

- stating personal facts (age, date and place of birth, address, family members)

- performing classroom routines (asking for permission, naming classroom objects, asking about assignments and homework)

- giving directions

- paraphrasing or summarizing a fictional text

- summarizing main ideas of a non-fiction text

- talking about personal activities (over the weekend, holiday period)

- presenting a project or task, following a model

Creating a French Classroom Environment

Taking the time to establish common, everyday, useful oral language expressions with students will assist in creating a French classroom environment that supports French-language development throughout the year and beyond.

The priority for teachers and students in FSL classrooms is to focus time on oral communication. To maximize classroom time spent on input and output, try to create an all-French classroom environment. You will need to model and practise on a regular basis, asking and answering questions about the date, weather, time of day, and school events.

Encourage students to come up with a list of regularly used language for situations that are common to them, for example, asking for permission to leave the classroom, go to the washroom, get a drink of water, sharpen a pencil, or go to a locker.

Make sure that classroom language includes examples of interactive conversations between students as well. For example, students should be able to ask a partner for a pencil, pen, or eraser, to share a resource such as a textbook or reading text, and ask to join a group.

Using French as the primary vehicle of instruction and of student participation is highly engaging and motivating for students.

What I Am Thinking Now

- In what ways are you involving your students in monitoring their own speaking in French? Which of these activities do your students respond to most positively?

- How do you prompt your students to take more risks in expressing themselves in French?

- What can you tell your students about your experiences in learning another language that will encourage them in their efforts?

From the Research

Research has demonstrated that input in the target language of instruction (TL) is crucial in leading to successful outcomes in the second-language classroom. According to Chaudron, "in the typical foreign language classroom, the common belief is that the fullest competence in the TL is achieved by means of the teacher providing a rich TL environment, in which not only instruction and drills are executed in the TL, but also disciplinary and management operations." (Chaudron, 1985)

To take these concepts one step further, Intensive French, a program born out of the 1960's concept of *un bain linguistique* and revitalized and retooled by Claude Germain and Joan Netten, "uses the target language as a means of communication and focuses on language learning rather than on the learning of subject matter in the second language." These principles, paired with an intense period of study in the target language, are characteristics of the most effective ways of learning a second language. (Netten and Germain, 2005)

For the 2008/2009 school year, approximately 375 Intensive French classes existed in Canada. Since 1998, provinces and territories piloting this approach have wanted to measure oral proficiency of students before and after participating in the five-month Intensive French experience. The New Brunswick Middle School Scale was chosen by jurisdictions across Canada to measure proficiency of young Intensive French-language students. To learn more about the scale and its application in your jurisdiction for FSL, contact the New Brunswick Department of Education.

For more information on Intensive French in Canada, visit the Canadian Association of Second Language Teachers (CASLT) online.

Collaborative Group Work

There are two basic types of oral interactions in the second-language classroom, already touched on in Chapter 6: transactional and interactive interactional communication. In transactional forms of communication, students will mostly listen to the model (you or the recording) and then respond, with the appropriate support, to what they have heard; and in interactive interactional forms, students listen and respond orally with another person.

While you play a pivotal role as a language model, make sure to allow students time to interact with one another. Time dedicated to student-to-student interaction that is properly scaffolded is of critical importance. Allowing for this type of interaction increases the number of opportunities that each individual student will have to communicate within the allotted French class. After you have modelled a concept with the class, have students practise in pairs or groups. Collaborative small group or partner work is an effective way of encouraging students to use French. Often pairs or groups can accomplish tasks that are too challenging for individuals.

From the Research

Interactive interactional communication is:

- Social and interpersonal
- Two-way communication
- Based on personal, daily information

Many researchers have observed the importance of "the collaborative nature of learning and language development between individuals, the interrelatedness of the roles of teacher and learner, and the active roles of both in the learning process." (Gibbons, 2002, p. 7) Collaborative work is most effective when tasks are properly scaffolded so students do not revert to their first language. (Kristmanson, 2007)

An activity such as a think-pair-share is a useful one for beginning language learners. Students first think of what they might want to say. Then they are paired together and exchange ideas. Next, the pair's ideas are shared with a larger group or even with the whole class. This interaction provides models for communication and another opportunity for multiple repetitions of output.

Oral Warm-Ups

One of the ways to incorporate oral practice into your classes is through regular oral warm-ups. Although the teacher starts out as the leader, over time, students will become confident enough to take turns leading the warm-up. Warm-ups are typically based on a routine and should be linked to the overall communicative outcomes.

Oral warm-ups include a great deal of repetition because repetition allows students multiple opportunities to hear and so learn routines quickly. It provides students with a comfort level that will lead them to take risks and participate in the classroom dialogue.

When oral warm-ups are part of the established classroom routine, they complement the main lesson by quickly preparing students for working in the target language.

Teacher Tip

Warm-ups should take no longer than five minutes. They are intended to break the ice and suggest ideas for the rest of the class, not to be the main activity.

If you are using entrance and exit passes, consider ways of incorporating students' responses to the entrance and exit passes as oral warm-ups.

Oral warm-ups do not have to be the first activity during class; they can precede the oral part of the class or be used as the final activity, especially if you are using them as part of the exit pass.

The most common type of oral warm-up, especially with beginner students or at the beginning of a new topic or theme, is a teacher-led question-and-answer session, usually following a routine. As students become more confident and familiar with the topic, consider incorporating games as oral warm-up activities as well. When games introduce a competitive element, they can motivate all students to participate.

CASE STUDY | Oral Warm-Ups: Improving Interaction

When Madame Brown began teaching FSL, she understood the importance of oral communication and included an oral warm-up in each lesson. She would consider the structures and vocabulary for the unit of study and carefully structure a list of questions to use for the oral warm-up each day. In this manner, she could reinforce the content of the unit while encouraging her students to talk in French. If, for example, the students were learning to tell the time, Madame Brown would develop a series of questions about the times of day when students might typically eat breakfast, finish school, or watch a favourite television show.

What Madame Brown found was a mediocre level of student engagement. While there were a handful of students who always participated eagerly and practised the structured questions she had designed, there were a large number of students who were not included in this activity. She decided to develop incentives for students to participate more fully, including participation points and «*prof du jour*». While these strategies improved the level of

participation of some of the students, Madame Brown was still unsatisfied with the authenticity of the oral communication she was striving to develop with her students. Understanding that listening and speaking are social skills, she needed to change the structure of the oral warm-up to engage all the students.

At about the time that Madame Brown was examining her practice and looking for better strategies to engage all her students in more authentic oral communication, a new active learning process called *Tribes* was being adopted by her school and school board. Madame Brown was particularly interested in the 'community circle' and how she might use this learning process in FSL to engage all her students and encourage a more genuine level of oral communication.

Rather than structuring questions to reinforce specific vocabulary or grammar concepts, Madame Brown decided to begin the oral warm-up with the simple question «*comment ça va?*». Even her most reluctant students were able to respond «*ça va bien*», or

Oral Warm-Ups: Improving Interaction (cont'd)

« Comme ci, comme ça ». When students responded *« Ça va mal »*, Madame Brown probed with *« Pourquoi ? »* Slowly, her students began to respond with more and more complex responses, and as new vocabulary was necessary for communication, Madame Brown would provide the students with the words or phrases required to express their ideas. Those new phrases and expressions were added to the Word Wall by the students themselves and, gradually, students began asking one another questions. The oral warm-up became longer, richer, and more inclusive, with students developing useful expressions and phrases to communicate their own ideas with genuine enthusiasm.

Today, all of Madame Brown's junior students are eager to participate in community circles, and the oral warm-up includes authentic oral communication for all her students. Similarly, Madame Brown knows her students so much better and can ask them how their hockey tournament went, or what movie they are going to see on the weekend.

What I Am Thinking Now

In the Case Study: Oral Warm-Ups: Improving Interaction, Madame Brown retools her oral warm-up routine so there is a greater level of inclusion and more dynamic interaction. What might you incorporate in your own practice to help improve the quality of oral production during oral warm-ups?

The following suggested warm-up activities can be adapted to suit the needs, level, or theme of your class. In all cases, encourage students to provide full-sentence responses rather than single-word answers. You might have to give a model of the sentence structure for their answers.

Teacher-Led Question and Answer

Use a question-and-answer format to review and revisit interactive "small talk" communication. Follow a recognized pattern and make changes based on the current classroom theme.

> *Madame Brown : Bonjour, mes amis !*
>
> *La classe : Bonjour, madame.*
>
> *Madame Brown : Comment allez-vous aujourd'hui ? Emily, est-ce que ça va bien ?*

Emily : Oui, ça va bien. Merci.

Madame : Qui peut me dire la date d'aujourd'hui ? James ?

James : Aujourd'hui, c'est lundi le 9 septembre.

Madame : Bravo ! Maintenant, qui peut me dire quel temps il fait dehors aujourd'hui ? Sam ?

Sam : Il fait soleil.

Madame : Oui, Sam. Merci. Qui peut me dire quelque chose d'autre à propos du temps ? Marlene ?

Marlene : Il y a du vent.

Madame : Merci, Marlene ! Est-ce que quelqu'un a entendu la météo pour demain ? Quel temps fera-t-il demain ?, etc.

Toss the Ball (*Lancer la balle*)

You will need a soft foam ball for this activity. Depending on your theme and vocabulary, explain that, when you throw the ball to the group, whoever catches it must say a word or a key expression as quickly as possible, and then throw the ball to someone else, who must say another word or expression as quickly as possible.

Variations: Play music and pause randomly as the ball is being tossed. Whoever has the ball when the music stops is out.

Divide the class into teams. If a player on one team repeats a word or expression used by the other team, that player is out. Track the results over a period of time to determine the winners.

Qui a… ? Moi, j'ai….

You will need double-sided cards or pieces of paper with the expression *Qui a…?* on one side and the words *Moi, j'ai…* on the other side. Each card will have a word or expression written for the *Moi, j'ai…* cards, for example, the leader will read: *Qui a un éléphant?* and the student with the card will respond, *Moi, j'ai un éléphant*! or *Qui a l'expression 'Il neige'? Moi, j'ai l'expression 'Il neige'.*

Charades (*Les charades*)

Divide the class into teams. You will need prepared cards with written words or expressions to draw from a hat. Determine which team goes first, and then one pair draws a word card. They have to act out the word or expression for the opposing team, who must guess the word or expression within a time limit. If they guess correctly, they win a point and then a pair from their team has a turn. If they guess incorrectly, the other team has a chance.

Variation: the partner pair draws the word or expression on the board.

Cut-Up Conversations (*Des conversations coupées*)

You will need to prepare a blackline master of typical conversations on a topic or theme. For example, if your students are talking about food, create a conversation between a customer and a waiter.

> *Bonjour, monsieur et madame. Comment allez-vous?*
>
> *Très bien, merci.*
>
> *Voici le menu. Qu'est-ce que vous désirez?*
>
> *Moi, je voudrais commander…*

Do not indicate the speakers. Cut the dialogue into strips and distribute one strip to each student. They must find the corresponding question or answer and reconstitute the dialogue.

Variation: Have groups create mini-dialogues on different topics and prepare and distribute their strips to other groups.

One-Minute Sentences (*Des phrases rapides*)

Ask students to create, within a time limit, sentences that use an element (vocabulary, expression, or language structure) that they have recently learned. Provide prompts, e.g., classroom objects or visuals.

Variation: Play a version of I Spy. Ask students to make up sentences based on classroom objects or classmates, using adjectives of colour, size, and shape. (If you are concerned about embarrassing students, then set the game rules to refer to only objects, not people.)

Message Rap (*Les raps*)

Create a rap or chant with your students based on recently learned vocabulary, expressions, or ideas. Start each class by performing the rap. If physical movements or gestures are appropriate, consider adding some.

Start by having the whole class perform the rap and then, as they become familiar with it, ask volunteers to take turns reciting lines.

What I Am Thinking Now

- List each of the foregoing activities on a chart and post it where students have access to it. Talk with your students about each of the activities and what they learned as a result of their participation. To what extent do the students' observations of the activities reflect what you intended them to accomplish?

Oral Activities to Motivate Your Students

The following activities are useful suggestions for including in lesson plans. The activities will not only be motivating for students and teachers, but also purposeful when part of a well-designed unit of study or lesson plan.

Ask-and-Answer Games (*Des jeux de questions et de réponses*)

There are many variations of ask-and-answer games. Twenty Questions, Seek and Find, *Qui suis-je?* are all useful and enjoyable in second-language classes. In each game, a student chooses a person, animal, or thing, and then others ask yes/no questions. Prepare students before the game so their questions will elicit the maximum amount of information in response, and not be random guesses.

In Twenty Questions, one student chooses a person or a thing while others, in groups or as a class, take turns asking answers beginning with the opening category question: Is it an animal? Is it a person? Is it a thing? (*Est-ce une personne? Est-ce un animal? Est-ce une chose?*) (You might wish to extend the categories to include places and events such as festivals if your students are learning about *la francophonie.*) The answers must be yes/no. Each answer should lead to the next question.

Limit the number of questions to 10, 5, and 3 and challenge groups to find the answers with the fewest number of questions.

As a further challenge, you might wish to encourage students to answer in complete sentences rather than with yes/no answers. Model complete answers first.

For younger students or visual learners, the game Seek and Find incorporates visuals. Find several thematically related visuals, for example, of animals. In groups or as a class, one student chooses a visual. Other students take turns asking yes/no questions to find the answer.

Est-ce une personne?

Non. (Non, ce n'est pas une personne.)

Est-ce un animal?

Oui. (Oui, c'est un animal.)

Est-ce que c'est un animal qui vole?

Non. (Non, ce n'est pas un animal qui vole.)

Est-ce que c'est un animal qui a quatre pattes?

Oui. (Oui, c'est un animal qui a quatre pattes.)

In *Qui suis-je?*, find several thematically related visuals. Tape a visual on each student's back with masking tape. Make sure that the student cannot see the visual. The visual should face outward so that others can see. Students circulate, asking each other one question to determine their animal identities. They circulate asking questions until they have enough information to make a guess.

Est-ce que je suis grand?

Est-ce que j'ai quatre pattes?

Est-ce que je peux nager?

Jeopardy

Choose a variety of different categories. Under each category there are 10 questions ranging in point values from $100 to $1000, according to their level of difficulty. Group students into teams. The team that earns the most money in the time allotted wins the game. Play the game for a few minutes at the end of class. Students often enjoy playing Jeopardy after they have learned about several themes, so that there are a variety of topics to use as categories.

Golden Egg (*Les oeufs d'orés*)

Golden Egg is similar to Jeopardy. Prepare 20 egg-shaped pieces of card-stock, numbered on the front and with envelopes taped to the back. Each envelope on the back has a money value written on it. The jackpot (*le gros lot*) amount is $500. One egg is the joker. If a player chooses this egg, team members lose their money. If one team is unable to answer a question, the question is returned to the egg in its original position.

TV Interviewer and Interviewee (*Des entrevues télévisés*)

In this game, students role-play a television interviewer and interviewee. You might wish to take the part of the interviewer until students get used to the format. Provide a script of the opening elements (greeting, description of the guest and the topic) until students become familiar with the format. To help students get started, suggest that the interviews include basic personal information (ask the interview subject his/her name, age, town, and one interesting fact about him/her, e.g., interests, hobbies, favourite movies, foods, animals, etc.). Interview topics can reflect any theme, e.g., sports, (the interviewee role-plays a famous athlete), movies, or music (the interviewee role-plays an actor or musician).

Musical Hands and Feet (*Des mains et pieds musicales*)

This game is a cross between the egg game and musical chairs. It incorporates both music and movement. Place numbered laminated hands and feet on the floor. There should be one less hand or foot than the number of students in the class. Turn on the music and have students walk around the classroom. When the music is turned off, students must stand on the nearest hand or foot. The student who does not have anywhere to stand is out. That student will choose a number and the student standing on that number will have to answer the question. Prepare a sheet of questions in advance and assign a point value to each question. If the student answers correctly, his or her team receives the points.

What Did You See? (*Que vois-tu?*)

Place a variety of objects (or visuals of objects) on a tray. Let students look at the tray for a few seconds. Students will then have to name as many items as they can remember, saying the names aloud to their partners. Encourage students to use articles and to speak in full sentences: *J'ai vu un lion, un ours, et un cheval. J'ai vu un chat et des singes.*

The individual or the pair with the highest number of correctly remembered items wins.

Surveys (*Les sondages*)

Survey skills involve creating questions, asking questions, and listening to and recording the responses of those being surveyed. Compile and display the survey results on charts, graphs, Venn Diagrams, and other graphic organizers. Surveys can be as simple as finding out the number and type of pets, musical instruments, etc. in each household. Other popular survey topics are current pop culture, sports, student interests, and extracurricular activities. Students are often interested in the results because they are relevant and immediate.

Quelles sont tes activités préférés ?

1. *Aimes-tu écouter de la musique ?*

2. *Aimes-tu parler avec tes amis au téléphone ?*

3. *Aimes-tu pratiquer des sports d'équipe ?*

4. *Aimes-tu participer à des activités physiques ?*

5. *Aimes-tu regarder des films DVD ?*

6. *Aimes-tu t'amuser avec tes amis ?*

7. *Aimes-tu jouer de la musique ?*

8. *Aimes-tu magasiner au centre commercial avec tes amis ?*

9. *Aimes-tu participer à des activités artistiques ?*

10. *Aimes-tu jouer à des jeux vidéo ?*

If you wish, model simple and more complex responses to survey questions, for example:

Aimes-tu écouter de la musique ?

Oui / Non

J'aime écouter de la musique. Je n'aime pas écouter de la musique.

Oui ! J'aime écouter de la musique. J'aime surtout la musique du groupe… la musique pop….

Oui, j'aime écouter de la musique, mais je préfère jouer de la musique. Je joue de la guitare.

Surveys can be an end in themselves or a preliminary step to preparing an interview, which more closely resembles an authentic conversation.

Collaborative Dialogues (*Des dialogues collaboratives*)

Collaborative dialogues incorporate both listening and speaking and are suitable with a variety of themes. Students can either interview each other about their own interests, role-play people to interview (e.g., famous athletes, movie stars, and musicians), or find people in the community with whom to speak.

Mingling to Music Interview

(Adapted from *Tribes*)

Preparation

You will need a CD player, a selection of music, and blank index cards.

Before the Activity

1. Perform any pre-activities necessary to activate prior knowledge and personal experiences, depending on the theme.

2. In pairs, have students write interview questions on index cards (or you can provide pre-made index cards).

Language learning is social in nature. Using games motivates students by providing a purpose for interacting and communicating.

During the Activity

1. Play the music and have partners mingle to the music by moving around the room.

2. When the music stops, students must turn to the person closest to them and ask the question they have written on their index card.

3. After the first student has answered, he or she asks a question.

4. Once all students have had a chance to ask and answer the questions, restart the music and repeat steps 1 to 3 until all students have as many questions and answers as necessary to create an interview. (The number of questions will depend on the theme or on your discussions with the class as part of the pre-activity.)

After the Activity

1. Invite students to share something positive that they learned from asking questions of their partners.

2. Discuss which strategies partners used to come up with the questions and then to ask and answer questions. What skills did they need to listen attentively while mingling? Were they respectful and did they listen to the question without interruption? Did they ask for clarification if it was required?

3. Discuss which strategies students used to create the interview format from the mingling to the music activity.

A completed interview might sound something like this:

A: Bonjour! Je suis ici avec une personne très intéressante. Comment t'appelles-tu?

B: Je m'appelle Michael Bradfield.

A : Bonjour, Michael. Comment vas-tu aujourd'hui?

B : Bien, merci et toi?

A : Très bien, merci. Michael, quels sont tes passe-temps préférés?

B : Je joue au hockey. J'adore le hockey.

A : Où est-ce que tu joues? ...etc.

Oral Presentations

Students have a tremendous sense of achievement in being able to speak in French and take part in a conversation. This might be the single most effective motivator for FSL students. Short oral exchanges such as those produced during oral warm-up activities are effective in relaxing students, but do not provide them with opportunities for sustained oral production over more than a minute or so.

In the FSL classroom, just as in the English Language Arts classroom, oral presentations play an important role in consolidating students' understanding of what they have just learned. Being able to communicate orally, by summarizing and paraphrasing and by identifying main ideas, is crucial to

Speaking activities and games are most effective when used within the context of a well-developed unit of study and lesson.

- laying down new knowledge in long-term memory

- making connections to other subjects

- increasing personal background knowledge that students can bring to bear on new subjects

Students should already be familiar with strategies for preparing and giving oral presentations from their English Language Arts and Social Studies classes. Ensure that students understand the purpose of the presentation and are clear about the steps involved. (See BLM 7.1 with strategies in French.)

- Is there a primary source? (This is usually a text, but in the second-language classroom this can sometimes be in a recorded aural format.)

- What steps should they follow to ensure that they have understood the primary source? (See the Listening, Reading, and Writing chapters.)

- Do they need to do research for the presentation? Which media are most appropriate for the topic (e.g., library books, Internet, interviews with peers or family, posters, or flyers)?

- Is the presentation collaborative? If so, do the group members or partners have defined roles and responsibilities?

- Do they have clear instructions on the parameters of the task?

- What planning will they have to do to carry out the task? Do they have or do they need to create checklists and graphic organizers?

- What are the criteria for the task?

The interactions students have in this setting help them solve routine language problems and in so doing, they can apply strategies such as noticing where they need help, generating possibilities for expression, testing the possibilities, and drawing upon their prior knowledge to help them deal with new material or familiar material that they now have to deal with in French. Swain notes that the communication demands of a task can push learners into thinking more strategically about the form of their oral expression. This kind of challenge, along with the teacher's support, helps extend the ability of the students to produce more effective talk. (Swain, 2005, p. 477)

Teacher Tip

An important consideration for the second-language teacher is the fact that students will do Internet and library research in L1 rather than in the target language. You can try to find ways to avoid this by:

· pre-researching the topic and suggesting French-language websites

· pre-researching search terms in French and providing these for students

· suggesting that students research French-language WebQuests and LQuests

· finding public libraries in your area that have French-language reference books

· suggesting government websites, which provide information in both official languages, as sources of information on topics such as nutrition, Canadian history, and physical fitness, etc.

There are many websites devoted to resources and websites for FSL teachers and their students. The Canadian Encyclopedia website provides information in both English and French.

Strategies to Use Before the Presentation

Encourage students to recall and use strategies from all facets of literacy. If the presentation is based on a reading text (e.g., a story or an informational text), students will use reading strategies to determine meaning. Remind them that the familiar words and cognates (*les mots-amis et les mots connus*) they should be looking for as they read might also be key words or expressions to convey the meaning of the text (the storyline, the main ideas) when they present.

Some useful strategies for students as they plan their oral presentation are

- What do I already know about the subject? *Qu'est-ce que je sais déjà à propos de ce sujet?*

- What have I learned about the subject by... reading the text/ listening to the recording/watching the DVD, etc.? *Qu'est-ce que j'ai appris quand j'ai lu le texte / quand j'ai écouté l'enregistrement / quand j'ai regardé le film?*

- What are the main ideas of my presentation? *Quelles sont les idées principales de ma présentation?*

- What interesting facts or supporting details do I want to mention? *Quels faits intéressants ou détails supplémentaires est-ce que je veux mentionner?*

- Can I find any key words or expressions that will help me express the main ideas in my own words? *Est-ce que je peux trouver des mots ou des expressions-clés qui vont m'aider à exprimer les idées importantes dans mes propres mots?*

- Are there any graphic organizers or checklists that I can use to organize my thinking? *Est-ce que je peux utiliser des graphiques pour organiser mes idées?* (See BLM 7.2 for an example.)

- Are there any visual aids or props that would help illustrate my ideas? *Est-ce qu'il y a des aides visuelles qui vont m'aider à expliquer mes idées?*

Summarizing and paraphrasing are difficult skills. Helping students rephrase in simple language might require giving them sentence starters such as: *Je pense que, À mon avis, Selon moi, Les idées principales sont...* and blackline masters that help them identify the main words or expressions.

Strategies to Use During the Presentation

Remind students that successful presenters rehearse many, many times. It might be helpful to pair students up with a peer who can listen to the rehearsal and provide suggestions. Suggest the following to help students when they rehearse:

- Are my ideas clearly organized? (If I am having problems moving from one section to another, that might indicate that my presentation does not flow logically.) *Est-ce que j'ai organisé mes idées clairement? (Si j'ai de la difficulté à passer d'une section à une autre, cela peut indiquer que ma présentation n'est pas dans un ordre logique.)*

- Do I need to prepare point-form notes of my main points to help me when I speak? *Est-ce que j'ai besoin de cartes aide-mémoire?*

- Am I speaking too quickly? Am I speaking clearly? *Est-ce que je parle trop vite? Est-ce que je parle clairement?*

- Am I looking at my audience when I speak? *Est-ce que je regarde les autres quand je parle?*

- Am I smiling? Am I making gestures? *Est-ce que je souris? Est-ce que je fais des gestes?*

- Am I using my visual aids to make points? *Est-ce que j'utilise mes aides visuelles pour illustrer mes idées?*

- Am I speaking with expression? *Est-ce que je parle avec expression?*

Strategies to Use After the Presentation

Prepare activities for self- and peer evaluation of the presentation. Encourage students to reflect on which strategies helped them succeed. (See BLMs 7.3 and 7.4.)

- Did the notes on my graphic organizers help me organize my work? *Est-ce que les graphiques m'ont aidé à organiser mon travail?*

- Did noting the key words or expressions help me organize my work? *Est-ce que les expressions-clés m'ont aidé à organiser mon travail?*

- Did making point-form notes help me present? *Est-ce que c'était utile de créer les cartes aide-mémoire?*

- Did I speak slowly and clearly? *Est-ce que j'ai parlé lentement et clairement?*

- Did I speak with expression? *Est-ce que j'ai parlé avec expression?*

- Did I look at my audience? *Est-ce que j'ai regardé les autres?*

Summary

The ability to communicate by speaking is the highest goal for FSL students to achieve, one that will allow them to travel, work, and communicate with Francophone speakers in many places around the world and in many different contexts in the present and future.

Achieving this goal is a multi-step process over time. Students will have to practise regularly in small, graduated steps through warm-up activities and games, through surveys and interviews, and through preparing and delivering oral presentations. It is essential that they be exposed to as intensive a French experience as possible. One way of accomplishing this is to create a French classroom environment and to remind students that "they do not need English to survive."

My Choices

- Make a tally of your responses to the foregoing checklist. What does the tally reveal about your approach to oral language activities?

- As you reflect on your students' participation in oral language activities, what observations do you have about the role of aptitude and the role of motivation in their learning?

- Talk is used to convey and negotiate meaning as well as to facilitate social interaction. How do you help your students build confidence in speaking French? When and for what purposes do you intervene to help your students improve the quality of their speaking in French?

Teacher Checklist			
The interaction in my classroom is predominantly student to student.	YES ☐	NO ☐	SOMETIMES ☐
Students have numerous opportunities to lead activities, assist in read-aloud activities, etc. in my classroom.	YES ☐	NO ☐	SOMETIMES ☐
Students interact in cooperative groups.	YES ☐	NO ☐	SOMETIMES ☐
Students participate in activities where they must interact in order to accomplish the task.	YES ☐	NO ☐	SOMETIMES ☐
Oral prompts are always provided to encourage students to speak in full sentences.	YES ☐	NO ☐	SOMETIMES ☐
Structures are scaffolded, modelled, and then practised repeatedly using variety.	YES ☐	NO ☐	SOMETIMES ☐
Students are encouraged to ask questions as well as to make statements.	YES ☐	NO ☐	SOMETIMES ☐
Games are used contextually to stimulate student interest.	YES ☐	NO ☐	SOMETIMES ☐
Role-playing is used to help students interact and make connections between their experiences and the new learnings.	YES ☐	NO ☐	SOMETIMES ☐

J'évalue mon expression orale

Nom : _____ Classe : _____ Date : _____

Faites la lecture de cette auto-évaluation avec l'élève. Avec le temps, l'élève va pouvoir remplir le formulaire sans aide.

	Oui ☺	Parfois 😐	Non ☹
Auto-évaluation — Mes comportements			
Je regarde la personne à qui je parle.			
Je parle clairement.			
Je parle assez fort, mais pas trop fort.			
J'essaie de ne pas changer de sujet.			
Je sais comment prendre la parole dans une discussion.			
J'envoie un signal à la personne pour montrer que j'ai terminé de parler.			
J'interromps la personne qui parle correctement.			

Un shéma circulaire pour organiser mes idées

Nom : _____   Classe : _____   Date : _____

_____ 6 _____ _____ _____	_____ 1 _____ _____ _____

Titre : _____
_____
_____
_____

_____ 5 _____ _____ _____	_____ 2 _____ _____ _____

_____ 4 _____ _____ _____	_____ 3 _____ _____ _____

Que penses-tu de ma présentation ?

Nom : _____ Classe : _____ Date : _____

Titre : _____

1. Je pense ta présentation _____

_____

_____

2. Cette présentation m'a fait penser à _____

_____

_____

3. Quand j'écoute ta présentation, je sens _____

_____

_____

4. À mon avis, ta présentation serait meilleure si _____

_____

_____

_____

Nom du ou de la partenaire

Ma présentation

Nom : _____ Classe : _____ Date : _____

Le sujet de ma présentation est :

_____

Voici ce que j'ai appris :

1.

_____

_____

_____

2.

_____

_____

_____

3.

_____

_____

_____

Chapter 8

Reading Strategies

"It's such a wonderful feeling to watch a child discover that reading is a marvellous adventure rather than a chore."
—*Zilpha Keatley Snyder*

My Thoughts

- What do you know about your students' reading attitudes and interests? From those observations, would you say that your students view reading as a "marvellous adventure"? Talk with your students about their reading activities both in and out of school. How can you use this awareness to support your students as they learn to read French?

- With a colleague, develop a pro and con chart to compare the adventure (pro) and chore (con) aspects of reading instruction. Observe which aspects—pro or con—are most apparent in your reading instruction. Why is this so? How do you think this situation will change over time?

In this chapter, we will discuss:

- Reading and Literacy in the L2 Classroom

- Reading Intention

- Scaffolding Reading

- Explicitly Teaching Reading Strategies

  ° Before-Reading Strategies and Activities
  ° During-Reading Strategies and Activities
  ° After-Reading Strategies and Activities

Reading and Literacy in the L2 Classroom

Reading is an essential aspect of literacy in the modern world. It is the foundation of much academic learning, and the basis of communication through 21st century media such as the Internet. In the second-language

Key to Success

Knowing that the four strands of language—listening, speaking, reading, and writing—are inter-related and inter-dependent ensures that you apply a communicative-experiential approach to instruction.

The Four Roles—
The student as:

· Code Breaker

· Text User

· Text Participant

· Text Analyst

(Luke, 1992)

classroom, however, the purpose of reading is integrally connected to oral communication. In past decades, second-language students read in the target language to improve their knowledge of language structures and vocabulary. But increasingly, we are realizing that students are highly motivated to read in the second language when they can communicate their responses by talking about what they have read.

As we discussed in Chapters 6 and 7, English Language Arts teachers are now learning a lesson from second-language teaching: that responding orally to a text is a vital way of internalizing the learning and demonstrating a deeper, higher-level understanding of it.

In this chapter, we will discuss lessons from L1 reading instruction, and how to enable students to transfer their pre-existing L1 skills to an L2 context. We will also discuss strategies specific to L2 reading instruction.

From the Research
Researchers in L1 reading instruction have developed a model, the Four Roles/ Resources, for describing the characteristics that all readers must have to be successful. 1. The student as code breaker must understand 　· the relationship between sound and written symbols 　· grammar 　· format and conventions of different text types 2. The student as text user must understand 　· that different text types have different uses and purposes 　· that purpose and format are related 　· that knowing about the text's purpose and format helps the reader to complete response activities 3. The student as text participant must create meaning through 　· personal experiences 　· prior knowledge 4. The student as text analyst must understand what is implicit in the text 　· the position of the writer or characters in the text 　· the way language use affects the presentation of ideas (Luke, 1992)

Reading Intention

Students should have a clear understanding of why they are reading a text. As with listening, having a purpose for reading helps motivate them, focuses their attention on the task, and reduces anxiety. (See BLMs 8.1 and 8.2 for attitudinal reading surveys.) Encourage students to realize that they do not have to understand every word, but that they can read for the main idea.

"If you don't have time to read, you don't have the time or the tools to write."

—Stephen King

In order for students to become effective readers, they must

• understand the purpose of reading

• prepare for the activity

• use appropriate reading strategies from their L1 experience

• learn how to use L2 reading strategies

(See BLM 8.3.)

Students need to be prepared before they can read. Before introducing a reading selection, consider the following questions:

• Is the purpose of the reading clear to them? For example, are they reading to find out how a story begins or ends? Are they reading an informational text for main ideas or details? Are they reading to research an individual or group project?

• Are there key words or expressions that they should look for?

• Are there contextual clues or information that will help them?

- Can students make predictions about the content or topic of the text?

- If the text is accompanied by visuals, are there clues that they can glean from looking at them?

Scaffolding Reading

"The goal for students is to eventually be able to successfully apply and monitor new strategies independently. The goal for teachers is to successfully offer varying levels of support to scaffold student learning." (Trehearne, 2006, p. 547)

Students learn best if their learning is scaffolded; that is, if the teacher supports them intensively at the beginning and then gradually allows them more independence as they are ready and able to take up new learning challenges. You can scaffold reading for students by continually making connections to their prior knowledge of the reading: thematic, cross-curricular, and personal. For example:

- Highlight text traits that are already familiar to students, such as features of informational texts.

- Point out familiar content from other subjects, e.g., remind them that they have read about *voyageurs* in Social Studies.

- Point out familiar words, language structures, and cognates.

- Teach students how to recognize patterns in word formation.

- Explicitly teach reading strategies during the three stages of reading (before, during, and after).

- Model reading through read-alouds.

- Model metacognitive strategies through think-alouds.

What I Am Thinking Now

Scaffolding is an application of steps in the Gradual Release of Responsibility model for instruction that has implications for both L2 and L1 teachers.

· With your students' English Language Arts teacher, discuss how scaffolding is incorporated in selected areas of English reading instruction; e.g., word recognition, making inferences, or reading non-fiction texts.

· Share observations about the students you both teach: Which students need lots of support and in which areas? Which students are best able to recognize when they encounter difficulties? What strategies do these students use to deal with the difficulties? Which students are comfortable talking about what they read and what they do as readers?

· How can you both demonstrate to your students the connections between what they are learning in French class and in English Language Arts class?

Explicitly Teaching Reading Strategies

In their first language, students have learned to decode text and are usually adept at making sound-symbol connections. In a second language, however, they will need explicit instruction on how to connect sound and symbol in learning French.

In order to be successful readers in a second language, learners must be able to

- recognize patterns in sound;

- recognize patterns in spelling;

- recognize morphemes (parts of words such as roots, and prefixes and suffixes that indicate grammatical relationships and that are affixed to roots);

- use contextual clues to figure out meanings of unfamiliar words and expressions;

- become aware of strategies to use when they encounter unfamiliar words and expressions.

Listening, speaking, and writing are all interconnected and essential for reading comprehension. Because students will not recognize sound relationships in French, it is essential that they hear, see, and then practise producing sound relationships in French. For example, vowel combinations such as *au* and *ou* will look like English diphthongs (a speech sound beginning with one vowel sound and moving to another vowel sound).

Students will also need to learn rules for recognizing silent final consonants and will have to be explicitly taught that French makes important meaning distinctions through the sounding of the final consonant after an *–e* in feminine endings.

Recognizing how vowels and consonants sound and how they appear in written form goes hand in hand. As students are seeing words, vowels, and silent consonants, they are also hearing them. Gradually, they will be able to make the connection between *au* on its own and *au* in *faux*, for example.

> Using flexible magnetic tape on the back of word cards, when you have access to a magnetic white or chalk board, can simplify the creation of a Word Wall if you are an itinerant teacher. Simply cut the tape from the roll in the length needed and apply to your word cards.

Teacher Tip

Compose a chant to help familiarize students with vowel sounds. Post the sounds on a Word Wall, and make sure that you connect the written and spoken forms.

For itinerant teachers, using Word Walls presents a challenge. The technique is invaluable to students and is worth the extra effort necessary to establish Word Walls as an itinerant French teacher. Some suggestions are to

- Negotiate space for the French Word Wall with the homeroom teacher.
- Create a removable Word Wall that can be posted at the start of each lesson. Use materials such as adhesive chart paper, pocket charts, or word cards with magnetic tape to apply to a magnetic chalk board. Establish a routine where French monitors know to post the Word Wall at the beginning of each French lesson.

Students are often unable to distinguish sounds that do not occur in their own language. For example, nasal vowels do not occur in English. Students might not to be able to distinguish words with nasal vowels and to reflect this in their written work, e.g., *an* is heard and written as *a*, and *en* becomes *à*; *–on* is heard as *–o*.

Making links between languages strengthens the development of all learners' languages. Cognates are words that share the same derivation and have the same meaning between two or more languages. Scanning a text for cognates helps students get a foothold in the text.

Finding cognates helps students

- make predictions about the topic or theme of the reading;

- overcome the anxiety of reading what, at first glance, looks like long, incomprehensible blocks of text;

- focus on the positive "What do I know?" rather than "There are so many expressions here I don't know! I feel overwhelmed!"

One useful before-reading strategy is to brainstorm thematically related cognates. For example, if students are going to be reading a non-fiction text about communication technology over the past century, then you might want to brainstorm words such as *la télévision, la radio, le téléphone, la technologie, la communication, le cellulaire*, etc. to demonstrate just how many words they already know.

In their first language in aural and oral communication, students have an almost unconscious awareness of lexemes and morphemes. They will need to be taught to recognize them in a second language. However, one of the L1 strategies they have learned to use in reading is to recognize parts of speech that indicate grammatical meaning (morphemes), and distinguish these elements from root and stem words that convey the dictionary meaning (lexemes).

From the Research

A lexeme is the root or stem of a word. It carries the lexical meaning of the word. A morpheme is the smallest unit of language that carries meaning. Morphemes usually convey grammatical information and cannot stand on their own.

For example:
The word "love" is a lexeme.
In the words "loving" and "lovable", "–ing" and "–able" are morphemes indicating grammatical meanings.
In the word *aimer*, *aim–* is the lexeme, and *–er* is the morpheme indicating a grammatical meaning.
In the word *aimable*, *–able* is a morpheme conveying grammatical meaning.

When students learn how to identify and separate the lexeme (*le sens*) from its morphemes, they will have discovered a strategy for making sense of words that, at first glance, might seem impenetrable. You do not have to teach grammar (although opportunities for teaching and reinforcing grammar can arise naturally through word analysis); you can encourage students to get the main idea of the meaning by identifying lexemes that they already know in other forms.

As students develop an understanding of how root words encompass larger meanings when morphemes are added, they will be able to expand their vocabulary. You can show them how to create families of words in this way, for example:

Adding –eur/-euse Jouer Joueur Joueuse	Adding –ment Probable Probablement
Adding –ateur/-atrice Dessiner Dessinateur Dessinatrice	Adding –ation illustrer Illustration
Adding –able Adorer Adorable	Adding –age rive rivage

Before-Reading Strategies and Activities

In order to be successful, students must be prepared to read. This is the time to remind them of familiar L1 reading strategies and give them the necessary background, historical, and cultural information.

From the Research
Before reading, effective readers: • have a purpose for reading: *Je connais le but de ma lecture.* • scan the title, illustrations, and other visuals: *J'examine le titre, les illustrations, et les autres aides visuelles.* • make predictions about what they will be reading: *Je fais des prédictions.* • look for repeated words, familiar words, cognates: *Je note les mots répétés, les mots familiers, et les mots amis.* • make connections to what they already know: *Je fais des liens avec mes propres connaissances.*

Activating Prior Knowledge (Personalizing): Students already have a concept of the world and real-life experiences in the context of their first language. Activating this frame of reference helps them make necessary connections in order to understand new topics. (See BLMs 8.4 and 8.5.)

For example, if students are about to read a party invitation, they already know that an invitation usually includes the time, date, location, and details such as theme and type of gift. If they are about to read a story, they already know that a story usually includes a beginning (a description of the characters and setting), a middle (an event that somehow evokes a conflict or problem for the main character), and an end (a resolution of that problem).

If they are about to read a non-fiction text, then they already know useful strategies from their L1 reading, e.g., scanning photos and captions, title and headings. They might already be familiar with some typical features of informational texts; non-fiction texts usually have an introduction that states the subject, a body of the text with more information, and a summary.

If students are reading a non-fiction informational text, then it is helpful to recall categories from their prior learning for thinking about the subject and ask them to be aware of those categories as they read the text. For example, if students are reading about animals, you might wish to have them recall categories and record them in a graphic organizer. For example:

- Is it a mammal or invertebrate? *Est-ce que c'est un mammifère ou un invertébré?*

- Is it two- or four-footed? *Est-ce que l'animal a 2 ou 4 pattes?*

- Can it fly? *Est-ce que l'animal peut voler?*

- How long does it take care of its young?, etc. *Pendant combien de temps est-ce que l'animal prend soin de ses petits?*

> ## Teacher Tip
>
> If there are repeated words, key expressions, cognates, and familiar words or expressions that are key to the reading, consider adding them to a Word Wall. Word Walls are most effective for second-language classrooms when the vocabulary included is accompanied by a visual.
>
> You might also consider creating a kinetic version of a Word Wall: actions that remind students of the vocabulary. Create an action routine of important words or expressions and perform the routine as a before-reading activity.

Predicting: Creating meaning from a text is an active intellectual process. Successful readers who enjoy reading find connections between what they read themselves and the world around them as they ask questions and make predictions. Explicitly teaching strategies for using visual and written clues before reading will prepare students for reading.

Examine visuals (cover, unit opener, illustrations, photos, and captions) and invite students to make predictions based on them. You might have to model making predictions or provide starter sentences for predictions. For example, if the text is fiction, discuss the book cover or the opening illustration. What details do they provide about the main characters? about the setting and story events?

Use the title, subtitle, key words or expressions, or the first sentence from the reading to elicit predictions through brainstorming. Write down ideas from the brainstorming in a web, concept map, or other graphic organizer. Have students self-assess their understanding of the text at this point. (See BLM 8.6.)

Predicting can be a whole class activity or it can be done in small groups. If students are working in small groups, then give each group a copy of the illustrations and a graphic organizer for recording ideas. (See BLM 8.7 and BLM 8.8.)

Questioning: Invite students to examine illustrations and then formulate questions that they would like to have answered as they read. This works particularly well with information texts. If students see that the text is about animals, for example, they might identify questions such as

- Where does the animal live? *Où est-ce que l'animal habite?*

- What does it eat? *Qu'est-ce que l'animal mange?*

- How long does it live? *Pendant combien d'années est-ce que l'animal vit?*

- Who are its predators? *Quels animaux sont les prédateurs de cet animal?*

What I Am Thinking Now

· What have you observed about your students' ability to make predictions prior to reading new material? How do they go about checking their predictions? In what ways is their ability to make successful predictions influenced by the type of reading material?

· What activities do you use to guide your students in making predictions about the selections they read? Which of these activities seems to be most effective for your students?

The following are suggested activities for engaging students in the act of reading. Some activities are intended to help focus on the purpose of reading, and some are intended to help provide context. Each one appeals to a different type of learner (e.g., kinesthetic, musical, visual).

Storytelling: Pre-tell students the story through a simplified outline, e.g., main plot points or one-line summary, orally or by scanning the illustrations, or through a storyboard.

Picture Books: Students bring a photo of themselves reading a favourite book or they draw themselves reading a favourite book. Invite them to explain why this book is special.

Personalized Bookmarks: Give students a bead or sticker for each contribution to the before-reading discussion. Ensure that every student has at least three beads or stickers by the end of the before-reading discussion. Have students string their beads on thread or ribbon or have them make a paper bookmark for the stickers. They can add to the ribbons or bookmarks as they continue reading.

Classroom-Door Book Covers: Examine the book cover and illustrations with students. Invite them to brainstorm ideas, words, and expressions they think might appear and make connections to the real world. Encourage students to visualize their predictions, interpretations, and real-world connections as pieces of art. Then have them decorate the classroom door as a giant book cover. As they continue reading, encourage them to add to or subtract from the classroom-door artwork to reflect how further reading has changed their initial predictions and impressions.

Sequencing/Story Map: If the text has visuals, make a photocopy and cut out the visuals from their accompanying text. Ask students to suggest a possible sequence. Once students have read the text, they re-read to confirm their predictions.

Scavenger Hunt: Divide the class into teams, each with a copy of the same book. Have them find the page numbers of particular objects, events, or people in the book.

Name That Book: Explain the importance of book covers and titles (how they create first impressions, tell something about the book's contents, create reader interest, etc.). Hide the cover and title as you read aloud a story. Ask students to imagine the cover image and draw it, and to suggest a title.

Story Webs: You will need a ball of string and a story. Have your students sit in a circle on the floor or at groups of desks. Ask one student to read aloud the first sentence, and then roll the ball of string to another student, who will read aloud the next sentence of the story. Continue until the story is finished. By the end, students will have created a web demonstrating the interconnections of story elements and the shared nature of storytelling.

For a variation, ask students to roll the ball of string from student to student only when certain conditions are met, e.g., whenever two characters interact; whenever a certain plot point is mentioned, etc.

During-Reading Strategies and Activities

The following are suggested instructional strategies to develop students' use of during-reading learning strategies. Both the read-aloud and the think-aloud featured below can be used by teachers to emphasize the learning strategy or strategies desired for student focus at a particular point in time during the school year.

Using Read-Alouds: In their first language, students often prepare for reading by first listening to teachers talk about the reading. Both reading and listening are reception skills, and involve comprehension as a necessary preliminary step before producing an oral or written response can occur.

Shared reading is an effective method of teaching reading to second-language students, especially beginning students. In shared reading, the teacher often leads the reading through a read-aloud. Using a big book, a copy of the text (students can have their own copies), or a copy projected on a transparency or a SMART Board, the teacher reads aloud the text. During a read-aloud, the teacher comments on the text in a variety of ways by

- drawing connections between the text and the visuals

- making predictions (What do you think happens next? What does the title tell us about this passage?)

- making connections to prior learning (What do we already know about this subject/story?)

- making connections to personal experiences (what does this remind you of in your life?)

- encouraging students to visualize elements of the text or story

At key points during the read-aloud, pause and invite students to anticipate the next section or the ending to the story. Encouraging students to make predictions helps focus their attention during reading and listening.

Read-aloud sessions should be short and the listening environment should be comfortable. Choose a reading selection at an age- and ability-appropriate level; perhaps a book that students are already familiar with in English.

You could also consider choosing more challenging texts for read-alouds. Using accessible texts slightly above students' reading level exposes them to language and ideas they might not encounter during independent reading. Select from various genres (fiction, non-fiction, poetry, plays, etc.) to demonstrate the unique features of different genres. This outlines for students how different genres sound. Students might also enjoy fiction and non-fiction texts on the same topic. Encourage them to participate in choosing read-aloud selections.

Researchers have documented the benefits of read-alouds in teaching literacy. The read-aloud enables teachers to offer texts with more challenging concepts and language than students can read independently. Read-alouds help second-language learners develop new vocabulary. It stimulates imagination while modelling good reading processes like predicting, making connections, inferencing, questioning, and visualizing.

Consult the CD-ROM for a short video segment on How to Use Think-Alouds in FSL to Support Reading Strategy Development.

Using Think-Alouds: Teach the during reading strategies first explicitly and then model them as a think-aloud. In a think-aloud, the teacher gives a running commentary on the strategies he or she is using. Commentary on the text features and the strategies are often interconnected.

You can mark places in the text where you will think aloud, or where you will prompt students to interact with the text. Ask a variety of questions to help students make personal connections to the story.

The development of the four skill areas (listening, speaking, reading, and writing) is intrinsically linked. Listening and reading are receptive skills that involve comprehension. To demonstrate comprehension, oral or written skills are typically employed.

Teach students ways of asking you to stop or slow down when they do not understand or need time to process new information and reflect. The listening skills of second-language students exceed their reading skills and this process ensures that they will all comprehend the material.

Think-alouds are opportunities for teaching students to reflect on the strategies that they will choose to use when they read independently or with other students.

For example, in the following think-aloud, the teacher reads aloud a *bande dessinée* about an adventure story, pointing out the characters, drawing attention to the speech bubbles, etc.

> *Regardez le titre dans cet épisode.* [pointing to the title on the page] *Connaissez-vous un mot dans le titre? Moi, je reconnais le mot é-pi-sode.* [repeat slowly, emphasizing syllables] *C'est un mot qui décrit une partie d'une émission de télé. Et regardez—il y a un poste de télé dans la photo ici.* [point to the TV in the photo] *Ces deux jeunes visionnent une émission de télé. À qui est-ce que le garçon parle-t-il?*

> *Quel geste fait-il* [imitate the welcoming gesture the boy is making to greet the girl] *à cette jeune fille qui entre dans la salle? Oui, c'est ça. Quel est le nom de l'objet dans lequel se trouvent les paroles?* [point out the speech bubbles] *C'est une bulle de dialogue. Dans quel genre de texte est-ce qu'on trouve ces bulles?*

> *Le garçon dit : Assieds-toi vite, Isabelle. L'émission Aventure X-trême a commencé! Regardez l'image sur l'écran de la télévision. Quel genre d'émission est-ce que les ados visionnent? Oui, merci, André. C'est un dessin animé. Vous connaissez le mot a-ni-mé?*

When developing a lesson or unit of study, consideration of the interplay of the skills is necessary. Focus assessment on the skill(s) identified as key for the block of learning. Be clear in planning and with students as to which skill(s) will be assessed and the method to be used.

Notice that the successful use of a read-aloud and think-aloud involves pausing to let the meaning sink in, physical gestures such as pointing and miming, repeating new or key words and expressions, and pronouncing new or key words slowly and in syllables to allow students to hear the phonetic similarities between cognates.

From the Research

During reading, effective readers monitor and repair comprehension by

- noticing when the text stops making sense: *Je note où j'ai des difficultés de compréhension.*
- slowing down and re-reading: *Je lis lentement et je relis.*
- looking at the visuals for clues: *Je regarde les images pour m'aider.*
- thinking about what would make sense: *Je note le contexte pour déterminer le sens.*
- reading ahead to see if the text makes sense later on (and then going back to make sense of the earlier part): *Je lis la fin de l'histoire pour m'aider à comprendre le début.*
- asking for help from the teacher, another student, from a dictionary, Internet, or other class resources: *Je cherche de l'aide quand c'est nécessaire. Je pose des questions au professeur ou à un(e) camarade de classe. Je consulte un dictionnaire, l'Internet, ou d'autres ressources dans la salle de classe.*
- making new predictions: *Je fais des prédictions.*
- reading on to see if predictions are correct: *Je vérifie mes prédictions.*
- using knowledge of the text type to aid comprehension: *Je note le genre du texte pour m'aider à comprendre.*
- asking questions about the text: *Je pose des questions.*
- visualizing the text during reading: *J'essaye d'imaginer l'histoire en images pendant que je lis.*

CASE STUDY | Success with Think-Alouds

Mme Taylor has taught Intermediate FSL for many years. Each year, she approached her reading lessons in the same way. After pre-reading activities that exposed her students to the vocabulary and themes that they would encounter in a text, she often proceeded to distribute a text or a reader. She often asked her students to identify the reading strategies that they were going to use to facilitate their comprehension of the text. As she approached her lesson in this way, she often received the same responses from the same students. Common responses included «*Je cherche les mots-amis et les mots connus, je regarde les illustrations et la poncutation*» and «*Je fais des*

prédictions». Mme Taylor assumed that all her students understood how these strategies help them and that they would apply these strategies effectively. However, the reading response tasks of her students revealed the same gaps. There appeared to be no improvement in comprehension. Her students needed something more.

It was time for a new approach. What Mme Taylor came to realize through student conferencing was that some of her students had not yet grasped the application of these strategies. Many of her students could recite the strategies but did not apply them effectively to help them understand the text.

She decided that it was time to implement think-alouds. Her colleagues had been discussing this strategy in other subject areas. Mme Taylor decided to model to her students the mental processes that she uses when she reads.

The next week, Mme Taylor brought in a reader at below-grade level. As she held the cover of the book in front of her students, she modelled her thought processes in words. Mme Taylor demonstrated strategies such as predicting, visualizing, and making connections. She used expressions such as: *je regarde, je me demande,* and *à mon avis.* As she spoke, she ensured that her students knew that she was modelling what she was thinking.

As Mme Taylor read the story, she continued to demonstrate her thought processes and literacy strategies. She pointed to the illustrations and the text and predicted what she thought was going to happen by describing her visualization. Expressions such as *je pense que* and *j'imagine* were used to demonstrate her thoughts. She made connections to her personal experiences so that students could see how stories can be linked to past experiences and help them better understand the text. Mme Taylor communicated her interpretation of the main character's feelings.

She also modelled questions to demonstrate the process of verifying predictions and conclusions.

Mme Taylor conferenced with her students and began to see improvement in their reading response tasks. Her students also communicated their awareness of their strengths and their own progress through metacognitive activities. They not only learned that good readers do a whole lot of thinking when they read, but they also learned a list of expressions to describe their thinking. At first it was difficult for students to express their thinking in French, but through encouragement there was significant improvement as their knowledge of expressions grew.

Mme Taylor realized that think-alouds are an important component of a literacy program. Reading strategies must be taught and modelled. In the beginning, Mme Taylor was not used to describing her thought processes as she read, but as this practice became more frequent, she saw the impact on student learning. Mme Taylor took a risk and incorporated a strategy that would cause a positive ripple effect in all subject areas. Her students are also cognizant of the impact on their learning.

What I Am Thinking Now

- In what ways are the instructional purposes of read-alouds and think-alouds different? Which of these instructional supports do you use most often and for what purposes?

- What opportunities do you provide for your students to engage in think-alouds?

- How confident are you that your students are familiar with strategies that effective readers use to monitor and repair their comprehension?

Ideally, texts used in the second-language classroom should be shorter than those used in the first-language literacy program. Chunking texts into smaller pieces makes them more manageable. Students find concentrating on long texts more demanding in a second language than in their first.

The following are suggested activities to engage students as they read.

Choral Reading: Read aloud a sentence as a model, and then have the class repeat it aloud together. Choral reading ensures that hearing is immediately followed by practice. It reinforces the connection between sound and symbol. If students are nervous about speaking aloud independently, then choral reading will help them overcome their anxiety.

Cutting Reading Apart (CRA): Photocopy and cut into sentence strips a short story that students have already read. Distribute one sentence to each student and then ask them collaboratively to put the story in sequence. Then encourage students to read aloud their sentences in the correct order.

> ## Teacher Tip
>
> Interactive white boards offer a range of possibilities for reading activities and for providing age-appropriate formats for reading. If students have outgrown sitting in circles, they will be more willing to read the text projected on the white board during shared reading activities. Try reading the text another day and cover (or delete) some of the words. Make sure you do not always choose the same part of speech.

Buddy-Reading: Have students re-read the text or a part of it with a partner, taking turns reading to each other. Buddy-reading provides an opportunity to understand through listening and reading, and then practise reading aloud.

Skimming and Scanning: Model how to skim a text for a specific piece of information for students. In order to learn how to skim a reading, it is important that students have a specific reading intention. For example, if students are reading a story, invite them to skim it to find one or two details about a character (See BLMs 8.9, 8.10, and 8.11.); if they are reading an informational text, invite them to read to find a particular fact. (See BLM 8.12.)

Jigsaw-Reading: Jigsaw-reading is organized around cooperative groups. You will need a different reading (or selection from a reading) for each group. Texts can be varied in length and subject matter.

Number students in each group (1, 2, 3, 4). Ask all students with the same number in each group (i.e., all number-one students) to regroup and read a text. After each group is finished reading, students return to their base groups and share the information from the text.

A graphic organizer for writing information helps students retain key details. Jigsaw-reading activities can take more than one class.

After-Reading Strategies and Activities

After the reading, effective readers use a variety of reading strategies. They

- decide if they have achieved their reading objective: *Je détermine si j'ai réussi à atteindre le but de ma lecture.*

- confirm predictions: *Je vérifie mes prédictions.*

- think about questions they still have: *Je determine si j'ai encore des questions.*

- compare the characters or events to themselves and their lives or to other books they have read: *Je fais des liens entre les personnages et les événements du livre et d'autres livres que je connais et mes propres expériences.*

- think about how the text is organized: *Je note l'organization du livre.*

- identify the main idea: *J'identifie l'idée principale.*

- identify details that support the main idea: *J'identifie les détails.*

- think about the message that the author wanted to convey: *Je réfléchis au message de l'auteur.*

- research additional information: *Je fais des recherches pour trouver des informations supplémentaires.*

The main reasons for reading for the second-language student should be a sense of achievement and enjoyment. Encourage students to extend their enjoyment and achievement through a variety of after-reading activities.

Retell or Recount: Invite students to summarize and retell key parts of the text, either as a whole-class activity or with a partner. Being able to talk about what they have learned helps students internalize and remember the reading. You can provide sentence starters to help them begin. Graphic organizers are useful supports. (See BLMs 8.13 to 8.19.)

Text Reconstruction: Photocopy a section of the text and cut it into sentences or paragraphs. Have students put the text strips into the correct order.

Matching: If the text has visuals, make a photocopy and cut out the visuals from their accompanying text. Students match the text with visuals.

Students can also sequence the story visually, by writing one sentence per event, or by illustrating it. (See BLMs 8.20 and 8.21.)

Bande dessinée : Have students draw the reading in comic-book format, with frames and speech and thought bubbles.

Timeline: Have students write down the main events of a story in the order and time (time of day, day, month, year, season), using a sequential graphic organizer.

Cloze Activity: Create a cloze activity from the reading text by omitting key words or expressions (or every seventh or eighth word) and replacing them with a line. Make sure to choose a variety of parts of speech for omission. Have students fill in the missing information individually, in pairs, or in groups and then check their answers against the text.

Readers' Theatre: Assign roles from a reading text (characters and narrators) and have students read aloud those roles with expression and in character. After they have rehearsed, ask groups to perform the passage for the rest of the class. (See BLM 8.22.)

True-False Questions: Create a true-false quiz based on the reading to check students' comprehension. Include both factual questions (where the answer is stated explicitly in the text) and inferential questions (where the answer is only implicitly stated).

What I Am Thinking Now

Fostering a love of reading is an important instructional goal in both L1 and L2 instruction.

- In what ways do the activities that you have students complete after reading focus on enjoying the selection, that is, seeing reading as a "marvellous adventure" rather than as a "chore"? To what extent do these activities involve students in talking about what they have read? What techniques do you use to scaffold their talk?

- How effectively are your students able to make connections between the text and their own experiences? between the text and other texts they have read? What kinds of instructional supports are useful to enhance your students' ability to make such connections?

Teacher Tip

Create a space in your school devoted to French-language resources, music and video resources, magazines, dictionaries (thematic, visual, and junior), reference works, games, posters, etc.). These spaces emphasize to all that learning French contributes to students' literacy skills.

Summary

Many reading strategies that students develop in English Language Arts have application as they learn to read French. However, students might not independently realize that they can use the strategies in both languages. For this reason, explicitly teaching strategies is important. Strategies enable students to gain control of their reading—to set purposes, to make predictions and to confirm them, to monitor their comprehension, and to regulate their reading by taking steps for correction or clarification.

Providing students an opportunity to talk about what they read is an essential feature of effective instruction in FSL classes. In all three phases of a lesson—before, during, and after reading—activities can be designed to engage students in listening and speaking. Read-aloud and shared-reading activities build awareness of the sounds and cadences of French that students can carry over to their own reading. Think-aloud presentations show students how to interact with a text. These supportive instructional practices combined with appealing content ensure that students will discover that reading selections in French is a "marvellous adventure."

My Choices

- What do you enjoy about teaching reading in your FSL classes? How do you communicate your enjoyment and enthusiasm to your students?

- Make a tally of responses to the Teacher Checklist that follows. What does the tally reveal about your approach to reading instruction?

- Reflect on the various activities for reading instruction that you have examined in this chapter. What insights have you gained that you want to add to your repertoire of teaching strategies?

Teacher Checklist			
I consider the three phases of reading when I plan.	YES ☐	NO ☐	SOMETIMES ☐
I plan for activities to activate students' prior knowledge of a subject before reading a new text.	YES ☐	NO ☐	SOMETIMES ☐
Students in my class have an intention for reading before they start to read a text.	YES ☐	NO ☐	SOMETIMES ☐
Students have the opportunity to read a text more than just once and in a variety of ways.	YES ☐	NO ☐	SOMETIMES ☐
Graphic organizers are used regularly.	YES ☐	NO ☐	SOMETIMES ☐
Strategies for reading in my classroom provide opportunities for students to read and think aloud on a regular basis.	YES ☐	NO ☐	SOMETIMES ☐
Individuals from the community are occasionally invited to read with my classes.	YES ☐	NO ☐	SOMETIMES ☐
Students are regularly invited to make predictions about readings before or during the reading of a text.	YES ☐	NO ☐	SOMETIMES ☐
My post-reading activities are designed to have students return to the original text.	YES ☐	NO ☐	SOMETIMES ☐
I use a variety of different ways for students to express comprehension of a text.	YES ☐	NO ☐	SOMETIMES ☐

Comment te sens-tu face à la lecture ?

Nom : _____ Classe : _____ Date : _____

1. Comment te sens-tu lorsque l'enseignant(e) lit une histoire à voix haute ?

2. Comment te sens-tu lorsque tu lis un livre à l'école en lecture individuelle ?

3. Aimes-tu lire pour le plaisir quand tu es à la maison ?

4. Aimerais-tu recevoir un livre en cadeau d'anniversaire ?

5. Comment te sens-tu lorsque tu vois un mot nouveau au cours d'une lecture ?

6. Que dirais-tu de faire de la lecture plutôt que de jouer ?

7. Comment te sens-tu lorsque tu parles avec ton enseignant(e) d'un livre que tu as lu ?

8. Penses-tu que tu aimeras lire plus tard, dans quelques années, ou lorsque tu seras adulte ?

Questionnaire sur la lecture

Nom : _____ Classe : _____ Date : _____

1. Pourquoi est-ce qu'on lit?

_____

2. Qu'est-ce qu'on doit faire pour être un(e) bon(ne) lecteur(trice)?

_____

3. Qu'est-ce que tu fais quand tu rencontres un mot que tu ne connais pas au cours d'une lecture?

_____

_____

4. Qu'est-ce que tu fais quand tu comprends les mots que tu lis, mais que tu ne comprends pas le sens général?

_____

_____

5. Quelles sortes de livres est-ce que tu aimes lire?

_____

_____

6. Comment est-ce que tu sais si un livre que tu a choisi sera « juste bien » pour toi?

_____

_____

7. Quels sont tes auteurs préférés?

_____

_____

8. Es-tu un(e) bon(ne) lecteur(trice)? Pourquoi?

_____

_____

9. Qu'est-ce qui pourrait t'aider à être un(e) meilleur(e) lecteur(trice)?

_____

_____

Quand je lis

Nom : _____ Classe : _____ Date : _____

Quand je lis	Pas souvent	Parfois	Souvent
• Je choisis des livres parfaits pour moi.			
• Je fais des liens.			
• Je fais des prédictions.			
• Je pose des questions.			
• Je crée des images dans ma tête.			
• Je sais quand je ne comprend pas.			
• J'utilise des stratégies correctices.			

Mes objectifs en lecture

_____

_____

_____

_____

_____

Je me prépare à lire

Nom : _____ Classe : _____

Titre : _____ Date : _____

❑ Je parle de la couverture du livre et de son titre avec un(e) camarade.

❑ À mon avis, ce livre parle de : _____

_____

❑ Je réfléchis à ce que je sais sur ce sujet :

_____

_____

1.

2.

3.

❑ Voici un dessin de ce qui arrivera dans l'histoire :

❑ Je fais un survol du texte avec un(e) camarade.

Chacun son tour

Nom : _____   Date : _____

Titre : _____   Auteur(e) : _____

Prédire	**Lire**	**Discuter**
_____	_____	_____
_____	_____	_____
_____	_____	_____
_____	_____	_____
_____	_____	_____
_____	_____	_____

Questions (dans le texte) (dans ma tête)

1. _____

2. _____

Résumé (jusqu'à présent)

_____
_____
_____
_____
_____
_____
_____

Évaluation des prédictions

Survoler un texte

Nom : _____ Date : _____

Titre : _____

Ce que je vois	Ce que cela me dit

Guide de prédiction

Nom : _____   Date : _____

Titre : _____

Genre : _____

Ma prédiction : _____

_____

_____

_____

_____

Avant la lecture de ce texte, j'aimerais savoir : _____

Après la lecture de ce texte, j'aimerais savoir : _____

QU'EN PENSEZ-VOUS ?

Ce texte est-il difficile à comprendre ?_____

Ce texte est-il intéressant ?

Un parcours de lecture en équipe

Noms : _____ Date : _____

Titre : _____ Auteur(e) : _____

1. Nous observons la page couverture du texte et nous prédisons que :

_____

_____

_____

2. Nous survolons les illustrations.

3. Voici un dessin pour représenter une de nos prédictions.

Notre prédiction

4. Nous lisons le livre en entier.

5. Notre prédiction s'est confirmée :

                          ☹

La fiche d'identification d'un personnage

Nom : _____ Classe : _____ Date : _____

Titre : _____ Auteur(e) : _____

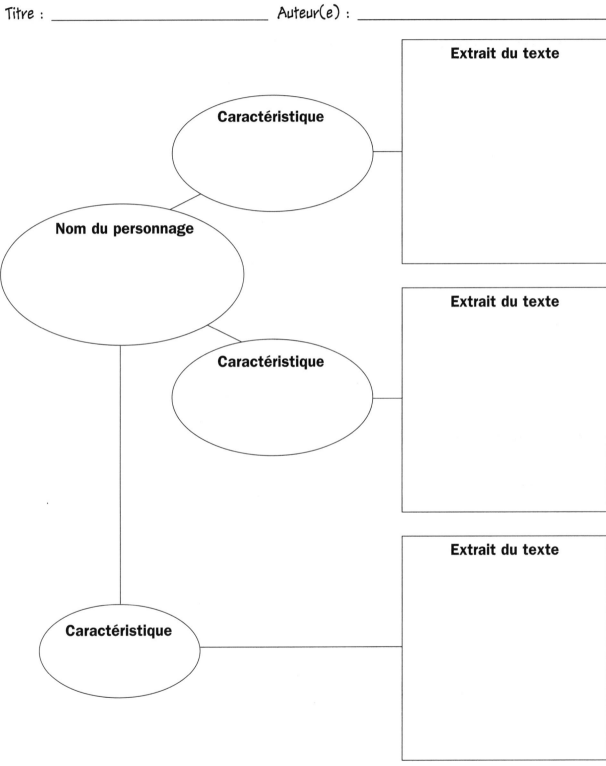

Qui est ce personnage ?

Nom : _____ Date : _____

Titre : _____ Auteur(e) : _____

Voici un dessin de mon personnage en pleine action :

Il ou elle pense :

Le nom de mon personnage est : _____

Il ou elle ressent :

_____

_____

Je le sais parce que :

_____

_____

Un personnage qui me ressemble

Noms : _____ Date : _____

Titre : _____ Auteur(e) : _____

Pouvez-vous nommer ce personnage?_____

Ce personnage ressemble à un autre personnage _____

tiré du livre _____.

Le compte-rendu

Nom : _____ Date : _____

Questions	Mes mots clés	Mes images clés
Qui ?		
Quoi ?		
Quand ?		
Où ?		
Pourquoi ?		
Comment ?		

La pyramide d'un personnage

Nom : _____ Classe : _____ Date : _____

Titre : _____ Auteur(e) : _____

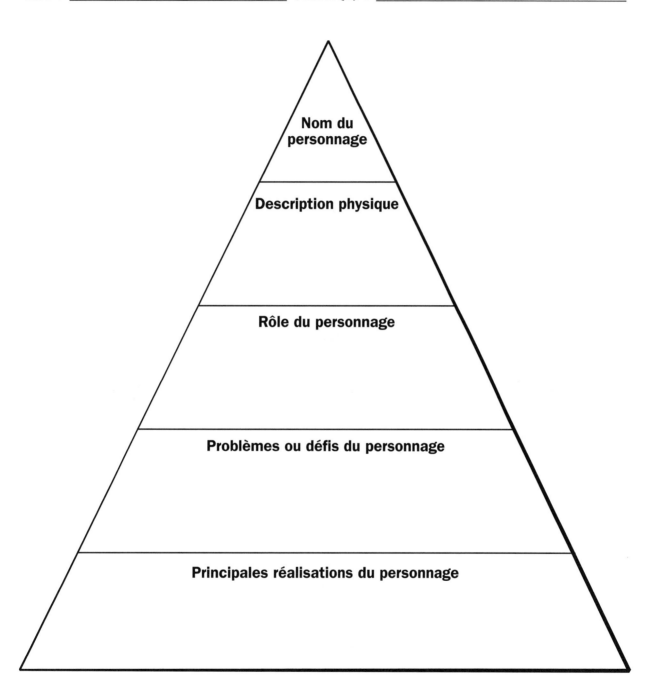

Nom du personnage

Description physique

Rôle du personnage

Problèmes ou défis du personnage

Principales réalisations du personnage

Trouver l'idée principale

Nom : _____ Date : _____

Titre : _____ Auteur(e) : _____

```
┌──────────────────────────────────────────────┐
│                                                │
│                                                │
│                                                │
│                                                │
│                                                │
│                                                │
│                                                │
│                                                │
│                                                │
└──────────────────────────────────────────────┘
```

Idée principale

Détail 1   **Détail 2**   **Détail 3**

Des pistes pour discuter à propos de nos lectures

Nom : _____ Date : _____

Titre : _____ Auteur(e) : _____

Sélectionne un commentaire parmi les suivants :

- Quelle est la partie du récit la plus excitante ?

- Quelle partie porte le plus à confusion ?

- J'ai aimé quand _____ parce que _____ .

- Je n'ai pas aimé quand _____ parce que _____ .

- C'était intéressant lorsque _____ parce que _____ .

- J'ai découvert que _____ .

- Cela me rappelle quand _____

_____

_____

_____

_____

_____

Une question que je souhaite poser au groupe :

_____

_____

_____

_____

_____

_____

_____

Le scénarimage

Nom : _____ Date : _____

Titre : _____

Début :

Milieu :

Fin :

Fiche de lecture

Nom : _____ Date : _____

Titre : _____ Auteur(e) : _____

Où et quand est-ce que le texte se passe?

_____

_____

Qui sont les principaux personnages?

_____

_____

Quel est le problème?

_____

Événement 1 : _____

_____

Événement 2 : _____

_____

Événement 3 : _____

_____

Le dénouement ou la solution du problème / la fin du récit _____

Le rappel d'un texte narratif

Nom : _____ Classe : _____ Date : _____

Éléments importants

_____

_____

Titre et auteur(e)

_____

_____

Où et quand est-ce que le texte décrit?

_____

_____

La situation au début de l'histoire

_____

_____

Personnages principaux

_____

_____

Le problème / le but poursuivi

_____

_____

Les principaux événements — dans le bon ordre

_____

_____

Le dénouement ou la solution du problème / la façon d'atteindre le but / la fin du récit

_____

_____

_____

Les impressions sur le récit

_____

_____

Mon compte-rendu de lecture

Nom : _____ Classe : _____ Date : _____

Le livre que j'ai lu s'intitule : _____ .

Ce livre est écrit par _____

et illustré par _____ .

Il s'agit d'un texte (coche une réponse)

❑ qui raconte une histoire

❑ qui donne de l'information

Le livre parle de _____

_____

_____

À mon avis, ce livre mérite un (choisis une réponse) :

☹ Ne lis pas ce livre.

😐 Tu peux peut-être aimer ce livre.

☺ Lis ce livre absolument !

Voici pourquoi : _____

_____

_____

Voici un dessin de mon passage préféré :

Un texte en diagramme

Nom : _____ Classee : _____ Date : _____

Un organigramme

Sujet : _____

Voici ce que je vois de la lecture de mon ou de ma camarade

Le ou la camarade : _____ Le ou la partenaire qui l'écoute : _____

Titre : _____ Date : _____

Après avoir écouté la lecture de mon ou de ma camarade, voici une image que j'ai faite :

Après l'avoir réécoutée lire de nouveau, j'ai choisi de modifier mon image comme ceci :

_____

_____

_____ . **Ça l'a rendue plus juste.**

J'évalue ma présentation au théâtre de lecteurs

Nom : _____ Classe : _____ Date : _____

Titre du scénario : _____

À l'aide des questions qui suivent, réfléchis sur ta présentation au théâtre de lecteurs. Ensuite, expliqui tes réflexions aux membres de ton groupe du théâtre de lecteurs.

Durant la représentation du théâtre de lecteurs...	Oui	Non
• est-ce que j'ai parlé assez fort et clairement ?		
• est-ce que ma voix était expressive ?		
• est-ce que j'ai lu couramment ?		
• est-ce que j'ai pris la parole au moment voulu ?		
• est-ce que mes gestes et mes actions étaient bien adaptés ?		
• est-ce que j'ai rendu mon rôle le mieux possible ?		

Le point fort de ma présentation a été _____

_____

_____

Je pourrais améliorer ma présentation en _____

_____

_____

Chapter 9

Writing Strategies

*"Writing is easy: All you do is sit staring at a blank sheet of paper
until drops of blood form on your forehead."*
—Gene Fowler

My Thoughts

- What was your initial reaction to this quotation? What does it suggest to you about Gene Fowler as a writer?

- Do you think this quotation carries a message about how students may view writing? Do you think they would appreciate the humour in the quotation?

In this chapter, we will discuss:

• Writing in the FSL Classroom

• From Speaking to Writing

• Scaffolding Writing

• Explicitly Teaching Writing Strategies

  ° Before-Writing Strategies and Activities
  ° During-Writing Strategies and Activities
  ° After-Writing Strategies and Activities

Writing in the FSL Classroom

Writing can be an important way of engaging the students' interest in the FSL classroom, especially when they are offered challenging activities of various types. (See BLM 9.1 for an attitudinal survey.) Writing both reinforces and extends students' oral knowledge of themes, topics, language structures, and vocabulary. Writing practice helps students understand the correlation between sounds and symbols as well.

Writing activities can provide many opportunities for students to use their imagination as they create their own stories, poems, skits,

Knowing that the four strands of language—listening, speaking, reading, and writing—are inter-related and inter-dependent ensures that you apply a communicative-experiential approach to instruction.

6+1 Writing Traits:

1. Ideas
2. Organization
3. Voice
4. Word Choice
5. Sentence Fluency
6. Conventions
+1 Presentation

—as identified by Ruth Culham

articles on topics of personal interest, poster and flyer text, advertisements, etc. Preparing for a writing task gives students time to process, reflect, write drafts, confer with peers, and self-assess. These steps break down the task into manageable chunks.

Ideally, writing should always be connected to listening and speaking opportunities. Students should be listening to you, one another, and to other recorded materials, and then talking about what they are learning as well as writing. Independent and group writing tasks should involve discussion and oral planning before students begin writing.

Few students will have occasion to write in French after elementary and high school, unless they continue French at the post-secondary level. Encourage students to develop their writing skills to practise and reinforce oral language, as extension activities for reading texts, and as preparation for oral presentations.

A comprehensive literacy focus encourages the gradual transfer of responsibility to students. Teacher support is essential during all stages of writing: shared, guided, and independent.

Writing traits are an effective way to teach students that writing is natural and comprised of many elements, some of which are basic to communication.

From the Research

A systematic search to identify the core elements defining exceptional writing was embarked on by a large number of teachers in the early 1980s. Over the course of many years, the core team examined a multitude of student writing samples with the purpose of finding common threads in the writers' success. Out of the quest came the concept of the six traits of writing that were soon expanded to the 6+1 Writing Traits by Ruth Culham. These traits are:

- Ideas: The meaning and development of the message
- Organization: The internal structure of the piece
- Voice: The way the writer brings the topic to life
- Word Choice: The specific vocabulary the writer uses to convey meaning
- Sentence Fluency: The way the words and phrases flow throughout the text
- Conventions: The mechanical correctness of the piece
- +1 Presentation: The overall appearance of the work

(Culham, 2003)

Teachers of L1 instruction use the writing traits to guide learning and assessment opportunities focused on writing. The traits assist in clarifying how to improve pieces of writing. As FSL teachers, it is important to be aware of the traits and student knowledge of the traits in order to transfer aspects of student learning from L1 to L2 writing situations.

You might wish to design a unit specifically around writing traits. Be sure to include modelled, shared, and guided writing with a specific theme before students write independently. Beginning second-language learners require both support and time in order to succeed as independent writers.

There are a number of differences between writing in a first language and in a second language. Students will have greater expressive capabilities in their first language. Their understanding of issues and ideas will exceed their ability to write about them in the second language. In choosing reading selections that lead to writing tasks, make sure to provide linguistically accessible, but not simplistic, texts.

Many of the strategies students are learning to use in L1 writing can be transferred to L2 writing. Students' content knowledge from other subject areas can also be transferred, although again their knowledge will exceed their ability to communicate it.

Students in L1 literacy experience focused instruction and are able to analyze writing traits such as tone, voice, word choice, etc. and reproduce these traits in their writing. In the second language, however, students will find this task much more challenging, thus requiring significantly more teacher support than in L1.

Most L2 writers will only consistently be able to demonstrate the traits of conveying ideas, organizing them logically, and using conventions accurately. However, depending on the task and on the model provided, they might be able to reproduce some of the other traits in their writing as well.

Issues of proficiency in the target language complicate the process of independent writing in a second language. In the second-language classroom, writing is often used as a way of practising language structures taught in class. In *Writing in a Second Language*, Alasdair Archibald explains:

"It is central to writing instruction that writers make progress as a direct result of the instruction they receive. In a general second language learning context, a student's progress in writing is often assumed to be simply a part of the overall increase in their language proficiency."

Instruction in writing and the integration and practice of its skills can effectively improve student proficiency in a number of key areas. Therefore, it is important to consider both strategy and language-skill

Refer back to Chapter 2: Effective Instructional Planning for tips on how to plan a unit of study.

development when working with students. Ongoing and effective feedback with regard to the development of writing skills is essential.

Successful writing programs are those where there is a school-wide approach and this includes L2 writing instruction. Talking with L1 and L2 teachers about the kinds of writing activities going on in their classrooms will help L2 teachers facilitate knowledge transfer for students.

Teacher Tip

It is challenging to teach voice, word choice, and varied sentence structure in the L2 classroom. However, there are some simple ways of helping students to develop an appreciation for voice and verbal expressiveness in French. If your class is reading a story with a strong narrative voice or character dialogue, you can demonstrate and model how simple language can convey voice.

- Read aloud the text expressively and dramatically, with gestures, to develop students' awareness of how voice is conveyed in French. Take them beyond understanding the literal meaning of the words.

- Invite the class to read aloud chorally and encourage them to imitate your intonation and expression.

- Adapt the text to dialogue form and invite students to perform a Readers' Theatre.

- Create a bank of short, expressive idioms and emphasize these whenever they appear in texts. Encourage students to use idioms from the idiom bank in their writing, especially in their creative story or dialogue writing. If their writing is based on a story, suggest that they include an expression or saying that aptly describes that character's personality in their stories.

- Encourage younger students to emphasize important words and expressions in their writing by colouring them, drawing them in shadow letters, underlining them, etc. When they are reading a text, ask partners to choose important words and expressions that they would emphasize graphically (but not in the textbooks!). Apart from photocopying selected texts, you might consider having students make lists on separate sheets of paper, or provide pairs of students with blank overhead transparency sheets and a marker to circle and underline overtop of a book.

- Encourage students to use exclamation marks, question marks, and ellipses to create tension, surprise, humour, etc., in their writing.

To give students options for developing word choice:

- Challenge them to find synonyms or antonyms for key vocabulary words to add to the Word Wall and then use in their writing.
- Suggest a contest in which students who use these synonyms win points.
- Ask peer editors to identify best examples of rich word choice from their sentences in graphically interesting ways. Post the sentences.

What I Am Thinking Now

- To what extent is writing an integral part of instruction in all subject areas in your school? What assumptions do you think other teachers have about teaching writing: Is writing the sole responsibility of the English Language Arts teacher? Is writing too time consuming for inclusion in other subject areas? What are the common concerns that teachers share about students' writing performance?

From Speaking to Writing

Students must be able to speak about a topic before they can write about it. Oral practice is essential to motivating students and then scaffolding writing. With your support, they can construct meaning and suggest appropriate ways of describing the topic. Once this step has happened orally, then students are better equipped to start a writing task on the same topic, either in pairs or small groups, and then independently.

The steps to move from speaking to writing are as follows:

1. Model the writing activity first and discuss strategies and organization as you write. (Modelled Writing)

2. Model writing, but this time invite students to comment on your model and make suggestions about the writing plan and content. Encourage students to think about strategies as you write. (Shared Writing)

3. Have students work together on a small task in pairs or small groups. Encourage them to discuss strategies they should use. (Guided Writing)

4. Have students work independently. After they have completed their work, encourage them to reflect on the strategies they used. (Independent Writing)

Scaffolding Writing

Students will require scaffolding at all stages of the writing process. In addition to the Gradual Release of Responsibility approach (using Modelled, Shared, and Guided Writing), there are other tools and techniques for scaffolding student learning, such as

- different types of graphic organizers designed for brainstorming ideas, discussion, organizing, and planning (See BLMs 9.2 and 9.3.)

- note-taking based on oral discussions and reading texts

- templates for text types such as cards, invitations, post cards, and recipes

- cloze passages from informational texts, letters, e-mails, book and movie reviews, with blanks for filling in key words and expressions

In a cloze passage designed to stimulate writing, students do not necessarily have to fill in given information, but can fill in their own ideas.

An anchor paper is a sample of student work that has been correlated to a specific level of performance. An exemplar is a sample of student work that shows the best or the expected level of performance for that task.

(Cooper, 2007)

Visual dictionaries, French-English dictionaries, and rubrics are also helpful support materials. Anchor papers, exemplars, and writing models are critical to successful writing at this stage. You can keep copies of student work to display as anchor papers or exemplars.

Graphic organizers are useful tools for supporting all aspects of literacy in L1 and L2. Use organizers with the whole class, groups, or individuals. Students might still need vocabulary brainstorming and support in order to use organizers effectively.

Before students begin writing, use graphic organizers, such as lexical webs and concept maps, as springboards for discussion and for brainstorming ideas and associations.

If the writing activity is based on a reading text, use graphic organizers to help students recount the narrative in writing. Include questions and spaces for students to summarize the beginning, middle, and end and describe characters. (See BLMs 8.9 and 8.16.)

To support visual learners, provide visuals from the text with sentences (cut out as strips or listed on the organizer) so that students can match images to text. Provide spaces for students to paraphrase the text and write beside the image.

Use Venn diagrams to generate and organize ideas through comparisons. Add a circle called *Moi* so that students can personalize their responses. After students have compared two different subjects or things, e.g., foods, fictional characters, family members, in a Venn diagram, they will have notes for writing a simple paragraph.

Have students create their work on computer, in PowerPoint, Word, or other computer programs. Such programs offer the opportunity for them to familiarize themselves with the French-language keyboard. Spell check and grammar check are also activated in adjusting the language setting. Students then need to be critical of the choices the programs provide them for corrections to their writing. The interactive support often is highly motivating to students. They can also add images to support their texts.

> Computer settings can be adjusted to allow toggling (using short-cut keys such as <alt> then <shift>) between English and French keyboard arrangements. Students quickly become familiar with both keyboard set-ups. Adjusting the language setting also allows spell check and grammar check to be used within computer programs.

Time spent conferencing with students also provides useful scaffolding. Conferences need only be brief. Focus on only one element or aspect of the writing. The goal of a conference is to encourage the student to discuss the task and reflect on the process. Encourage the student to talk by asking questions, such as

- Can you explain the purpose of the writing? What do you want to accomplish? *Quel est le but de l'activité d'écriture? Quel message est-ce que tu veux transmettre?*

- Is there a writing trait that you are focusing on? Show me examples in your draft or in your notes. *Tu te concentres sur quelle technique d'écriture? Montre-moi des exemples dans tes notes.*

- Try reading aloud that part of the piece. Do you think it flows well? Have you described a certain character in your writing? *Lis à haute voix cette section de ton travail. Est-ce que les idées sont dans un ordre logique? Est-ce que tu as décrit ce personnage dans ton travail?*

Give specific feedback when you praise. Identify strong points and explain why. If there are weak points, ask questions to prompt students to see how they could improve. (Trehearne, 2006)

- Graphic organizers are tools that many teachers use to scaffold student learning. To what extent are your students familiar with different types of graphic organizers and how to use them effectively?

- What other kinds of scaffolding activities have you found to be most effective with your students?

- How frequently are you able to schedule individual conferences with your students? How informative are these meetings for you? for the students? What changes, if any, would you like to make in the conferences?

Explicitly Teaching Writing Strategies

In order to develop as writers regardless of the language of instruction, students need to know the parameters of quality writing. They also need to be explicitly taught strategies they can employ to apply the writing traits.

One important aspect to teaching writing is to expose students to a large variety of text types. The text types read by students later become models for student writing. There are many text types that L2 students can produce effectively. These include short poems, invitations, voicemail messages, e-mail messages, cartoons, letters, post cards, birthday greetings, thank-you cards, Valentine's Day messages, posters, school event notices, labelled community maps, advertisements, and flyers.

Point out the features of each text type and make sure to provide models that show all of those features when you model the writing task. For younger students, choose text types that use sentence fragments (e.g., invitations, posters, school event notices).

For older students, using a graphic organizer with a visualization strategy can help them approach writing in a non-threatening way. Consider using an interactive white board or a computer and projector for shared writing. Compile a bank of images as visual supports for written activities.

Before-Writing Strategies and Activities

Before they begin writing, encourage students to start thinking about what strategies they might use during the task. You should discuss how to use the strategies as you model the writing task.

Introduce writing strategies to students and prompt them to look for how you use the strategies as you model the task. For example:

- Gather together your ideas on the subject, theme, or reading text. *J'identifie mes idées sur le sujet, le thème, ou le passage de lecture.*

- Examine a model (from a reading text; from the teacher). *J'examine un exemple (un passage de lecture, un exemple de l'enseignant(e)).*

- Plan your writing. Organize ideas. Create a timeline (of events in a story or events in an informational text). *Je planifie les étapes de mon écriture. J'organise les idées. Je crée un schéma du temps (une liste des événements qui se passent dans une histoire ou dans un texte informatif).*

Demonstrate the writing task first for the class. As in a think-aloud for a reading text, discuss the purpose of your writing, how you intend to start, and your plan for the writing.

Model all the steps in the writing process, breaking up the process by stages and inviting students to continue with guided practice before you model the next stage. Show or model for students your preparations before you begin the writing, e.g., your notes and writing plan or organizer.

Using think-alouds, you show students how to

- Choose an idea. *Je choisis une idée.*

- Make notes and plan their writing. *Je crée des notes et je planifie les étapes de mon écriture.*

- Find a word or expression on the Word Wall (or from a dictionary or other classroom resource). *Je trouve des mots et des expressions sur le mur des mots (ou dans un dictionnaire ou dans d'autres ressources).*

- Use conventions (commas, capitals, periods, paragraph breaks). *J'utilise les virgules, les lettres majuscules, les points. Je crée des paragraphes où il faut.*

- Come up with a title and subtitles. *Je crée un titre et des sous-titres.*

- Add expressive details through word choice, dialogue, punctuation, whenever possible. *Je choisis bien les mots, la ponctuation, et les passages de dialogue pour ajouter des détails.*

- Re-read to see if the writing makes sense. *Je relis pour m'assurer que mon travail est bien fait.*

- Revise. *Je fais des révisions.*

Modelled writing is an essential and effective strategy to use with beginning second-language learners. As you are writing and vocalizing your thought processes, students develop an awareness of the details of letters, sounds, and words while constructing meaningful text. This will include everything, from which word to select, to which genre to use. You can model the use of the support materials, such as the Word Wall or vocabulary lists, as well as the structures and vocabulary in use with the theme. During this time, some first-language literacy skills such as the use of conventions can be demonstrated to allow students to make connections and transfer from their first-language knowledge.

What I Am Thinking Now

- What is your "comfort level" with writing? How frequently do you write, for what purposes, and with what degree of satisfaction or confidence?

- How can you help your students to appreciate the value of writing activities in French class?

Teacher Tip

Visual aids are essential in the L2 classroom for suggesting vocabulary and ideas. Consider bringing in or asking students to bring in small props (food, clothing, toys or regular sports equipment, stuffed animals, etc.) that relate to the writing themes. Use these as springboards for before-writing discussions.

For example, if your class is discussing foods, suggest that students write about their favourite foods. Find relevant vocabulary from the Word Walls or other classroom resources. Bring props if appropriate. Model note-taking in preparation for writing. Model some sentence starters and expressions that they will find useful.

As well as props, use visualizing to help students get started. If students are describing something or someone, ask questions to help them visualize. For example:

Imagine ton animal ou l'animal de ton ami(e). Est-ce qu'il est grand ou petit?

Quelle est sa couleur? Est-ce qu'il est brun, noir, blanc, ou d'une autre couleur? Imagine que tu touches ton animal. Est-il doux ou rugueux? Est-ce qu'il a de la fourrure? Pense encore à ton animal. Est-ce qu'il a une queue? Est-ce qu'elle est longue ou courte? Qu'est-ce que ton animal mange? etc.

Follow the visualization exercise with a modelled writing piece incorporating the same descriptors.

For example, a teacher working on descriptive language in writing could discuss the topic with students while pointing to props or visuals in the classroom while saying:

On discute de la nourriture dans la classe de français. Je pense que j'aimerais écrire une description de ma nourriture préférée. J'aime manger! J'ai toujours faim. Moi, j'aime les sandwichs. Je vais décrire mes sandwichs préférés.

Quels mots est-ce que je vais utiliser dans ma description? Est-ce qu'il y a des mots sur notre mur de mots qui peuvent m'aider? Est-ce qu'il y a des mots dans ce dictionnaire visuel?

D'abord, quels sont les ingrédients de base? Je vais dresser une liste de ces ingrédients. [Make notes on the board]

Pour faire un sandwich, j'ai besoin :
· *de pain*
· *de beurre*
· *de la mayonnaise*
· *de la moutarde*

Dans mon sandwich, je vais mettre :
· *du poulet*
· *du jambon*

Et j'aime ajouter :
· *des tomates*
· *de la laitue*
· *des cornichons…*

Quoi d'autre? Je déteste le concombre. Je ne mets pas de concombre dans mon sandwich.

Quelles sont les expressions qui vont être utiles? Je vais dresser une liste :

· *J'aime*
· *Je n'aime pas*
· *Je déteste*
· *Dans mon sandwich préféré, il y a…*
· *Je mets…*
· *Je ne mets pas…*

Maintenant, je suis prête à faire une description de mon sandwich préféré.

Before-writing activities should enable students to make connections to their personal experience about the topic and their prior knowledge about the topic as well as the writing skills that they will require.

As with all other activities, students will be more motivated if they have a purpose for writing. Are they learning to write a particular genre (a personal e-mail or letter, an invitation, a flyer or poster, a story) or are they writing in response to another text (reading or listening)? Establishing an intention for writing is also part of the oral before-writing discussion as you model the writing task. During your modelling, you will be showing how to write certain features of the genre, for example, or pointing out how the writing should be structured.

First, if the topic is open, brainstorm ideas orally. If the writing task is based on a story students have read, brainstorm ideas about or variations on the plot events, or on the motivations or actions of characters.

If the topic is based on a non-fiction text or topic, brainstorm ideas, themes, and categories for describing the topic. Ask questions of students to remind them of what they already know from L1 literacy classes about the features of certain texts. For example, discuss and list the features of

- a personal written communication (a letter, an e-mail, a post card)

- a book or movie review

- a menu

- a poster advertising an event

- an article for the school newspaper

Some oral brainstorming questions will call forth key words and expressions relating to the topic that you might wish to include in a Word Wall.

During-Writing Strategies and Activities

When students are ready to begin writing, whether in shared, guided, or independent contexts, remind them of strategies that they should be using and discuss how to implement the strategies.

Remind students to

- Make a draft from their notes or graphic organizer. *Je crée un brouillon. J'utilise mes notes ou un schéma graphique.*

- Have a partner read the draft. *Je demande à un(e) camarade de classe de lire le brouillon.*

- Discuss the draft with the teacher. *Je discute du brouillon avec l'enseignant(e).*

- Make changes to their plan and draft based on feedback from classmates and the teacher. *Je fais des révisions à partir des commentaires de mes camarades et de l'enseignant(e).*

- Add new ideas. *J'ajoute de nouvelles idées.*

- Prepare the final draft. Check spelling, punctuation, and other language conventions. Use a dictionary or other resources. *Je prépare la copie finale. Je vérifie l'orthographe, la ponctuation, et d'autres techniques d'écriture. J'utilise un dictionnaire et d'autres ressources.*

Revising is a challenging skill to learn. The best way to show students how to revise is to model the process with your own writing. Consider keeping student before- and after-writing pieces from previous years as well.

Explain that revision is not simply re-writing a text to correct spelling and punctuation errors. Revision involves analyzing and asking questions about the text:

- Are the ideas clear? Does my partner understand my message? If the message is not clear, should I... *Est-ce que les idées sont claires? Est-ce que mon/ma camarade comprend mon message? Si le message n'est pas clair, est-ce que je dois...*
  - ...add more details or information? *...ajouter des détails ou des informations supplémentaires?*
  - ...re-order some paragraphs? *...changer l'ordre des paragraphes?*
  - ...change the title and subtitles? *...changer le titre et les sous-titres?*
  - ...make the beginning and closing sentences more effective? *...réviser la première et la dernière phrase?*
- Have I checked all the steps in the task instructions? Do I need to add anything? *Est-ce que j'ai vérifié toutes les étapes dans les instructions? Est-ce qu'il y a quelque chose que je dois ajouter?*

Once students are finished the revision process, you could check that they have revised their work during a brief conference. Ask the following:

- Do you think that the message is clear now? *Est-ce que tu penses que ton message est clair maintenant?*

- Is your opening sentence effective? *Est-ce que ta première phrase est réussie?*

- Do you have a favourite part in your work? Which one? Why? *Est-ce que tu as une partie préférée dans ton travail? Laquelle? Pourquoi?*

- Do you have a least favourite part? Why? *Est-ce que tu as une partie que tu aimes moins dans ton travail? Laquelle? Pourquoi?*

(Adapted from Trehearne, 2006)

After you have modelled the writing process, the next step is to invite students to participate in shared writing. Students will be familiar with shared writing from their experiences in the L1 classroom, but will require more scaffolding in the L2 classroom.

Shared writing gets students excited about writing without making them anxious about having to create a text on their own. The production acts of speaking and writing are the most anxiety producing in L2 communication, and your students will benefit from support to avoid developing writer's block.

In shared writing, you are still providing a model and guiding the process, but now you ask students questions to involve them in the task. Students should help you take notes, plan the task, find useful vocabulary and expressions, and transform starter sentences and key expressions into personalized written text.

For example, if your class is discussing or reading about sports, a possible subject for a writing task is to describe a favourite sport. After the class has discussed the topic, purpose, and suggested some sports (perhaps based on a reading text), you can begin the model.

Consult the CD-ROM for a short video segment on How to Use Shared Writing Experiences in FSL.

> *On va discuter un peu au sujet du sport. Moi, je vais parler du cricket. J'ai choisi le cricket parce que c'est le sport national du pays de mes parents. J'ai joué au cricket lorsque j'étais jeune. J'aime regarder les matchs de cricket à la télé.*
>
> *Et vous, mes amis? Quels sont vos sports d'équipe préférés? Jouez-vous à ces sports? Regardez-vous des matchs de ce sport à la télé? De quels sports d'équipe aimeriez-vous écrire? On va dresser une liste de sports. Cameron? Quel est ton sport préféré? [pause while student answers] Le soccer? Très bien.*
>
> *Et vous autres?*
>
> *De quoi est-ce qu'on a besoin pour jouer à un sport? Par exemple, pour jouer au cricket, on a besoin d'une balle et d'une batte.*
>
> *De quel équipement est-ce qu'on a besoin pour participer à un sport... etc.*

Ask questions to guide students as a group to think of categories for describing sports, e.g., equipment, game location (indoors or outdoors), playing field (rink, diamond, pitch, court). Their examples can refer to their own sports, or you can ask them to help you with one sport that you can be reasonably sure most of them will be familiar with, e.g., a school sport.

> *Quelles sont les catégories pour décrire un sport? Aidez-moi à écrire ces catégories sous forme de question.*
>
> *De quel équipement est-ce qu'on a besoin?*
>
> *Où est-ce qu'on joue à ce sport?*
>
> *Il y a combien de joueurs dans une équipe?*

In guided writing, students will practise the strategies they have seen modelled and have tried during shared writing. Guided writing allows more independence in that students will be writing their own text. Since this is still a step toward independent writing, consider having students work collaboratively in groups or with a partner on a writing task. They will still require teacher support in the form of

- guided questions and prompts from you

- graphic organizers developed specifically for the task

- sentence starters

- cloze passages

- teacher conferencing

When students are ready to undertake independent tasks, remember that some stages, such as brainstorming ideas, can still be helpful and motivating to do collaboratively. If students are having trouble getting started, they can be overwhelmed by the task or simply draw a blank when they have to generate ideas. To unblock them, start with tiny chunks of the task, or by asking them to free-associate ideas.

- Write a one-sentence thought about the topic.

- Answer one question about the topic.

- Think of one key word related to the topic. What other words does that word call to mind?

- Look at a visual.

- What resources are available for your students to use during writing? What have you noticed about their use of these resources?

- What have you observed about how your students cooperate during writing? Do these observations indicate that any changes are needed—in student groups? in your participation during writing?

After-Writing Strategies and Activities

After they have completed a writing task, students should reflect on the strategies they have used and assess whether they were useful and how they could improve for the next writing task. If possible, have them compare their writing texts with those of other students. What areas could they improve on? You can establish guidelines for the comparisons beforehand.

Compare your writing with a partner. Consider:

- Is the message clear? Did you understand it? *Est-ce que le message est clair? Est-ce que tu l'as compris?*

- Are the opening and closing sentences effective? *Est-ce que la première et la dernière phrases sont réussies?*

- Is it well organized? *Est-ce que le travail est bien organisé?*

- Are the words and voice well chosen? *Est-ce que les mots et la voix sont bien choisis?*

- What is your favourite part of your partner's work? Why? *Dans le travail de ton ou ta camarade, quelle est ta partie préférée? Pourquoi?*

- Would you recommend that a friend read this work? Why? *Est-ce que tu recommenderais à un(e) ami(e) de lire ce travail? Pourquoi?*

Post student work and discuss with the class. Sharing texts aloud connects writing and reading. Then send their work home to their parents, if possible, with a note explaining the task. It is important to show parents and family that students are successfully communicating in French.

If students enjoyed the writing task, extend their learning with related activities. Some extension activities based on fiction include

- Write another episode, e.g., alternate ending, back story, prequel.

- Create a Readers' Theatre version.

- Create an illustrated version, e.g., Big Book, *bande dessinée*, storyboard.

Some extension activities based on non-fiction include

- Research and write about another aspect in an informational text that interests students.

- Create a version of the text in another genre, e.g., if the text was about a period in history, invite students to translate their research into a newspaper article or a journal account of the day in a life of a *voyageur*. (See BLM 9.4.)

- Create a poster or ad in another medium about the subject of the non-fiction text, e.g., if the text is about the environment, invite students to create an Earth Day poster.

- Create a crossword puzzle with clues based on the text information.

Make sure that the extension ideas involve text types and activities that students have already had experience doing in class or have seen modelled.

Teacher Tip

Brain research on how we learn has underlined the importance of frequent, focused practice. All skills must be practised many times before we can become adept at them. In the L2 classroom with its focus on oral communication, it can be challenging to make time for frequent writing practice.

Consider ways of incorporating regular, brief writing activities in your classroom. For example:

- Invite students to keep a French journal. At a specified time during each class, give them a question to answer briefly. As a warm-up activity for the next class, ask them to compare their answers.

- Ask students to write entrance and/or exit passes.

- Invite students to play a collaborative story-writing game. Start a story by writing a sentence on a piece of paper. Pass the paper around the class over the course of several days and ask students, either individually or in groups, to add a sentence to the story. Writers are allowed to read only the last sentence, not the work in progress. When everyone has contributed a sentence, ask a volunteer to read aloud. Invite groups to act out the story.

What I Am Thinking Now

- What do you consistently look for in your students' writing samples? How do you use this information to help students make decisions about their progress as writers in French?

- How do you ensure that "after-writing" activities do not overwhelm the students? How do you use such activities to build students' interest and confidence in writing?

Summary

Although writing is often listed last within the strands of language learning, this placement should not imply that writing is an afterthought—something to be done when listening, speaking, and reading activities have been completed. On the contrary, writing is an integral part of activities in the other three skill areas; it extends students' knowledge of oral vocabulary and helps them understand the sound-symbol relationships. In addition, writing activities are outlets for imagination, reflection, and exploration of new topics and ideas. Although students have greater expressive capacity in their first language, they do possess an understanding about the writing process that will support their development as writers in another language.

Writing instruction practices in FSL classes parallel those used in English Language Arts classes. Teacher support is provided in shared, guided, and independent writing activities where students can learn about writing traits—ideas, organization, voice, word choice, sentence fluency, conventions, and presentation. Generally, the focus for L2 writers will be on the traits of conveying ideas, organizing them logically, and using conventions accurately.

Modelling is an essential feature of L2 writing instruction—a feature that encompasses listening, speaking, and reading as parts of the process of learning to write. Listening and reading activities present students with examples of different types of writing (e.g., story, report, dialogue, poetry, recount). Speaking provides the oral rehearsal of ideas and vocabulary necessary to construct passages in writing. The structure of writing lessons can parallel that of reading lessons—before, during, and after writing activities that allow the teacher to provide explicit instruction in writing strategies. Within each segment of the lessons, opportunities exist for students to talk, listen, and read in response to their own writing or that of their peers. Writing is another way to foster students' engagement with the new language they are learning.

My Choices

- Reflect once again on the quotation at the beginning of this chapter. What new insights about writing have you gained from this chapter that make you more confident in your instruction?

- What do you think are the key messages you should share with your students' parents/caregivers about their writing in French? What could you do to help these adults understand how the students' writing helps them use French more effectively?

- What does it take for you to become inspired about writing? Does this personal understanding help you in working with your students?

Fiche d'auto-évaluation : Mon opinion sur l'écriture

Nom : _____ Date : _____

	Oui ☺	Un peu 😐	Non ☹
1. Est-ce que tu aimes écrire? Explique pourquoi. _____	❏	❏	❏
2. Est-ce qu'écrire est difficile? Explique pourquoi. _____	❏	❏	❏
3. Je pense que j'écris bien. Voici pourquoi : _____	❏	❏	❏

4. J'aime écrire sur les sujets suivants : _____

_____

5. Quand je ne sais pas comment écrire un mot, je

_____

_____

6. Je pense que cet(te) auteur(e) ou ce(tte) camarade de classe :

_____ écrit bien parce que _____

7. À la maison, j'écris sur les sujets suivants :

_____

_____

_____

Le schéma du récit

Nom : _____ Classe : _____ Date : _____

Titre : _____

Contexte (où et quand) :	Personnages (qui) :

Intrigue

Problème (quoi) :	Solution (comment) :

Un napperon

Noms des élèves : _____

Classe : _____ Date : _____

En groupes, écrivez le thème ou le sujet de votre discussion au centre du napperon. Faites un remue-méninges en utilisant les quatre quadrants pour vous aider à organiser vos idées.

Catégorie 1	**Catégorie 2**
Sujet	
Catégorie 3	**Catégorie 4**

Mon article de journal

Nom : _____ Date : _____

Je prépare mon article :

Qui : _____

Quoi : _____

Quand : _____

Où : _____

Pourquoi : _____

Comment : _____

Mon article :

Titre : _____

Par : _____

Phrase à mettre en évidence, le chapeau de l'article : _____

Les faits :

Fait	**Fait**	**Fait**

Conclusion : _____

_____

_____

_____

Conclusion

Keys to Success: My Thoughts and Choices

Drawing upon their knowledge of second-language instruction and classroom experience, the authors and contributors of *Strategies for Success* have assembled a resource filled with guidelines and suggestions for best practice. The knowledge and skill that teachers bring to the instructional setting are vital factors affecting how and what students learn. Learning a second language can present challenges to both teachers and students. However, it is our belief that well-planned instruction that builds on the students' experiences and fosters communication will lead to visible accomplishments that minimize the challenges. Language learning can and should be a rewarding experience for both teachers and students.

At the beginning of each section, we have identified Keys to Success. In summary, these keys focus on the instructional leadership teachers provide because of the knowledge they possess about teaching and the learning needs of their students. Through their example, teachers instill confidence in their students—confidence that will enable their students to acquire sufficient proficiency in French to participate in social conversations and events. The primary keys to successful practice in the second-language classroom include

Keys to Success

- Creating a classroom climate that is conducive to communication and in which experimentation is expected and honoured.

- Planning instruction with both short-term and long-term goals in mind—today's lessons are the foundations for future success.

- Knowing that students' intellectual and emotional development influence the ways in which they participate in learning activities.

- Having confidence in your professional capacity to identify student learning needs enables you to make timely and appropriate instructional decisions.

- Knowing that the four strands of language—listening, speaking, reading, and writing—are inter-related and inter-dependent ensures that you apply a communicative-experiential approach to instruction.

As evidenced by the book's title, *Strategies for Success*, strategic teaching and learning are core principles in second-language instruction. Teachers and students both need strategies. Strategies focus attention on goals, purposes for learning, behaviours needed to achieve goals, expected learning outcomes, and the means to determine the extent of learning accomplishments. These factors apply to teachers as they plan and provide instruction; they apply to students who need to acquire strategies that will enable them to become independent learners.

As you read this book, you had occasion to reflect on the content and messages implicit in that content. At the beginning of each section and chapter, quotations and "My Thoughts" were presented to prompt exploration of positions related to teaching and learning. Throughout the chapters, you encountered "What I Am Thinking Now" segments that suggested that you pause and verbalize your agreement, disagreement, or perhaps confusion about the ideas the authors have presented. At the end of each chapter, "My Choices" placed you in the decision-making role. Now, at the conclusion of the book, you might want to return to the thoughts you had and the choices you made in the course of reading this resource and share its contents with friends and colleagues. What are your Keys to Success and how do you plan to use them?

My Choices

It is time to look back at the year that has gone by and to begin planning for the year ahead.

- Read the Case Study: End-of-Year Reflection. What would your plans for next year include?

- Use BLMs C1 and C3 to reflect on this year and plan for next year. You might want to share the forms with colleagues for school-wide planning purposes. Consider focusing on one or two keys to success in the Annual Action Plan.

CASE STUDY | End-of-Year Reflection

This year, one of the primary goals of Mme Hynes' Annual Learning Plan was to organize events that would enable her Core French students to learn and appreciate the French language, develop an understanding of French culture, and provide an opportunity to use their French-language skills both in and out of the classroom.

For years, she observed other teachers organizing field trips and events in the school that made their subjects come alive. In this manner, Mme Hynes felt that students were enriched, inspired, and motivated to learn more about the specific subject. She wanted to do more for her students and create a different perspective for them. Looking back on the year, Mme Hynes was glad she took the time to plan activities that promoted cultural awareness. Overall, the plan had been a success.

The weekly French club Mme Hynes started was a good example of the plan in action. Students were invited once a week during break time to participate in various French activities. In this club, students played vocabulary games, watched French movies, made seasonal crafts, and read newspaper articles and comic books in French. They also sang songs, listened to French music, and practised mini skits. Mme Hynes began to see more junior students each week as Grade 8 students became leaders of the activities. Although Intermediate student attendance was lower than expected, plans for next year would focus on incorporating more Intermediate level activities or even a separate French club day for this age group.

In the winter, Mme Hynes planned a Winter Carnival that engaged students in seven different activities throughout the school. The day commenced with a kickoff assembly. At the assembly, students sang traditional *Carnaval* songs and watched a movie on the history of *Carnaval* and how it is celebrated in Québec. The students in Grades 4–7 were divided into seven groups with Grade 8s leading carnival-type activities at each station. Mme Hynes planned a variety of activities that addressed various learning styles: a music station, a reading station, a traditional folk dance station, a cooperative games station, a craft station, and the most popular, a hot chocolate station!

The entire day was spent in a traditional French atmosphere with even a visit from *Bonhomme Carnaval* to share in the festivities. Many staff members assisted the students to make it truly a wonderful day. Teachers commented on how much fun the students had at each station and how the Grade 8 leaders took their roles seriously and spoke in French! The following day, Mme Hynes was approached by many students eagerly requesting to do it again for the following year. Although it required many hours to prepare for this event, Mme Hynes could see that her efforts paid off in the form of promotion of cultural awareness and student motivation that continued, to her great pleasure, well beyond the Carnival day.

At the end of a long year, Mme Hynes reflects positively on the great efforts that resulted in positive change. Next year, she plans to look for events to engage students in authentic cultural experiences. As she looks at her jot notes for next year's plan, she sees her idea to invite a chef to prepare a recipe in French. In conjunction with the music teacher, Mme Hynes is aspiring to host a French café involving parents and students speaking and singing in French. She will continue to strive to make French a living language that goes beyond the walls of her classroom.

My Year in Review

Grades: _____   Date: _____

1. This year was:

❏ Very successful   ❏ Successful   ❏ Somewhat successful   ❏ Not very successful

2. Three new things that I tried this year.

_____

_____

_____

3. This year, I did the following:

Activity		Yes	No	Sometimes
1.	I set up a profile chart for each of my students to determine how they learn best.			
2.	I differentiated my instruction on a regular basis to provide choices for my students.			
3.	I ensured that the work we did was age appropriate and related to topics that interested my students.			
4.	I provided my students with daily opportunities to interact with each other in French.			
5.	I broke up my teaching lessons and my activities into Before, During, and After.			
6.	I taught my students how to use strategies to enhance their learning.			
7.	I helped my students develop new skills in all four areas: listening, speaking, reading, and writing,			
8.	I adjusted my teaching to meet the needs of all my students.			
9.	I added a great deal of novelty and variety to my lessons.			
10.	I gave my students responsibilities to help me as an itinerant teacher.			
11.	By means of scaffolding lessons and explicitly teaching learning strategies, my students were gradually able to work more independently at the end of the year than at the beginning.			
12.	I added assessment tools to my toolkit to help my students learn better.			

Activity	Yes	No	Sometimes
13. I used technology to interest my students.			
14. I taught my students how to reflect on their learning and why they should do so.			
15. I provided a risk-free environment for my students.			
16. I provided appropriate feedback to my students so that they could improve their learning.			
17. I worked with my colleagues to help my students see the link between L1 and L2.			
18. I used French when talking to my students and gave them the tools to understand.			
19. I provided a warm and nurturing classroom where students were encouraged to respect each other.			
20. I used think-alouds and read-alouds to help my students develop their reading skills.			
21. I was able to report to parents about their child's progress in a way that helped them understand what was happening in our classroom.			
22. I made an effort to inform my colleagues about what the students were doing in French so that they would value our French work.			
23. I set up a French area in the school so that visitors to the school would see what was happening in French class.			

4. The following teaching activities worked really well this year, and will definitely be part of my teaching next year.

_____

_____

_____

5. Next year, I want to try these three new teaching, planning, or communication activities.

_____

_____

_____

J'évalue mon année

Nom : _____ Classe : _____ Date : _____

1. **J'ai terminé ma _____ année ! Cette année, j'ai appris à** _____

   _____

   _____

   _____

2. **Au début de l'année, je ne savais pas comment** _____

   _____

   _____

   mais maintenant, je sais _____

   _____

   _____

3. **J'ai revu tous les éléments de mon portfolio. Le document qui me donne le plus de fierté est** _____

   _____

   _____

   parce que _____

   _____

   _____

4. **L'an prochain, je veux apprendre à** _____

   _____

   _____

   _____

5. **Le conseil que je donne aux élèves qui vont être dans cette classe l'an prochain est de** _____

   _____

   _____

Annual Action Plan

Name _____ Year: _____

- This plan should be completed at the beginning of the year, altered in the middle of the year, as needed, and finalized at the end of the year.
- You may wish to keep copies of your plans from year to year to support your teaching.
- Complete one BLM for each grade that you teach.

Teaching Assignment (Grades taught): _____

Part A: To be completed at the beginning of the year.

- Identify objectives that you hope to meet this year.

Objectives	What is involved? List the steps.	Who else needs to be involved for you to meet this objective?	How will you know when you have met this objective?	What are the next steps?

Part B: To be completed part-way through the year.

- Which objective(s) that you identified at the beginning of the year need(s) to be adjusted?

_____

_____

_____

_____

_____

- Why is this adjustment needed? Circle any answers that are applicable.

  a) This objective will take more time than my students and I have this term.

  b) I need to break the objective down into more manageable chunks.

  c) Some of my students are not yet ready for us to meet this objective.

  d) I need to match my objectives with those of my students.

  e) We completed this objective so fast, that I need to add another one to my list.

  f) I want to add a sub-section to this objective.

  g) I do not have the budget to purchase the resources that I need to meet this objective.

  h) I need to add an objective that all teachers have been asked to meet in our school or Board.

  i) Other: _____

- Insert the new or changed objectives in this chart.

New or Changed Objectives	What change is needed from information included at the beginning of the year?	Who else needs to be involved for you to meet this objective?	How will you know when you have met this objective?	What are the next steps?

Part C: To be completed at the end of the year.

Professional Objectives

· What were your objectives for this year?

· How well did you meet each objective?

Objectives	Very well	Well	Somewhat well	Not very well

· For the objectives that you met well or very well, explain why this was so.

_____

_____

· Are the objectives that you did not meet still valid? Check off the appropriate one.

❑ All are valid   ❑ Some are valid   ❑ None are valid

· For those objectives that you did not meet and that are still valid, explain what needs to be done so that they can be met (e.g., by you, by others).

_____

_____

· What changes do you intend to make for next year?

_____

_____

Professional Learning

· What professional learning events did you participate in this year?

· How effective were they in helping you with your teaching?

Professional Learning Events/Activities	Very helpful	Helpful	Somewhat helpful	Not very helpful

· What professional learning would you like to experience/pursue/take advantage of? Can you "receive" professional learning? receive it next year? Provide specific examples, and explain why these are important to you.

_____

_____

Enjoy your summer!

Glossary

Assessment AS Learning (*n.f. Évaluation en tant qu'apprentissage*) Assessment that emphasizes self-reflection and metacognition. Students learn how to reflect on how they learn and how to use learning strategies effectively.

Assessment FOR Learning (*n.f. Évaluation au service de l'apprentissage*) Assessment designed primarily to promote learning and determine students' next steps. This form of assessment is designed to improve students' most recent work, through descriptive feedback, not marks.

Assessment OF Learning (*n.f. Évaluation de l'apprentissage*) Assessment to determine student achievement at any given point (e.g., grades, marks) intended for parents, students, and school and board administrators.

Assessment Strategy (*n.f. Méthode d'évaluation*)An assessment strategy is the activity that the teacher sets for the student. These can take many shapes, e.g., games and activities that are catalysts for role-play or dialogues, songs and rhymes, learning logs, journals, entrance and exit passes. Basically, an assessment strategy is the action that a teacher takes to learn more about a learner's behaviour.

Assessment Tool (*n.m. Outil d'évaluation*) An assessment tool provides feedback to the students, helps teachers make instructional decisions, and compiles data for reporting. Basically, an assessment tool is a resource that illustrates or records what the behaviours reveal.

Aural (*adj. Audio / sonore - selon le contexte*) This term refers to auditory, and is used to describe listening tasks.

Backward Design (*n.f. Planification à rebours*) The goal of a lesson or a unit of study, which starts by identifying what is expected of the students at the end. Once the student learning outcomes are defined, teachers can then plan their assessment, and what students should know, understand, and be able to do.

Basic French (*n.m. Français de base*) The name given to the French-as-a-second-language program in some parts of the country. For example, Manitoba uses this term to describe its FSL program.

Bloom's Taxonomy (*n.f. Taxonomie de Bloom*) A system developed by Benjamin Bloom that classifies cognitive skills and objectives. Bloom wanted to encourage students to develop higher-order thinking skills beyond recognition and comprehension, such as analyzing, evaluating, synthesizing, and creating new meanings. Bloom's Taxonomy defines three domains of learning: the cognitive domain skills (mental), the affective domain skills (emotional growth), and the psychomotor domain skills (physical).

Brain-Based Learning (*n.m. Apprentissage compatible avec le cerveau*) Understanding how the brain functions is critical to understanding how students learn. Brain research helps us understand why certain FSL instructional practices work, and how to make them even more effective. Brain-based learning in based on five principles: each brain is unique, emotions impact learning, time is needed for processing new learning, time is needed for reflection, and the need to develop higher-order thinking skills in order to process and think about new learning.

Cognate (*n.m. mot-ami*) A cognate is a word that shares the same derivation and has the same meaning between two or more languages. Cognates also have similar spelling between languages. For example, students immediately recognize the words *téléphone*, *télévision*, and *radio* because the words are the same in English as they are in French. Cognates that are similar, such as *maman*, *papa*, *papier*, etc. rarely cause a problem for students.

Common European Framework of Reference (CEFR) (*n.m. Cadre Européen Commun de Référence (CECR)*) The CEFR is a common scale developed in Europe for assessing proficiency in the target language. The CEFR allows for common assessment criteria to enable a better understanding of language proficiency regardless of the target language or the locale, or even the age of the learner.

Concept Maps (*n.m. Schéma conceptuel*) A concept map is an arrangement of key words and concepts on a specific subject or topic. Concept mapping is a process used by students to visually represent what they know about a topic. Students begin with a central idea or topic, and by means of a visual chart they insert words and ideas related to the central idea, linking them together by means of lines. Concept maps are used to organize information, find patterns and similarities, compare and contrast, sequence stories and timelines, and plan.

Core French (*n.m. Français de base*) This is the name given to the French-as-a-second-language program in some parts of the country. For example, Ontario uses this term to describe its FSL program.

Corrective Feedback (*n.f. Rétroaction corrective*) Corrective feedback is feedback provided to students that leads to student self-correction.

Descriptive Feedback (*n.f. Rétroaction descriptive*) Descriptive feedback is provided to students as they work on tasks to help them improve their learning. Through a variety of assessment tools, such as conferencing, checklists, etc., teachers provide feedback to students so that they can identify what they know, what they need to work on, and what comes next in their learning.

Differentiated Instruction (*n.m. Enseignement différencié*) Differentiated instruction (DI) is an approach to learning and teaching that acknowledges and honours students as individuals. Differentiated instruction is aligning instructional practice with students' needs to ensure that all students have equal access to the same learning. Teachers use differentiation in their classrooms to differentiate for content, process, product and learning environment, and use readiness, interests, and learning profiles to do so. The basic premise of DI states that no two students are alike, and no two students learn in the same way. A classroom where this premise is accepted respects these differences and allows students' choices to enhance their learning.

Entrance and Exit Passes (*n.m. Billets d'entrée et de sortie*) Entrance and exit passes include sample questions that students have to fill out before class in order to enter and, at the end, before they leave. The questions are usually, but not limited to, reflection questions, often inviting students to jot down what they have done, what they have tried to do, and how they feel about what they have done. These passes are valuable tools in an effective assessment toolkit.

European Language Portfolio (ELP) (*n.m. Portfolio Européen des Langues (PEL)*) The ELP is a strategy used by language learners to record their progress and reflect on their learning of language(s). The ELP combines three sections: the passport (an overview of the learner's proficiency in the target language at a particular point in time), the language biography (a personal record created by the learners whereby the learner reflects on his or her learning process and progress in the target language), and the dossier (personally created materials that demonstrate achievement and experiences outlined in the first two sections).

Evaluation (*n.f. Évaluation*) Typically, the stage of assessment that is graded and used for reporting purposes. More and more, this term has been replaced by "Assessment OF Learning."

Extended French (*n.m. Programme intensif de français*) This is a French program, offered primarily in Ontario where French is taught as a subject and also serves as the language of instruction for 25 per cent of the time—for at least one other subject.

French Immersion (*n.f. Immersion française*) This is a French program, offered across Canada, where French is taught as a subject and also serves as the language of instruction for at least for 50 per cent of the time. Typically, students are exposed to French for 100 per cent of the time in the early years; this gradually lessens as students progress through school. By the end of elementary school, most French Immersion students spend 50 per cent of their day in French.

French-as-a-Second-Language (*n.m. Français langue seconde*) Typically, this is a course of studies offered in schools across Canada where French is taught to non-Francophone students. These FSL programs generally include Core/Basic French, Intensive French, Extended French, and French Immersion.

Gradual Release of Responsibility (*n.m. Transfert graduel de responsabilité*) The process by which teachers and students collaborate to create autonomous student learners is called the Gradual Release of Responsibility. At the beginning, the teacher is the focus of the instruction, but over time, modelled, shared, and guided practice prepare the students to become independent learners and guide their own learning.

Guided Practice (*n.f. Pratique guidée ou dirigée*) Guided practice happens after shared practice and can be used for speaking, reading, or writing. In these instances, students work together on the task, generally, after it has been modelled by the teacher and shared with the rest of the class or group. Together, students discuss the strategies they should use. Frequently, teachers will pause in the middle of a shared activity to allow students to work together on a section of the task. This allows teachers to observe how well students have understood what they should be doing. Once students have spent time together, the teacher may wish to return to the shared activity. Guided practice is the final stage of the Gradual Release of Responsibility model before independent practice.

Independent Practice (*n.f. Pratique autonome ou indépendante*) Students work independently on tasks, mainly reading or writing, when the teacher feels that they can cope with working alone. However, working independently does not imply that the teacher and other students are not involved. Prior to working independently, students will have seen the task modelled, have participated in shared and guided activities, and following the Gradual Release of Responsibility model, will be ready to work independently.

Intensive French (*n.m. Français intensif*) This is a program for students used in some parts of the country, to increase students' exposure to French. Typically, in either Grade 5 or Grade 6—depending on the province—60–80 per cent of the student's day is spent on French from September to January. In this instance, the curriculum for the rest of the year is compacted. During this period, students study only French.

Itinerant Teacher (*n.m. Enseignant itinérant*) An itinerant teacher is one who does not have his or her own classroom and must travel from class to class to meet students. A high percentage of elementary French teachers across the country are itinerant, and travel with their carts within a school. In many instances as well, itinerant teachers might teach in more than one school during a given year.

K.U.D. (*vt. Connaître, comprendre, faire*) An acronym for Knowledge, Understanding, Doing. As teachers begin to plan a lesson or a unit of study, they should identify the K.U.D., that is, what students should know, what they should understand, and what they should be able to do.

L1 (*n.f. L1 (langue maternelle)*) L1 refers to the first language of instruction, generally English in Canada.

L2 (*n.f. L2 (langue seconde)*) L2 refers to the study of a second language, in this case, French. Links can be made between L1 and L2 to facilitate second-language learning.

Lexeme (*n.m. Lexème*) A lexeme is the root or the stem of a word. It carries the lexical meaning of the word. For example, in the word *aimer*, *aim*– is the lexeme, and *–er* is the morpheme (see definition below).

Modelled Practice (*n.m. Modélisation*) The stage of learning where the teacher models the tasks that are given to students. During this phase of learning, students observe and prepare for the next step, shared practice. Think-alouds and read-alouds are examples of modelled practice. The modelled stage of learning is the first step in the Gradual Release of Responsibility model.

Morpheme (*n.m. Morphème*) A morpheme is the smallest unit of a word that when broken down still holds meaning. For example, in the word bicycles, the morphemes are bi, cycle, and s.

Multiple Intelligences (*n.f. Intelligences multiples*) This theory was espoused by Howard Gardner. It states that the concept of multiple intelligences is a way of understanding how students can learn using a variety of abilities and skills. He identified the following learning profiles: verbal/linguistic; logical/mathematical; visual/spatial; bodily/kinesthetic; musical rhythmic; interpersonal; intrapersonal. Identifying a student's intelligence(s) helps the teacher to create a student's profile in order to meet the student's needs.

Oral (*adj. Oral*) This term refers to speaking and listening tasks, the two forms of oral communication.

Performance Tasks (*n.f. Tâches signifiantes*) Performance tasks are also known as culminating tasks. They provide opportunities for students to demonstrate their abilities to synthesize and apply their learning. They often complete the end of a unit.

Prior Knowledge (*n.f. Connaissances antérieures*) This term refers to the knowledge and experiences that students bring to a topic before it is studied. For example, students who know about hockey will feel comfortable beginning a unit of study on hockey.

Read-Alouds (*n.m. Lire à haute voix*) This activity happens in class as students prepare to read. The teacher reads the text aloud, either by using a big book, a copy of the text, or a copy of the text projected on a transparency or a SMART Board, as students listen. During a read-aloud, the teacher comments on the text and asks questions of the students to help them consider various strategies to use as they read.

Scaffolding (*n.m. Étayage*) Scaffolding activities are created as steps that allow the students to gradually work their way up a "ladder" toward independence. Along the way, teachers provide varying degrees of support until students are able to tackle a task independently. Scaffolded activities can be used following the Gradual Release of Responsibility model in that, at the beginning, students require a great deal of scaffolding and as they develop their skills, the scaffolding becomes suggestions, or one-word ideas. Graphic organizers are excellent tools that can be used for scaffolding.

Shared Practice (*n.f. Pratique partagée*) Shared practice happens in a classroom that is preparing for speaking, reading, or writing. In each case, the teacher models the task, and through questioning, involves the students in the task (sharing). Questions are usually aimed at strategy development, encouraging students to think about what they have to do in order to speak, read, or write. Shared activities are one of the first stages of the Gradual Release of Responsibility model.

Skill (*n.f. Compétence*) Students begin their learning by developing strategies to help them learn. Once students use these strategies frequently enough so that they become automatic, the strategy becomes a skill. Skills are developed in all four skill areas: listening, speaking, reading, and writing.

Strategy (*n.f. Stratégie*) A strategy is a deliberate action that enables students to control and modify their efforts at learning. Strategies can be taught and can be learned. Once they become automatic, they are no longer considered strategies, but skills.

Think-Alouds (*n.m. Penser à haute voix*) A think-aloud is a form of teacher modelling to help students understand. In a think-aloud, the teacher gives a running commentary on the strategies he or she is using. By pointing out the cover of a book that the students are about to read, the teacher uses a think-aloud to describe the strategies that he or she needs to understand—I wonder what the story is about? I'm not sure I know why there's a dog in the corner, but we'll find out; this reminds me of …, etc. Think-alouds help students listen for information, make connections to their personal experiences, and develop an understanding of some of the strategies they need to understand what they are about to read.

Triarchic Theory of Intelligence (*n.f. Théorie triarchique de l'intelligence*) Sternberg's triarchic theory of intelligence contends that successful intelligence arises from a balance of analytical, creative, and practical abilities, and that these abilities function collectively to allow students to achieve success. According to Sternberg, intelligence is a person's ability to adapt to the environment. Determining whether students are analytical, creative, or practical learners helps teachers create a learning profile of their students.

Visualization (*n.f. Visualisation*) A technique that encourages students to picture a scene before reading about it or discussing it. While visualizing, students consider the sights, sounds, and smells of the scene. Visualizing before and during reading helps students understand better, remember what they have read, and identify places or words in the text that they are having difficulty understanding.

References

Alberta Education. *French as a Second Language Classroom Assessment Material —Grade 4 to Grade 6.* Calgary: Alberta Education, 2006.

Anderson, B., J. Netten, and C. Germain. *The Intensive French Interprovincial Teachers' Guide.* Fredericton: New Brunswick Department of Education, 2005.

Archibald, A. *Writing in a Second Language.* Southampton, UK: Subject Centre for Languages, Linguistics and Area Studies, University of Southampton, 2004. http://www.llas.ac.uk/resources/goodpractice.aspx?resourceid=2175

Arpin, L. and L. Capra. *L'apprentissage par projets.* Montréal: Chenelière/McGraw-Hill, 2001.

Asher, J. *Learning Another Language through Actions.* 6th ed. Los Gatos, CA: Sky Oak Productions, 2000.

Bennett, B., and C. Rolheiser. *Beyond Monet: The Artful Science of Instructional Integration.* Toronto: Bookation Inc., 2001.

Bernard, I. *Acti-vie Program Guide.* Toronto: Gage Education, 1998.

Brandt, R. *Powerful Learning.* Alexandria, VA: Association for Supervision and Curriculum Development, 1998.

British Columbia Education. *Core French Grades 5 to 12. Integrated Resource Package 2001.* Ministry of Education, British Columbia, 2001.

Buehl, D. *Classroom Strategies for Interactive Learning.* 2nd ed. Newark, DE: International Reading Association, 2001.

Caine, R.N., and G. Caine. "How To Think About the Brain: A set of guiding principles for moving cautiously when applying brain research to the classroom." *The School Administrator.* Arlington, VA: American Association of School Administrators, January 1998. http://www.aasa.org/publications/saarticledetail.cfm?ItemNumber=4268.

———. *Making Connections: Teaching and the Human Brain.* Nashville, TN: Incentive Publications, 1990.

Callella, T., S. Samoiloff, and D. Tom. *Making Your Word Wall More Interactive.* Huntington Beach, CA: Creative Teaching Press, 2001.

Cameron, S. *Recueil d'activités de lecture.* Laval, Québec: Groupe Beauchemin, éditeur ltée, 2005.

Canadian Association of Second Language Teachers (CASLT). *Assessment Instruments for French as a Second Language, Français langue seconde, Beginner Level.* Ottawa: CASLT, 1998.

Canadian Association of Second Language Teachers (CASLT). "Summary of Findings—Canadian Youth Forum on Bilingualism." Ottawa: CASLT, January 2008.

Chapman, C., and R. King. "11 Practical Ways to Guide Teachers toward Differentiation." *Journal of Staff Development.* Volume 26, Number 4, Fall 2005: 20–25.

———. "11 Practical Ways to Guide Teachers toward Differentiation (and an Evaluation Tool)." T3: Teachers Teaching Teachers, *Journal of Staff Development.* Volume 1, Number 6, March 2006: 8–9.

Chaudron, C. *A Method for Examining the Input/Intake Distinction* in *Input in Second Language Acquisition.* ed. S. M. Gass and C.G. Madden. Rowley, MA: 1985: 285–302.

Cogswell, F., and P. Kristmanson. *French Is a Life Skill: A Summary of Research, Theories, and Practices.* Toronto: Thomson Nelson, 2007.

Cogswell, F. « *Êtes-vous prêt(e)s pour les cyberquêtes ?* » *Journal de l'immersion,* Volume 29, Number 2, Summer 2007.

Conseil atlantique des ministres de l'Éducation et de la Formation (CAMEF). *Trousse d'appréciation de rendement en lecture : immersion française, quatrième à sixième année.* Halifax: CAMEF, 2004.

Cooper, D. *Talk About Assessment: Strategies and Tools to Improve Learning.* Toronto: Thomson Nelson, 2007.

Cooper, H., J. C. Robinson, and E. A. Patall. "Does Homework Improve Academic Achievement? A Synthesis of Research." American Educational Research Association (online): *Review of Educational Research,* 76, 2006: 1–62.

Council of Europe. *European Language Portfolio.* Strasbourg, France: Council of Europe, 1997.

Cunningham, P.M., D.P. Hall, and C. Sigmon. *The Teacher's Guide to the Four Blocks.* Greensboro, NC: Carson-Dellosa, 1999.

Davies, A., C. Cameron, C. Politano, and K. Gregory. *Together Is Better: Collaborative Assessment, Evaluation & Reporting.* Winnipeg: Peguis, Classroom Connections International, 1992.

Diamond, M.C. *The Brain ... Use It or Lose It.* This article first appeared in Mindshift Connection, Zephyr Press Publication. Ed. Dee Dickinson, Volume 1, Number 1, 1996. http://www. newhorizons.org/neuro/diamond_use.htm.

Dicks, J., and S. Rehorick. *Maritime Oral Communication Assessment Portfolio (MOCAP): Evaluation Techniques for French as a Second Language.* Halifax, NS: Maritime Provinces Higher Education Foundation, 1992.

Earl, L., and S. Katz. *Rethinking Classroom Assessment with Purpose in Mind.* Manitoba Education, Citizenship and Youth, 2006.

Earl, L.M. *Assessment as Learning: Using Classroom Assessment to Maximize Student Learning.* Thousand Oaks, CA: Corwin Press, 2003: 24.

Echevarria, J., M.E. Vogt, and D.J. Short. *Making Content Comprehensible for English Learners: The SIOP Model.* 2nd ed. Boston: Pearson Allyn and Bacon, 2003.

Edwards, V., P. Kristmanson, and S. Rehorick. *Manuel pour la formation des enseignants et des enseignantes : L'enseignement des langues secondes d'après une approche communicative / expérientielle.* Fredericton: l'Institut en recherche des langues secondes au Canada (Centre didactique des langues secondes). Université du Nouveau-Brunswick, 2000.

Fogarty, R., and J. Bellanca. *Patterns for Thinking: Patterns for Transfer.* Arlington Heights, IL: Skylight Training and Publishing, 1991.

Fountas, I.C., and G.S. Pinnell. *Word Matters.* Portsmouth, NH: Heinemann, 1998.

Gibbons, P. *Scaffolding Language, Scaffolding Learning: Teaching Second Language Learners in the Mainstream Classroom.* Portsmouth, NH: Heinemann, 2002.

Gibbs, J. *Tribes, A New Way of Learning and Being Together.* Santa Rosa, CA: Centre Source Systems, 1995.

Giedd, J., J. Blumenthal, N. Jeffries, F. Castellanos, H. Liu, A. Zijdenbos, T. Paus, A. Evans, J. Rapoport. "Brain development during childhood and adolescence: a longitudinal MRI study." *Nature Neuroscience.* 2 (10), New York: Nature Publishing Group, a division of Macmillan Publishers Limited, 1999: 861–863.

Gregory, G.H., and L. Kuzmich. *Data Driven Differentiation in the Standards-based Classroom.* Thousand Oaks, CA: Corwin Press, 2004.

Gregory, G.H., and T. Parry. *Designing Brain Compatible Learning.* Thousand Oaks, CA: Corwin Press, 2006.

Gregory, G.H., and C. Chapman. *Differentiated Instructional Strategies: One Size Doesn't Fit All.* Thousand Oaks, CA: Corwin Press, 2002.

———. *Differentiated Instructional Strategies in Practice: Training, Implementation, and Supervision.* Thousand Oaks, CA: Corwin Press, 2002.

Gregory, G.H., and L. Kuzmich. *Differentiated Literacy Strategies for Student Growth and Achievement in Grades K–6.* Thousand Oaks, CA: Corwin Press, 2005.

Guskey, T.R. "How Classroom Assessments Improve Learning. Using Data to Improve Student Achievement." *Educational Leadership.* Volume 60, Number 5, Alexandria, VA: Association for Supervision and Curriculum Development, February 2003: 6–11.

———. *Evaluating Professional Development.* Thousand Oaks, CA: Corwin Press, 2006.

Hatton, N., and D. Smith. *Reflection in Teacher Education.* Sydney, Australia: University of Sydney, 1995. http://alex.edfac.usyd.edu.au/LocalResource/ Study1/hattonart.html.

Hendrickson, J.M. "Error Correction in Foreign Language Teaching: Recent Theory, Research, and Practice." *Modern Language Journal.* 62, Monterey, CA: John Wiley & Sons, 1978: 387–398.

Herrell, A., and M. Jordan. *Fifty Strategies for Teaching English Language Learners.* Upper Saddle River, NJ: Pearson Education, 2004.

Hill, J., and K. Flynn. *Classroom Instruction That Works with English Language Learners.* Alexandria, VA: Association for Supervision and Curriculum Development, 2006.

Howden, J., and M. Kopiec. *Cultiver la collaboration.* Montréal: Chenelière/McGraw Hill, 2002.

Jensen, E. "Enriched Environments and the Brain," *Teaching with the Brain in Mind,* Alexandria, VA: Association of Supervision and Curriculum Development, 1998.

————. *A Fresh Look at Brain-based Education*. Phi Delta Kappa International, 89(6), February 2008: 408–417.

————. *Arts with the Brain in Mind*. Alexandria, VA: Association of Supervision and Curriculum Development, 2001.

Johnson, D., and R. Johnson. *Learning Together and Alone: Cooperative, Competitive, and Individualistic Learning*. Boston: Allyn and Bacon, 1999.

Johnston, P.H. *Choice Words: How Our Language Affects Children's Learning*. Portland, ME: Stenhouse Publishers, 2004.

Kagan, S. *Cooperative Learning*. San Juan Capistrano, CA: Kagan Cooperative Learning, 1994.

Koenraad, T., and G. Westhoff. *Can you tell a LanguageQuest when you see one? Design criteria for TalenQuests*. Paper presented at the 2003 Conference of The European Association for Computer Assisted Language Learning, 2003.

Kristmanson, P. *Beyond Time on Task in Second Language Teaching and Learning: A Case Study of Cognitive Processing in Intensive French*. unpublished Ph.D. dissertation, University of New Brunswick, 2006.

Leblanc, J.C. "The Fundamentals of Second Language Instruction." Volume 5, Number 1. London, ON: Mosaic Press, 1997.

LeBlanc, C., C. Courtel, and P. Trecases. *Étude nationale sur les programmes de français de base (National Core French Study): Syllabus culture*. Ottawa: Raymond LeBlanc, 1990.

Luke, A. *Reading and Critical Literacy: Redefining the "Great Debate"*. Paper presented at the 18th Annual New Zealand Conference on Reading, May 1992.

Lyster, R., and L. Ranta. "Corrective Feedback and Learner Uptake: Negotiation of form in communicative classrooms." *Studies in Second Language Acquisition 19*, New York: Cambridge University Press: 1997: 37–66.

Manitoba Education. *Français de base de la 4e à la 6e année, Programme d'études : document de mise en œuvre*. Manitoba Department of Education, 2006.

Maritime Provinces Education Foundation. *Maritime Oral Communication Assessment Portfolio (MOCAP)/ Dossier d'évaluation de la communication orale aux Maritimes (DECOM)*. Maritime Provinces Education Foundation, 1992.

Markowitz, K., and E. Jensen. *The Great Memory Book*. Thousand Oaks, CA: Corwin Press, 1999.

Marzano, R.J., D.J Pickering, and J.E. Pollack. *Classroom Instruction That Works: Research-based Strategies for Increasing Student Achievement*. Alexandria, VA: Association of Supervision and Curriculum Development, 2001.

Marzano, R.J., and D.J. Pickering. "The Case For and Against Homework." *Educational Leadership*. Volume 64, Number 6, Alexandria, VA: Association for Supervision and Curriculum Development, March 2007.

Maxwell, W. *Research into the Effectiveness of the Accelerative Integrated Method*. (unpublished thesis), 1999.

McKenzie, J., and H.B. Davis. "Classroom Strategies to Engender Student Questioning." *Educational Technology Journal*. Bellingham, WA: From Now On (FON), 1986.

McKenzie, J. "The WIRED Classroom: Creating Technology Enhanced Student-Centered Learning Environments." *Educational Technology Journal*. Volume 7, Number 6, Bellingham, WA: From Now On (FON), March 1998.

National Capital Language Resource Centre. *The Essentials of Language Teaching*. Washington, D.C.: Teaching Listening, 2004.

National Institute of Mental Health. *Teenage Brain: A Work in Progress*. Bethesda, MD: NIH Publication Number 01-4929, 2001.

Netten, J., and C. Germain. "Pedagogy and Second Language Learning: Lessons Learned from Intensive French." *Canadian Journal of Applied Linguistics/ Revue canadienne de linguistique appliquée*, 8(2), 2005: 183–210.

New Brunswick Department of Education. *Assessing the Oral Proficiency of the Junior Learner—New Brunswick Middle School Scale*. Fredericton: New Brunswick Department of Education, 1984.

————. *Français langue seconde, français de base 9-12*. Fredericton: New Brunswick Department of Education, 2004.

———. *New Brunswick Middle School Oral Proficiency Scale*. Fredericton: New Brunswick Department of Education, 1984.

———. *Français langue seconde : français de base : Programmes d'études et guide d'enseignement*. Fredericton: New Brunswick Department of Education, 2004.

Norris-Holt, J. "Motivation as a Contributing Factor in Second Language Acquisition." *Internet TESL Journal.* Volume VII, Number 6, June 2001. http://iteslj.org/Articles/Norris-Motivation.html.

Nunan, D. *Learning to Listen in a Second Language.* Prospect 5 (2). 1990: 7–23.

Nunley, K. *Differentiating the High School Classroom: Solution Strategies for 18 Common Obstacles.* Online: Sage Publications, Inc., 2005.

Pryor, W.B., and C.R. Pryor. *The School Leader's Guide to Understanding Attitude and Influencing Behavior: Working with Teachers, Parents, Students, and the Community.* Thousand Oaks, CA: Corwin Press, 2004.

Richard-Amato, P.A. *Making It Happen: From Interactive to Participatory Language Teaching Theory and Practice.* Essex, UK: Longman UK, 2003.

Richards, J.C. *The Language Teaching Matrix.* New York: Cambridge University Press, 1990.

Saskatchewan Education, *Core French: A Curriculum and Resource Guide for the Elementary Level.* Saskatchewan Education, September 1994.

———. *Core French: A Curriculum and Resource Guide for the Middle Level, Evaluation.* Saskatchewan Education, 1995.

Sharpe, D. E "Effective Communication." *Common Sense Business & Technology Perspectives for Educators.* http://www.k4uconsulting.com/index.cfm.

Sigmon, C. *4-blocks literacy model.* Greensboro, NC: Carson Dellosa, 1997.

Sousa, D. *How the Brain Learns: A Classroom Teacher's Guide.* Thousand Oaks, CA: Corwin Press, 2001.

Sparks, D. "Assessment Without Victims: An Interview with Rick Stiggins." *Journal of Staff Development,* Volume 20, Number 2, Oxford, OH: National Staff Development Council, 1999.

Sternberg, R.J. "Allowing for Thinking Styles." *Educational Leadership.* 52(3), Alexandria, VA: Association for Supervision and Curriculum Development, 1994: 36–40.

Stiggins, R. *Assessment Crisis: The Absence of Assessment for Learning.* Bloomington, IN: Phi Delta Kappa International, 83(10), 2002, 758–765.

———. *Assessment, Student Confidence, and School Success.* Phi Delta Kappa International, Volume 81, Number 3, November 1999: 191–198. http://www.pdkintl.org/kappan/k9911sti.htm.

———. "Assessment Through the Student's Eyes." *Educational Leadership.* Volume 64, Number 8, Alexandria, VA: Association for Supervision and Curriculum Development, May 2007.

———. *Evaluating Classroom Assessment Training in Teacher Education Programs.* Hoboken, NJ: Educational Measurement: Issues and Practice, 18(1), 1999: 23–27.

Stratman, G. "Ten Subtle Ways to Create a Positive Learning Environment." Wrightwood, CA: Echo. Association for Environmental and Outdoor Education, Summer 2000.

Strickland, C. (n.d.). *Success with Differentiated Instruction.* Online professional development course. Association for Supervision and Curriculum Development. Course preview available at http://pdonline.ascd.org/pd_demo/table_c.cfm?SID=72.

Swain, M. *The output hypothesis: Theory and research* in *Handbook of Research in Second Language Teaching and Learning.* ed. E. Hinkel. Mahwah, NJ: Lawrence Erlbaum Associates, Publishers, 2005: 471–483.

Tate, M. *"Sit & Get" Won't Grow Dendrites.* Thousand Oaks, CA: Corwin Press, 2004.

Tedick, D.J., and B. de Gortari. "Research on Error Correction and Implications for Classroom Teaching." *ACIE Newsletter.* Volume 1, Number 3, Indianapolis, IN: University of Minnesota, May 1998.

Tomlinson, C.A. "Deciding to Teach Them All." *Educational Leadership.* 61(2), Alexandria, VA: Association for Supervision and Curriculum Development, October 2003: 6–11.

———. "Invitations to Learn." *Educational Leadership.* Volume 60, Number 1, Alexandria, VA: Association for Supervision and Curriculum Development, September 2002: 6–10.

———. *How to Differentiate Instruction in Mixed-Ability Classrooms.* 2nd ed. Alexandria, VA:

Association for Supervision and Curriculum Development, 2001.

―――. *Fulfilling the Promise of the Differentiated Classroom*. Alexandria, VA: Association for Supervision and Curriculum Development, 2003.

―――. (traduction : Bernard Théorêt) *La classe différenciée*. Montréal: Chenelière Education, 2004.

―――. *The Differentiated Classroom. Responding to the Needs of All Learners*. Alexandria, VA: Association for Supervision and Curriculum Development, 1999.

Tomlinson, C.A., and J. McTighe. *Integrating Differentiated Instruction and Understanding by Design*. Alexandria, VA: Association of Supervision and Curriculum Development, 2006.

Trehearne, M. *Comprehensive Literacy Resource for Grades 3–6 Teachers*. Toronto: Thomson Nelson, 2006.

―――. *Grades 1–2 Teacher's Resource Book*, Toronto: Thomson Nelson, 2004.

―――. *Littératie en 1re et 2e année : Répertoire de ressources pédagogiques*, Toronto: Thomson Nelson, 2006.

Turnbull, M. "There is a Role for the L1 in Second and Foreign Language Teaching, But …," Toronto: *Canadian Modern Language Review*, 57, 4, 2001. Valentino, C. *Flexible Grouping*. www.eduplace.com/science/profdev/articles/valentino.html.

Vandergrift, L. *Listening: Theory and Practice in Modern Foreign Language Competence. Guide to Good Practice*. Southampton, UK: Subject Centre for Languages, Linguistics and Area Studies, University of Southampton, 2002. www.lang.ltsn.ac.uk/resources/goodpractice.aspx?resourceaid=67

―――. *Proposal for a Common Framework of Reference for Language for Canada*. Ottawa: Canadian Heritage-Official Languages, 2006.

Varlas, L. *Getting Acquainted with the Essential Nine, Curriculum Update*, Alexandria, VA: Association for Supervision and Curriculum Development, Winter 2002: 4–5.

Vygotsky, L. *Mind in Society: Development of Higher Psychological Processes*. 14th ed. Boston: Harvard University Press, 1978.

Vygotsky, L., and A. Kozulin. *Thought and Language. Revised ed.* Cambridge, MA: MIT Press, 1986.

Wiggins, G. *Educative Assessment*. San Francisco: Jossey-Bass, 1998.

Wiggins, T., and J. McTighe. *Understanding by Design*. Alexandria, VA: Association of Supervision and Curriculum Development, 2000.

Wilson, L.M., and H.W. Horch. "Implications of Brain Research for Teaching Young Adolescents." *Middle School Journal*, National Middle School Association, Volume 34, Number 1, September 2002: 57–61.

Wolfe, P. *Brain Matters: Translating Research into Classroom Practice*. Alexandria, VA: Association of Supervision and Curriculum Development, 2001.

―――. *Brain Research and Education: Fad or Foundation?* Tempe, AZ: Maricopa Centre for Learning and Instruction, Forum: teaching, learning and assessment, 2003.

Zahar, R., T. Cobb, N. Spada. "Acquiring Vocabulary through Reading: Effects of Frequency and Contextual Richness." *Canadian Modern Language Review*. 57, 4 (June), Toronto: University of Toronto Press—Journals Division, 2001.

Zull, J.E. *The Art of Changing the Brain*. Alexandria, VA: Association of Supervision and Curriculum Development, 2004.

Credits

We have made every effort to trace the ownership of all copyrighted material and to secure permission from copyright holders. In the event of any question arising as to the use of any material, we will be pleased to make the necessary corrections in future printings. Thanks are due to the following for permission to use the material indicated.

Cover

Photos: Main: © Jim Craigmyle/Corbis; top left: Image 99/Jupiter Images; top right: Comstock Images/Jupiter Images
Except where indicated, all interior photos © Nelson Education Ltd.

Text Credits
Section 1: Preparing for Success
Chapter 1

8: Source: Living and Learning in a Bilingual Canada: Regional Youth Forums. Adapted with permission of the Society for Educational Visits and Exchanges in Canada (SEVEC); **14:** Adapted with permission from George Stratman, Director of Shady Creek Outdoor School; **17:** Source: "Deciding to Teach Them All," by Carol Ann Tomlinson in the October, 2003, issue of Educational Leadership, 61(2), pp. 6–11. © 2003 by ASCD. Used with permission. Learn more about ASCD at www.ascd.org; **23:** Adapted with permission from George Stratman, Director of Shady Creek Outdoor School.

Chapter 2

45: Figure adapted from Miriam P. Trehearne's *Nelson Language Arts Grades 3–6 Teacher's Resource,* 1E, p. 459 © 2006 Nelson Education Ltd. Reproduced by permission. www.cengage.com/permissions; **50–51:** Howden, Jim and Marguerite Kopiec. 2002. *Cultiver la collaboration.* Montreal: Cheneliere/McGraw-Hill. **58:** From David R. Johnson and Roger T. Johnson's *Learning Together and Alone: Cooperative, Competitive, And Individualistic Learning,* 5/e. Published by Allyn and Bacon/Merrill Education, Boston, MA. Copyright © 1999 by Pearson Education. Reprinted by permission of the publisher.

Chapter 5

154: From Damian Cooper's *Talk About Assessment,* 1E, p. 11 © 2006 Nelson Education Ltd. Reproduced by permission. www.cengage.com/permissions; **155–156:** From Damian Cooper's *Talk About Assessment,* 1E. © 2006 Nelson Education Ltd. Reproduced by permission. www.cengage.com/permissions; **156:** Adapted with permission of the National Staff Development Council, www.nsdc.org, 2009. All rights reserved; **162–163:** Adapted with the permission of Roy Lyster, Leila Ranta, and Cambridge University Press; **172, 175–176, 186:** From Damian Cooper's *Talk About Assessment,* 1E, pp. 13–14, 45, 195–198. © 2006 Nelson Education Ltd. Reproduced by permission. www.cengage.com/permissions.

BLMs

1.10, 1.11, 1.12, 5.6, 5.7, 5.8: Miriam P. Trehearne's *Litteratie en 1re et 2e annee—Repertoire de ressources pedagogiques.* © Groupe Modulo, 2006, pp. 124, 631–633, 761, 762.; **1.5:** Miriam P. Trehearne's *Litteratie de la 3e a la 6e annee—Repertoire de ressources pedagogiques* © Groupe Modulo, 2006, p. 532; **2.3, 2.4, 2.5, 5.2, 5.3, 5.4:** From Damian Cooper's *Talk About Assessment,* 1E, pp. 301, 302, 303, 299, 300, 359 © 2006 Nelson Education Ltd. Reproduced by permission. www.cengage.com/permissions.

Section 2: Literacy Development Strategies
Chapter 6

Photo: 204: © David Buffington/Photodisc/Getty Images; **216:** Adapted from the National Capital Language Resource Centre (NCLRC). (n.d.). *The essentials of language teaching.* Retrieved 2009 from http://nclrc.org/essentials; **224:** Adapted by permission of McREL from Classroom Instruction that Works by Robert J. Marzano, Debra, J. Pickering, Jane E. Pollock. Copyright 2001. Alexandria, VA: Association for Supervision and Curriculum Development.

Chapter 7

241: © Raymond LeBlanc, Ottawa, 1990.

Chapter 8

268: Used with permission by Allan Luke.

Chapter 9

312: Adapted from *6+1 Traits of Writing: The Complete Guide Grade 3 and Up* by Ruth Culham. Scholastic Inc./Teaching Resources. Copyright © 2003 by Northwest Regional Educational Laboratory. Reprinted by permission of Scholastic Inc.; **327:** From Miriam P. Trehearne's *Nelson Language Arts Grades 3–6 Teacher's Resource,* 1E, pp. 235–236 © 2006 Nelson Education Ltd. Reproduced by permission. www.cengage.com/permissions.

BLMs

6.1, 6.3, 7.1–7.3, 8.1–8.19, 8.21, 9.1, 9.4: Miriam P. Trehearne's *Litteratie en 1re et 2e annee—Repertoire de ressources pedagogiques.* © Groupe Modulo, 2006, pp. 96, 98, 103, 104, 123, 355–357, 376, 385, 456, 458, 461, 464, 466–469, 473, 476, 481, 501, 502, 658; **8.3, 8.9, 8.13, 8.22, 9.2:** Miriam P. Trehearne's *Litteratie de la 3e a la 6e annee—Repertoire de ressources pedagogiques* © Groupe Modulo, 2006, pp. 186, 187, 193, 218, 543.

Conclusion
BLM

C.2: Miriam P. Trehearne's *Litteratie de la 3e a la 6e annee—Repertoire de ressources pedagogiques* © Groupe Modulo, 2006, pp. 541.

Index

A

Acting out, 69
Activities
  for analytical ability, 138
  Ask-and-Answer Games (Des jeux de questions et de réponses), 250–251
  as assessment strategies, 164–165
  cloze, 223–224, 285, 316
  Collaborative Dialogues (Des dialogues collaboratives), 254
  for creative ability, 138
  Golden Egg (Les oeufs d'orés), 251–252
  for higher-level thinking, 63
  information gap, 222
  inquiry-oriented, 44
  Jeopardy, 251
  jigsaw, 224
  learning styles and, 63
  listening, 210. See Listening activities
  Mingling to Music Interview, 254–255
  Musical Hands and Feet (Des mains et pieds musicales), 252
  name tag, 126
  for practical ability, 138
  to raise profile of FSL, 11
  read-aloud, 212–213, 271, 278–279
  reading. See Reading activities
  Surveys (Les sondages), 253–254
  think-aloud, 211–212, 271, 319–320
  TV Interviewer and Interviewee (Des entrevues télévisés), 252
  warm-up. See Warm-up activities
  What Did You See? (Que vois-tu?), 252–253
Adaptability, 137
Age
  and FSL, 13–14
  and learning styles, 83
  and readiness to learn, 83
  and risk-taking, 13–14
Amygdala, 81
Analyzing, 96
Anderson, Lorin, 106–109
Anecdotal data sheets, 171–173

Anxiety reduction, 21
Archibald, Alasdair, 313
Asher, James, 52
Ask-and-Answer Games (Des jeux de questions et de réponses), 250–251
Asking-for-help strategies, 218
Assessment. See also Ongoing assessment; Peer assessment; Self-assessment
  anecdotal data sheets for, 171–173
  backward design and, 157, 159–160
  BIG ideas, 155–156
  of communicative strategies, 178
  confidence and, 161
  definition of, 153, 154
  diagnostic, 153, 154
  direction cards and, 173
  feedback and, 161–162
  goals and, 158
  graphic organizers and, 166–167
  instructional planning and, 65, 66, 156–158, 176–177, 186
  AS learning, 154, 156
  FOR learning, 154, 156
  OF learning, 154, 156
  of listening skills, 178–179
  observation and, 165–166, 171
  performance tasks and, 169–170
  of portfolios, 167
  purposes of, 156
  of reading skills, 179–180
  rubrics, 173–176
  of speaking skills, 181–182
  strategies, 164–165
  student involvement in, 153, 161–166, 186
  terminology, 153, 154
  toolkit, 164–166, 183–186
  trust and, 161
  of writing skills, 182–183
Auditory learners, 133
Authentic communication, 241
Authentic documents, 19–20
Autonomy, 22

B

Backward design
  and assessment, 159–160
  and instructional planning, 65–

66, 156, 159–160
Bandes dessinées, 285
Bar graphs, 94
Barrier games, 227–229
Behaviour, management of, 14
Bilingualism, positive beliefs about, 7–8
Bloom's Taxonomy, 106–109
Bodily/kinesthetic intelligence, 135, 136
Bookmarks, personalized, 277
Brain
  age and, 83
  in children/adolescents vs. adults, 83–84
  development of, 83
  environment and, 80
  and higher-order thinking, 105–109
  individual uniqueness of, 82–84
  learning function of, 78–79
  and new learning, 90–102
  novelty and, 23, 90
  parts of, 81
  plasticity of, 78, 82, 83, 134
  and practice, 328
  and principles of learning, 82–109
  research on, 77–78
  second-language learning and, 9
  stress and, 23
Brainstorming
  of cognates, 273
  graphic organizers for, 95
  visual materials and, 100
  for writing, 322, 326
Buddy-Reading, 283

C

Carte de l'histoire, 96
Cerebellum, 81
Cerebral cortex, 81, 105
Charades (Les charades), 248–249
Choice, student
  in instructional planning, 63
  and product, 125
  relevance and, 85
Choral reading, 283
Classroom
  interaction, 17–18
Classroom-Door Book Covers, 277

Classroom organization, 14, 120
Cloze activities
    for listening, 223–224
    for reading, 285
    for writing, 316
Cognates, 272–273
Collaboration. *See also* Cooperative
    learning; Group work
    instructional planning and, 64, 69
    language for, 88–89
    social aspect of learning and, 87
Collaborative Dialogues *(Des dialogues
    collaboratives),* 254
Colour-coding, 132
Communication. *See also* Oral
    communication
    assessment of strategies, 178
    classroom, in 17–20
    instructional planning and, 64–65
    interactional, 208–209, 218, 244
    purpose of, 64–65
    questions and, 18
    reading and, 19
    transactional, 208–209, 218, 244
    writing and, 19
Comparing and contrasting, 68, 95
Computers, 317
Concept maps, for new learning,
    93–96
Connections, making. *See also*
    Experiences; Prior knowledge/
    learning
    brain and, 78, 80
    cross-curricular connections and,
        10
Constructivist-based pedagogies,
    59–61
Content
    defined, 124
    mastery of, 80
Conversation, 181–182
Cooper, Damian, 155–156
Cooperative learning, 57–59. *See also*
    Collaboration
Cross-curricular connections, 9–10
    brain and, 80
    constructivist approach and, 60
    PBP and, 51
Culham, Ruth, 312
Culture/cultural studies, 15–17
Curriculum
    and differentiated instruction, 121
    and instructional planning, 65, 66

quality of, 121
Cut-Up Conversations *(Des
    conversations coupées),* 249
Cutting Reading Apart (CRA), 283

D

Diagnostic assessment, 153
    definition of, 154
    and differentiated instruction, 123
    for readiness, 126
Differentiated instruction (DI), 55–
    59, 116–119
    acrostic for, 139–140
    brain and, 83
    classroom environment and,
        120–121
    curriculum and, 121
    diagnostic assessment and, 123
    framework for, 124–138
    grouping and, 122
    learning preferences and, 83
    learning profiles and, 132–133
    and listening, 219
    multiple intelligences and, 133–
        136
    readiness and, 126
    and respectful work, 122
    and tiered instruction, 126–129
    Triarchic Theory of Intelligence
        and, 137–138
Differentiation, 118, 119–124
Diphthongs, 272
Direction cards, 173
Discovery-based approach to learning,
    59

E

Emotions, and learning, 84–90
Entrance passes, 69, 120, 126
Environment
    and brain, 80
    and differentiated instruction,
        120–121
    enriched, 80
    for positive emotions, 84
    risk-free, 120–121
Une esquisse, 96
Une étoile, 95
European Language Portfolios (ELPs),
    168
Evaluation, definition of, 154
Exit passes, 120, 126
Experiences

learning from, 78
and new learning, 62, 91
and patterns, 91
spiralling and, 92
and writing, 322

F

Feedback
    and assessment, 161–162
    on goal attainment, 69
    instructional planning for, 64
    and new learning, 104–105
    praise and, 317
    and reflection, 104–105
    for writing, 314, 317
First language
    research in, 258
    second-language learning and, 6
    transfer of knowledge from, 238
    writing in, vs. in second language,
        313
First-language instruction
    collaboration with teachers, 10
    and oral communication, 211
Formative assessment, 153, 154
FSL
    activities to raise profile of, 11
    age and, 13–14
    attitudes toward, 7
    positive classroom atmosphere
        and, 12–25
    positive school atmosphere and,
        9–12
Full sentence-answers, in tiered
    instruction, 128–129

G

Games, TPR and, 53–54
Gandhi, Mahatma, 21–22
Gardner, Howard, 133–136
Goals
    and assessment, 158
    backward design and, 65
    in instructional planning, 65
    oral communication, 242
    and product, 125
    students setting own, 62, 69
    teacher, 6–7
Golden Egg *(Les oeufs d'orés),* 251–
    252
Gradual Release of Responsibility
    (GRR), 44–48, 90, 127, 239, 312
Grammar, 19

Graphic organizers, 94–96
    for assessment, 166–167
    in instructional planning, 68, 69
    and readiness, 126
    for survey results, 253
    visual learners and, 132
    in writing, 316, 318
Group work
    and bar graphs, 94
    differentiation and, 122
    and oral communication, 244–245
    participation in French language
        during, 89
    scaffolding and, 244
    as team work, 89
    and writing, 312, 326
Grouping. *See also* Small groups
    and cooperative learning, 57, 58
    and differentiated instruction, 122
    itinerant teaching and, 125
    student-led groups, 122
    teacher-led groups, 122
    whole-class, 122
Guided practice, 47
Guided writing, 326

H

Higher-order thinking
    brain and, 81, 105–109
    instructional planning for, 63
Hippocampus, 81
Home links, 25–26
Homework, 69
Hypothalamus, 81
Hypotheses, 69, 78

I

Independent learning
    Gradual Release of Responsibility
        and, 44, 47
    group work vs., 122
    skills for, 8
    writing, 312, 326
Information gap activities, 222
Input, 239–241
Inquiry-oriented activities, 44
Instructional materials, development
    of, 91–92
Instructional planning, 43–76
    and assessment, 156–158, 176–
        177, 186
    backward design and, 156, 159–
        160

and curriculum, 65, 66, 121
    principles of, 61–69
Intelligence
    brain and, 79
    interpersonal, 135, 136
    intrapersonal, 135, 136
    Sternberg's definition of, 137
Interaction, 14
    classroom, 17–18, 20
    in conversation, 181–182
    instructional planning and, 64, 65
    and oral communication, 244
    oral warm-ups and, 246–247
Interest
    relevance and, 129–130
    technology and, 130–131
Internalization, 87
Internet, 19–20, 99, 258
Interviews
    questions, 181
    for readiness, 126
    in tiered instruction, 128
Itinerant teaching, 9, 24, 125

J

Jeopardy, 251
Jigsaw listening, 224–226
Jigsaw-Reading, 284
Journals
    for pre- and post-assessment, 123
    review/reflection on learning and,
        103, 170–171
    and self-assessment, 170–171

K

Kinesthetic learners, 133
K.U.D. (know, understand, be able to
    do), 65, 69, 124, 126

L

Language
    biographies, 168
    and culture, 15
    importance of, 207
    integration of skills in learning, 13
    levels, and instructional planning,
        64
    listening and, 207, 229
Learner-centred approaches, 44
Learning
    brain and, 78–79
    as continuous process, 77–78
    emotions and, 84–90

social aspect of, 84, 87
Learning preferences/profiles, 10, 63,
    82–83, 132–133
Learning styles, 10
    age and, 83
    in instructional planning, 63
Level of actual development, 87
Level of potential development, 87
Lexemes, 273
Libraries, use of, 20
Lifelong learning, 5, 18
Ligne du temps, 96
Liste en gradins, 95
Listening
    assessment of skills, 178–179
    bottom-up, 216
    as communicative goal, 67
    and differentiated instruction, 219
    instructional planning for, 62
    intention, 209–211
    and language, 207, 229
    metacognition and, 217
    and oral communication, 206–208
    purposes for, 219, 220
    self-assessment of skills, 219
    strategies, 214–218
    teacher, 18
    teacher talk for, 211–214
    top-down, 216
    and writing, 312
Listening activities, 210, 220–229
    and barrier games, 227–229
    cloze activities and, 223–224
    jigsaw, 224–226
    matching games and, 226
    music and, 223
    riddles and, 226
    sequencing games and, 226
    and writing, 329–330
Logical/mathematical intelligence,
    134, 136
Logs, learning, 170. *See also* Journals
    for pre- and post-assessment, 123
Lyster, Roy, 162–163

M

MacLean, Paul, 80
Marzano, Robert, 68–69
Matching, 285
Matching games, 226
Message Rap *(Les raps),* 249–250
Metacognition
    and GRR approach, 47–48

instructional planning and, 62
and listening, 217
strategies developed by students, 68
and think-alouds, 271
Mingling to Music Interview, 254–255
Modelling
reading, 271
of strategies/skills, 46
of writing, 318–320, 329
Monitoring of own learning, 62–63, 89. *See also* Self-assessment
Morphemes, 273–274
Motivation, 12–13
constructivism and, 59
cultural studies and, 15–19
emotions and, 84
instrumental, 15
integrative, 15
listening activities for, 222–229
and purpose for writing, 322
variety in classroom life and, 13
Multiple intelligences, 83, 133–136
Music, 100–101, 223
Musical Hands and Feet (*Des mains et pieds musicales*), 252
Musical/rhythmic intelligence, 135, 136

N

Name tag activities, 126
Name That Book, 277–278
National Core French Study (NCFS), 49–50
on culture, 15
Neuron networks, 82, 91, 110
New learning
brain and, 79
concept maps and, 93–96
experiences and, 62, 91
feedback and, 104–105
graphic organizers and, 93–96
music and, 100–101
practice and, 101–102
prior knowledge and, 62, 91
processing of, 90–102
reflection and, 102–105
repetition and, 101
and rote memorization, 44
spiralling and, 92
variety and, 97–98
visual literacy and, 98–100

warm-up activities for, 120
Norris-Holt, Jacqueline, 15
Note-taking, 68
and jigsaw activities, 224
visual learners and, 132
for writing, 316
Novelty
brain and, 23, 90
and new learning, 97
in review and reflection, 103

O

Observation
for assessment, 165–166, 171
checklists, 171
One-Minute Sentences (*Des phrases rapides*), 249
Ongoing assessment
diagnostic, 123
PBP and, 51
by students, 62
Oral communication. *See also* Communication; Speaking
authentic, 241
collaborative, 14
collaborative group work and, 244–245
first-language instruction and, 211
goals, 242
listening and, 206–208
and literacy, 238
question-and-answer activities and, 247–248
and reading, 238, 268
and second-language learning, 238
and self-assessment, 238
skills, 19
stress and, 85-86
student-to-stdent interaction and, 244
think-pair-share activity and, 245
warm-up activities and, 245–256
and writing, 238, 329
Oral participation
criteria for, 61–62
instructional planning and, 61–62
and learning environment, 120
Oral presentations, 256–261
Output, 239–241

P

Parents/guardians, 25–26
Patterns

brain and, 78, 79
concept maps and, 93–94
in development of instructional materials, 91
new learning and, 91–92
recognition and finding of, 91–92
Peer assessment, 170–171
Performance tasks, 169–170
Personalization
activating prior knowledge and, 274–275
of topics, 85
Personalized Bookmarks, 277
Picture books, 277
Portfolios, 167, 168
Positive classroom atmosphere, 12–25
Positive school atmosphere, 9–12
Practice
brain and, 328
and new learning, 101–102
and production, 101–102
Praise, 14, 22, 68, 317
Predicting
brain and, 78
in instructional planning, 69
and reading, 275–276
Prior experience. *See* Experiences
Prior knowledge/learning
access strategies, 62
concept maps and, 93–94
constructivist approach and, 60
early humans and, 78
new learning and, 62
and patterns, 91
and readiness, 126
and reading, 274–275
spiralling and, 92
and top-down listening, 216
and writing, 322
Process, defined, 124
Product, defined, 125
Project-based pedagogy (PBP), 50–52
Projects, long-term, 122

Q

Question-and-answer activities, 247–248
Questions
bottom-up, 216
and classroom communication, 18
constructivist approach and, 60
interview, 181
and prior knowledge, 69

and reading, 276–277
for reflection, 103–104
in shared practice, 46–47
in tiered instruction, 128
top-down, 216
varying, 22–23, 97–98
Qui a... ? Moi, j'ai...., 248

R

R.A.F.T. (Role, Audience, Format, Topic), 130, 131
Ranta, Leila, 163
Read-aloud activities, 212–213, 271, 278–279. *See also* Reading aloud
Readers' Theatre, 285
Readiness
  age and, 83
  brain and, 83
  defined, 126
  and differentiated instruction, 126
  prior learning and, 126
Reading
  activating prior knowledge for, 274–275
  activities, 277–278
  assessment of skills, 179–180
  attitudinal surveys on, 10
  and communication, 19, 67
  comprehension, 99, 272
  explicit teaching of, 271–274
  intention, 269–270
  and literacy, 267
  oral communication and, 238, 268
  picture books and, 277
  predicting and, 275–276
  questioning and, 276–277
  scaffolding, 270–271
  shared, 278–279
  storytelling and, 277
  think-alouds and, 211–212, 279–282
  visual materials and, 99
Reading activities, 277–278
  Bande dessinée, 285
  Buddy-Reading, 283
  choral reading, 283
  classroom-door book covers, 277
  Cloze Activity, 285
  Cutting Reading Apart (CRA), 283
  Jigsaw-Reading, 284
  Matching, 285
  Name That Book, 277–278

personalized bookmarks, 277
Readers' Theatre, 285
Retell or Recount, 285
Scavenger Hunt, 277
Sequencing/Story Map, 277
Skimming and Scanning, 283
story webs, 278
Text Reconstruction, 285
Time Line, 285
True-False Questions, 286
and writing, 329–330
Reading aloud. *See also* Read-aloud activities
  auditory learners and, 133
  of writing, 317, 327
Real-world connections, PBP and, 51
Recognition
  in instructional planning, 68
  and self-efficacy, 22
Reflection
  and new learning, 102–105
  question-and-answer routine for, 103–104
  and self-assessment, 170–171
  on skills, 62
  on writing, 327
Relevance
  interest and, 129–130
  and student choice, 85
Repetition, and new learning, 90, 101
Respectful work, 122
Responses, varying, 22–23, 97–98
Responsibility for own learning
  assessment and, 153
  classroom organization and, 120
  constructivism and, 59
  grouping and, 122
  past instructional practices and, 80
Retell or Recount, 285
Retention, cooperative learning and, 57
Reviews of lessons, 103
Riddles, 226
Risk-taking, 21–22
  age and, 13–14
Role-playing
  in cooperative learning, 58–59
  kinesthetic learners and, 133
  in tiered instruction, 128
Rote memorization, 44
Rubrics, 166, 173–176

S

Scaffolding
  and collaborative work, 244
  conferencing with students and, 317
  constructivism and, 60
  and group work, 89
  instructional planning for, 64
  modelling and, 46
  reading, 270–271
  writing, 315, 316–317
  for writing, 317
Scavenger Hunt, 277
Second-language learning
  and academic success, 9
  affective aspect of, 4, 8
  attitudes toward, 7
  and brain, 9
  and differentiated instruction, 55
  and first language, 6
  NCFS principles, 49–50
  oral communication and, 238
  reasons for, 5–8
  teaching challenges in, 9
  transfer of knowledge from first language in, 238
Self-assessment, 170–171
  of listening skills, 219
  oral communication and, 238
  for readiness, 126
Self-efficacy, 21–22
Self-esteem, cooperative learning and, 57
Sentence starters, in tiered instruction, 128
Sequencing, 95–96
  games, 226
Sequencing/Story Map, 277
Shared practice, 46–47
Shared writing, 324–326
Similes, 68
Situation cards, 182
Skills
  integration of, 13, 61
  modelling of, 46
  multiple intelligences and, 134–135
  social, 57, 59
Skimming and Scanning, 283
Small groups
  cooperative learning and, 57
  and differentiated instruction, 122
  predicting in, 276

Social skills, in cooperative learning, 57, 59
Sound relationships, 272
Speaking. *See also* Oral communication
    assessment of skills, 181–182
    as communicative goal, 67
    stress regarding, 85–86
    writing and, 312, 315–316, 330
Spider maps, 94
Spiralling, 90, 92
Stakeholders, 5
Sternberg, Robert J., 137–138
Story webs, 278
Storytelling, 277
Stress, 23, 85–86
Summarizing, 68
Summative assessment, 153, 154
Surveys *(Les sondages),* 253–254

T

Tableau action / réaction, 96
Tableau avant / aprés, 96
Le tableau T, 95
Teacher talk, for listening skills, 211–214
Teams, learning, for long-term projects, 122
Technology, 130–131
Tests, and level of actual vs. potential development, 87
Text Reconstruction, 285
Thalamus, 81
Themes/topics
    and instructional planning, 65
    personalization of, 85
Think-aloud activities
    and reading, 271, 279–282
    teacher talk and, 211–212
    and writing, 319–320
Think-pair-share activity, 245
Tiered instruction, 126–129
Time Line, 285
Tomlinson, Carol, 17, 130
Toss the Ball *(Lancer la balle),* 248
Total Physical Response (TPR) approach, 52–54
Transitions, TPR activities as, 53
Triarchic Theory of Intelligence, 132, 137–138
Triune Brain Theory, 80

True-False Questions, 286
TV Interviewer and Interviewee *(Des entrevues télévisés),* 252

V

Variety
    of contexts for learning strategies, 48
    and motivation, 13
    and new learning, 97–98
    of questions, 22–23, 97–98
    of responses, 22–23, 97–98
    of text types for writing, 318
Venn diagrams, 94, 317
Verbal/linguistic intelligence, 134, 136
Verbs, strong, 130, 131
Visual, auditory, and kinaesthetic (VAK) learning style, 132
Visual aids
    and listening activities, 223
    predicting and, 276
    in second-language learning, 99
    and writing, 133, 317, 320
Visual learners, 132–133
Visual literacy, 98–99
Visual/spatial intelligence, 134–135, 136
Visual synectics, 100
Visualization, 96, 99–100
    for writing, 318, 320–321
Vygotsky, Lev S., 10, 87

W

Warm-up activities
    charades *(Les charades),* 248–249
    Cut-Up Conversations *(Des conversations coupées),* 249
    kinesthetic learners and, 133
    Message Rap *(Les raps),* 249–250
    for new learning, 120
    One-Minute Sentences *(Des phrases rapides),* 249
    oral, 245–256
    question-and-answer, 247–248
    Qui a… ? Moi, j'ai…, 248
    Toss the Ball *(Lancer la balle),* 248
    TPR activities as, 53
What Did You See? *(Que vois-tu?),* 252–253
Whole-class instruction, 122

Writing
    assessment of skills, 182–183
    attitudinal surveys on, 10
    brainstorming for, 322, 326
    cloze activities for, 316
    collaborative group work, 326
    and communication, 19, 67
    and computers, 317
    exceptional, 312
    experiences and, 322
    explicit teaching of strategies in, 318–329
    extension activities, 328
    feedback for, 314, 317
    in first vs. second languages, 313
    graphic organizers for, 316, 318
    group, 312
    guided, 326
    importance of, 311–315
    independent, 312, 326
    instruction in, 313–314
    listening and, 221, 312, 329–330
    modelling of, 318–320, 329
    note-taking for, 316
    oral communication and, 238, 329
    prior knowledge and, 322
    purpose for, 322
    reading aloud, 317, 327
    reading and, 330
    reflection on, 327
    revising of, 323–324
    riddles, 226
    scaffolding of, 315, 316–317, 317
    school-wide approach, 314
    shared, 324–326
    speaking and, 312, 315–316, 330
    text types for, 318
    think-alouds for, 319–320
    Venn diagrams for, 317
    visualization for, 318, 320–321
    visuals and, 317, 320

Y

Y charts, 94

Z

Zone of proximal development (ZPD), 87
Zull, James, 82, 110